MIDDLEMAN BLUES

And One Hell of a Life

By W. JACK MAYBEE

Publisher: GWN Publishing
Cover Design by: Kristina Conatser

ISBN: 978-1-965971-42-0

*For those whose lives were
compromised by what happened to
them when they were children.*

Table of Contents

Preface

The following narrative tells the story of my life in the best way that I can tell it with the passage of time. Others may have interpreted shared circumstances and events differently. I won't disagree, argue or attempt to deflect from the truth. By nature I am merely a miner in search of meaning. The story of my life is full of ugly details, and so unflattering, I hate to share it with anyone and do so only out of a sense of duty.

A reader may also see questionable facts and unsubstantiated opinions, sprinkled rather freely I admit, but they are not those of a self-proclaimed expert, nor are they conclusive. They are the assumptions of someone who has spent a lifetime trying to figure out what it means to live on this planet. Facts and opinions are always subject to revision and change upon receipt of better evidence. I am almost never sure about anything. Although, it's also true, I usually think I'm right.

After our marriage ended my ex-wife said to me, "You know, people do want to hear what you have to say." This perplexed me and I thought about it for two years. Finally I determined, no they don't, which is why I'm inclined to keep my ideas and opinions to myself. Just not all of them and not forever. Many may think they would be interested, but experience has shown me they are seldom genuine and sincere, and are only out to prove they're right and I wrong. Again, I won't argue.

People overwhelmingly resist outsiders. They are rarely receptive to alternative points of view that threaten their preconceived ideas. Their resistance is apparently due to the human condition. It's why humanity evolves, if it does at all, at a snail's pace. History provides many examples.

It's why there was an American Revolution, a Constitution, a Civil War, 100 years of Jim Crow, and a civil rights movement with violence before many Americans were finally willing to admit that black people, just like them, are people too. People who look different, act different, or think different, face an uphill battle for recognition and acceptance among mainstream society. That's one of the few truths I'm sure of.

However it's hard to imagine me threatening anybody. I'm a free-thinking individual, and despite unconventional viewpoints, not a revolutionary. Threats and arguments embody hostility, which I want no part of. Also, largely as a result of living with little ego and a lot of humility, it goes against the grain for me to criticize anyone who is not obviously evil. Besides, I never wanted to change the world; I merely wanted to understand it, albeit while wanting the world to be a better place. Frankly, despite thinking about it a great deal throughout my life, I wouldn't know where to begin to make the world better. Except in one way.

What I do know about is the harm that can be done to children when they're young, and how those children, when they become adults, can in turn do more harm to more innocent victims - too often to more young children - throughout their lives. A greater commitment to prevent harm to children, to strike a balance by encouraging them without overly protecting and thereby suffocating them, and starting with infants as soon after birth as possible, I'm positive would make life on this planet better for everyone. That's my motivation to write about me.

It's not in my personal interest to share the story of me. Scrutiny begets attention that can only disrupt and destroy privacy and peace, obtained after many years of struggle to find them. No thank you to fame, fortune, awards or a mega book deal. No amount of money can offset their true costs.

Ironically, and there will be more irony to follow, the story about me isn't even about me. That's not my reason for writing. The story that follows is not self-promotion, which as will be seen is ridiculous. Hopefully a reader will come to understand that I set myself up as a straw man to advance a philosophy, not a biography, that readers can if they so choose use as a mirror to reflect upon their own lives and habits. For that reason, I don't care if readers find fault or disagree. I'm not soliciting commentary. And please no sympathy either, which quite frankly misses the point.

It will also not displease me if no one reads about me. I'm just trying to help others while believing life is always best if there are choices. Nonetheless, in a best-case scenario I will reach two select groups of people. One of them consists of those who suffer as a result of their childhood past, who fight every day to maintain their strength and their sanity. I hope they'll find something useful in my story that will help them to carry on until they too find the peace they deserve.

My story is also essentially a long letter to my descendants and to my ex-wife, the other select group. I hope to help them understand me, my origins, and impacts on them as a result, providing a modicum of long overdue closure with more peace.

One foundational belief I acquired along the way is that life is a precious gift. As a consequence, every newborn child deserves to enjoy a long life here on earth, while they are still here among the living.

PART ONE
In the Beginning

What Was He Thinking?

It wasn't often that I called my father in his advanced years. Still it was enough to know what to expect. Inevitably someone at one of his assisted living facilities would tell me he was outside smoking and to call back in an hour. That always made me wonder. In his time alone, did Father think about why his children were scattered to the wind? Did he search for a unifying theme that would explain everything? Did he assess his life and consider himself a failure?

After he fell asleep with a lit cigarette in his apartment, and started a fire that almost killed him, liabilities wiped out his nest egg. Then he was passed around from one assisted living facility to another. Father was so hard to please. My guess is that he complained a lot and care givers were relieved to transfer him to somewhere else. But that's just conjecture on my part. Certainly life was hard for Father after the fire. It's never easy to go from feeling like a king to being a powerless pawn.

The possibilities for what he was thinking were endless. There was so much negativity under our roof, and our relationship knots were so tangled, none of us understood why. Our pain had such deep roots that every household member had to develop a strategy to endure their personal heartaches.

Although we didn't meet up, many years ago I called my older sister from a truck stop, one town over from where she lived. That's been our only contact since 1983. The first thing we did was agree that we grew up in hell. Then my sister told me her childhood experiences were why she decided to never have children. This saddened me because she would have been a great mother anyway. She just didn't believe in herself. Of course, who would want to risk living through the same nightmare twice.

The following year, in a different part of the country, I called my other sister, also from a truck stop one town over from where she lived, and we also only talked on the phone. It was apparent that neither sister was enthusiastic to hear from me. My younger sister, two years older than myself, somehow became an important nurse at a famous hospital.

A few years before that phone call, my younger sister told me that our grandmother who had died when I was in the service and out in California, died as a result of falling down stairs, and if the quack doctor had diagnosed her correctly she would have been saved. Recently I was handed a copy of the death certificate stating Grandmother's cause of death as lung failure. That was the determination of the quack doctor who we never trusted, the doctor that told all three of us in 1983 that our mother only had three more days to live but then she lived another ten years. That was when we all flew back to New York and met for the last time. I still believe my younger sister was right. Her explanation of water on the brain is consistent with Grandmother's gradual lingering death on the sofa. Nevertheless, before her fall, Grandmother told my sister that she hoped to die in the next five years and she got her wish.

There are two words that best describe our mother. One of them is miserable. The other is martyr, which is what my sisters always called her because she accepted the blame for everything that was wrong. That was her domestic role though it garnered her neither respect nor love. Mother's strategy was to isolate in her room where she smoked and drank her way to an early grave.

Father survived Mother's death by twenty years and estrangement from his children by thirty years. Whatever his thoughts were, he had many years to think about everything. Or about nothing. Just as I have had many years to think about him. However, once the riddles of my past were solved, to the extent it was possible to solve them, I seldom looked back anymore. When I did, Father was not the cause of our dysfunctional household. No. He too was a victim just like the rest of us.

Where the Heart Is

Memories to the start of my life at Esperance, New York remain vivid despite only living there until age seven. Esperance was so small, not even big enough for a traffic light, one could drive right through it on U.S.20 and not even notice it was a town. Esperance was a sleepy place enjoying a peace dividend after a world war. After moving away, it became a symbol of peace that was taken away from me.

The move downstate, that occurred abruptly when I was in second grade, divided childhood in half. With what happened immediately after moving, it made the first half seem better than it actually was. By comparison Esperance gained in stature.

The foremost reason early memories remained etched in my mind though, was because in those first seven years I had a weak sense of self-identity. Without that basic foundation, I felt compelled as a young child, and in much of my adult life, to look backward to gather the strength to go forward. Psychologically, Esperance had me trapped in a labyrinth.

One source of confusion was not particularly troubling but it did make me wonder what impact, if any, it may have had. My mother told me I was a blue baby. That shouldn't have mattered, and it probably didn't, but in conjunction with other factors it was one more piece of the puzzle. If there was relief among household members that I had survived a birth ordeal, I never felt an inkling of that sentiment. Instead mostly what I felt was a mix of indifference and resentment. Everyone in the household was older than myself but there appeared to be no protection or consideration for a vulnerable youngest child.

My mother also told me that I had contracted mumps, whooping cough, chicken pox, and had more than one bout with pneumonia. Could that much illness in a young child, before memory, have a lasting deleterious effect on a developing child's psyche?

For years I asked myself an endless stream of questions as I wrestled with a lack of identity, low self-esteem, and underlying fear. There had to be a cause, or perhaps several root causes. It bears emphasis, however, that it was never the case that I felt sorry for myself. Nor was there ever a desire, or need, to blame others for anything. Rather I was merely stuck in a groove, only wanting to understand myself. The questions either had no answers, or the answers were lost to the sands of time, but the questions continued just the same.

Most people begin life after birth with their mother. This was especially true in the 1950's. Something ended in the relationship with my mother, but I was never able to identify exactly what it was, or evaluate its significance. As far back as I can remember my mother saw me as a burden. She often told me outright in these exact words: "Well, your father wanted a boy." Perhaps she was abused in the past and didn't want any boys. That was one possibility. Or, since she had three miscarriages in addition to my two sisters before me, maybe she resented pressure from my father to try again.

Her feelings toward me could not have been clearer. My deep-rooted fear of humiliation is traceable to our relationship. My mother often humiliated me, not with vindictiveness, but with careless indifference. And she always wanted to be rid of me. For example, she appealed to the local elementary school to make sure they would accept me into kindergarten before age five. Then on the first day of school she persuaded a girl who lived next door to show me where the kindergarten classroom was. A few years later, when I was eight and hospitalized following a bicycle mishap, on the morning of my release a doctor removed the last stitches from my face, leaving unsightly and embarrassing temporary scars. That same morning my mother picked me up from the hospital and drove me directly to fourth grade. It was September and the first day of school. She claimed that she didn't want my perfect attendance to be ruined. But she was already too late and it didn't matter. At the end of the school year my report card showed my absence for one half day.

Whenever people have asked me, "You love your mother, don't you?" I was never able to give an honest answer. Which was, "Not really," because no one could have understood. However, I did not dislike my mother. She did what a mother needs to do for a child. She fulfilled her responsibilities. There was enough food to eat. There were clothes to wear. She applied iodine and put on band-aids when they were necessary. Later in childhood she was a reliable chauffeur. There wasn't any hostility between us. Moreover, although I could never figure out the cause, there was soul-crippling despondency underneath the surface of my mother's personality. It's impossible to dislike someone one feels so sad for.

Enduring my mother, though, always came with a price. Challenges began in early childhood. One day, when I was still too young for school and there were just the two of us, she sent me on an errand to buy unpasteurized milk from a nearby farm. I knew how to get there, through a gully, then a patch of woods, between strands of a barbed wire fence, and across a field. On the way back one of the worst things that has ever happened to me happened. I was a victim of sexual abuse. When I got back, either because it was she who sent me on the errand, or it was me, a boy, she showed no interest in my account or concern for my welfare. Subsequently, while trying to distinguish between negative impacts on my life, the event and my mother's indifference added substantially to the confusion I spent years trying to unravel.

Halfway through adulthood, mentally paralyzed while unable to stop asking myself questions without answers, I was sure that that event and the affectionless relationship with my mother were important, but they were only partial explanations. By themselves they didn't explain alienation inside a family unit, profound neglect, and immobilizing fear.

Although we lived under the same roof in a house of average size, I can't recall a single memory of my grandmother until after we had moved downstate. Likewise my father played almost no role in my upbringing during the early years. After he stopped working for GE in Schenectady, and it was always a mystery to me whether he quit or was fired, my father found a job in Kingston. He lived down there and only came home sporadically on weekends. In dysfunctional families an unfavored child will often form a strong bond with a sibling. That didn't happen with me. I was a youngest child with the status of an outsider.

A child doesn't think in adult terms. It's only in looking back that I realize the extent to which I was neglected was a huge hurdle to overcome. Carol was a mature girl who lived across the road. She often walked over to visit with my sisters. With a sixth sense that told me she was coming, before she knocked on the door I would climb up on a counter. The second she stepped inside, I jumped on her and forced her to catch me. It was a regular routine and a stupid stunt on my part. She was nice enough to tolerate me with merely a sigh of displeasure. It's shameful for me to remember this, but now I know, I wanted assurance from somebody that they would catch me. No one else would have.

After the kindergarten and first grade teachers terrified me, the second-grade teacher, Mrs. Pinto, was a model of kindness and encouragement. She walked up behind me one day and noticed I was still writing with a closed fist. With gentle persuasion that astonished me and overcame my resistance, she convinced me that, yes, I could write while holding a pencil properly just like all the other kids. In every possible way, from knowing how to tie my shoes or how to blow my nose, there was always a gap in knowledge between myself and what other kids already knew.

It's incredibly difficult to admit cowardice, which is why it's rarely done. Was it emotional detachment from a mother, illnesses, sexual abuse, neglect, or something else that robbed me of innate courage? However, just as a big bad alligator never loses fear that is ingrained, when as a baby it is prey to every other creature, I too always had deep-rooted fear without knowing why. Children aren't born that way.

On a spring day in first grade, when warm weather arrived and kids were sent outside to the playground, I got in line for the slide. When it was my turn, I climbed the four steps to the top, looked down, and couldn't move. I had to back down against the grain of kids waiting their turn. That much fear in a young child, if not redressed, can ruin a life before it starts. Years later it was torturous to try to figure out where that fear came from. Without a rudimentary amount of courage it's impossible to achieve anything in an adult world. That's why I had to spend the rest of my life dealing with fear the hard way, teaching myself to take chances only after calculating risks in advance.

The darkest mystery of my past, though, is related to my paternal grandfather. His nebulous image haunted me like a ghost. We lived in his house until he died. I was between age three and four at the time. I later came to believe he had beaten and abused my father, but my only direct memory of him is fleeting and seemingly meaningless.

When I was suicidal and barely hanging onto sanity, I tried endlessly to focus on a faint memory. I was in a crib in an attic-like room over the garage. Someone was whipping me. I was too young for disobedience but not quite old enough to establish a clear memory. By process of elimination, my grandfather was one of two people who could have beaten me in a crib. The other possibility was my mother, perhaps after being pressured to shut the kid up.

That happened in the 1950's when children were more likely than livestock to be beaten on a whim. For unclear reasons, this particular beating seemed to hold significance. Maybe directly, or indirectly, my grandfather was the root of all evil and the cause for the inner fear and submissiveness that I've had to live with. Unfortunately, in regards to my grandfather, none of my soul-searching questions ever produced answers. Ultimately I had to settle for best guesses as substitutes for actual truth.

Nevertheless, despite ominous signs, my start to life in Esperance was not a nightmare. That came afterwards. Unless weakened by severe physical or mental handicaps, and sometimes even then, children like the young of all species are incredibly resilient. I was no different. I was neither despondent nor depressed in Esperance. Figuratively I was a top with a lot of spin but beginning to wobble. Like every other kid, I looked forward to a full life and a chance to make dreams come true.

In the meantime, I had friends to play with next door and within shouting distance just down the road. It was easy for me to walk across the bridge and into the village for Sunday School. My Great Aunt Amy, who always made me feel wanted, often came over from Syracuse to visit. Finally I had a nice second grade teacher with whom I felt comfortable. What I had in Esperance in those first seven years was a place to belong, a modicum of stability, and just enough belief in myself to feel like a real person with a real life.

After leaving Esperance, with no choice in the matter, I went without these essential elements for almost sixty years.

Shadow Boxing

Our house in Esperance, New York was probably paid for and owned by my grandfather. I was too young to know important details. Little effort was made to inform me. I lived in the house along with my grandfather until he died, my grandmother, father, mother, and two older sisters.

Only one adult showed genuine interest in me. Great Aunt Amy, my grandmother's sister, didn't live with us but she often came to visit. Her husband had died and they were childless. That may explain her interest in me. However, I also believe she saw how I was neglected, and out of a sense of responsibility and compassion tried to steer me in a better direction. Certainly she was the only adult I trusted to confide in.

The only recallable memory I have of my grandfather is vague. One warm sunny day he took me for a walk and showed me a chestnut tree on the other side of the road. Strangely, that's it. What I remember with more clarity, though, is that after he died no one said anything to me. But I noticed he was missing. The next time Aunt Amy came to visit I asked her where my grandfather was. She took me by the hand, led me behind the stairwell, pointed to a grate on the floor, and before walking away said, he's down there. I was a three-year-old toddler and this confused me. So, I got down on my hands and knees and tried to see him through the grating. It took a few more years for Aunt Amy's hidden message to sink in.

She was telling me my grandfather was burning in the furnace of hell. In time I came to believe she was probably right.

My father was an alcoholic. After we had moved downstate and into a different dwelling, several times a week he stopped after work at the house of his coworker and drinking buddy. It was common for him to arrive home in mid evening in a mood best described as jolly drunk. My grandmother, always sensitive to his feelings, would practically push me out the door saying, go meet your father. I'm ashamed to say I was happy to see him in that mood. Jolly drunk meant he was neither demanding or threatening.

Sometimes on Friday nights my father continued drinking after he got home. If he did, his moods went through stages. If he drank whiskey, which fortunately he did infrequently, he was unpredictable and dangerous. He didn't take a belt to his children but he would lose all sense of himself and forget where he was. All objects within his reach, including heavy pieces of furniture, were potential missiles. One time he grabbed a glass plate and smashed it on my grandmother's head. I watched as blood cascaded down the side of her face.

There were rare instances, though, when my father drank beyond the anger stage and regressed in his mind to being a child again. That's when I saw him crying like a baby as he begged his father to stop beating him. Knowing there had to be a cause and effect, I understood at an early age why my father was an alcoholic. I doubt he ever knew why himself. Ironically he harbored resentment, and apparently buried anger towards his mother, but he never had a bad word to say about his father. I believed his state of denial was huge.

My grandfather was born in Fine, New York, far upstate in the North Country. The tiny town is the epitome of the expression out in the sticks. The rural setting, it seems, was insufficient for his larger aspirations. My grandfather was a WW1 veteran. My father once told me he tried to reenlist for WW2 but was turned away for being too old. He made his living, or the bulk of his money as an oil driller in Texas and Mexico, before buying a chicken farm. Grandfather might be burning in hell as Aunt Amy suggested, but he knew what it meant to work like a dog and sweat like a pig here on earth. He was a man in a man's world when men were held to different standards.

All of my information about my grandfather is second hand. I am not qualified to judge him. There was no recourse but to figure him out, as best I could, from scattered pieces of evidence. After Grandfather died other members of the household seldom mentioned him. That was one clue. He continued to exist only as a shadow cast over much that went on later.

By contrast, either by force, coercion, or despite my reluctance, an enormous amount of my childhood was spent in the company of my father. What was actually a survival tactic, I was able to scrutinize and analyze my father. I didn't doubt that my grandfather had beaten my father, thereby radically altering the course of his life. However, if my theory is right, and I believe that it is, there is another dimension to the relationship between the two of them.

Nothing ever justifies child abuse. It should never be swept under the rug the way it was so often in the past. In most instances of violence, though, there are important factors worth noting beyond a determination of right and wrong. Compelled to unearth important impacts on my own life, the relationship between my grandfather and my father, one of whom was dead and the other fraught with contradictions, was crucial for me to understand.

Doing the math, when Father was born his mother and father were in their thirties, an age in which parents are usually thrilled to have a child. His parents were middle class and had disposable income, even in the Great Depression. They never had more children making my father an only child. Is it possible for a child to be both physically abused and at the same time spoiled? I believe it is. Observing my father extensively and exercising some deductive reasoning, his demanding hard-to-please nature was consistent with a child who had no competition from siblings, one whose parents probably loved him, even as his father often beat him.

How then, does a child rationalize a father that loves him, spoils him, but also beats him, other than to bury the pain and confusion within himself? That can explain a huge state of denial, becoming an alcoholic, and why my father was an incredibly conflicted man.

Once in passing, my father mentioned that his grandfather had beaten him. He did not beat me, so maybe he did want to break the chain, but he took his frustrations out on me in other ways. My father didn't hesitate to swear at me in crass language. He engaged in mind games and tricks designed to elevate himself and make me out to be a fool. He sometimes humiliated me in drastic ways, and he was capable of unspeakable acts. On the other hand most of the time my father was warm, friendly, helpful, and on occasion surprisingly thoughtful. And he was a master at self-deprecating humor. But for being unpredictable, and at times intolerable, I always thought my father's good traits outweighed the bad. I respected him too, though no doubt he never knew this.

My father struggled with loneliness. More often than not I was his designated companion, although I never wanted to be near him. We had an ongoing tug of war. I did what was necessary to satisfy him, then ran like the devil away from him as soon as freedom was granted. This in turn established a pattern and set me up for a life on the run. Perpetual motion equaled freedom. Looking back, I believe my father was a very good man, trapped by his own personal history, which was probably, or may have been, hidden even to himself.

The specter of my grandfather posed an entirely different set of problems. What he may have done to me personally factored into the equation, but he seemed to mean even more than that. The metaphoric picture of him that sticks in my mind is of someone who rolled a bowling ball through time causing destruction and dysfunction in future generations. That's not a conclusion. It's only guesswork.

Half a lifetime ago, synonymous with climbing out of suicidal depression, I stopped thinking about my grandfather. I had reached a point, finally, where I concluded there are childhood mysteries that are unknowable. If only the journey to reach that point hadn't been so convoluted and gut wrenching.

Glimmer of Hope

It's impossible for me to imagine how my life would have turned out if it wasn't for my Great Aunt Amy. One parent repeatedly let me know I was a burden to her. The other parent wanted me to share his exact name, to like what he liked, and in essence to be a carbon copy of himself. That was not the same thing as wanting me. Emotional detachment from parents, grandparents, and sisters, began early. I was rudderless when Aunt Amy stepped in to fill a void.

Her contributions to my development were numerous and immeasurable. She gave me encouragement that was sorely lacking. She taught me to read, which thanks to her I could do quite well by age four. Aunt Amy convinced me to practice good manners, not to impress her, but for the rest of my life because it would earn me more respect. I would not have seen the connection otherwise. She gave me the game *Sorry* that we played when she came to visit. It was a game two people, one old and one young, could play together in a relaxed atmosphere; she thereby gave me companionship and my only good adult relationship. For my fifth birthday, Aunt Amy gave me a green dump truck that was so big and nice, I couldn't believe it was mine. To somebody, I mattered.

After the move downstate Aunt Amy gave me a subscription to *Life* magazine. The wisdom behind this gift was profound. *Life* magazine was famous for its amazing photography.

With pictures alone the magazine could tell subscribers about the Cold War, cutting-edge science, the civil rights movement, assassinations, Vietnam, and the race to the moon. So much happened in the 1960's and I had a front row seat to it all. How does one begin to calculate the value of that gift, as I, a young impressionable and vastly ignorant child, was stimulated to think about the bigger themes of life on this planet? And in a time of upheaval?

Two years later, when I became interested in sports, Aunt Amy added a subscription to *Sports Illustrated* magazine. She also gave me my first bicycle, that I relied on and used constantly to escape a dreadful domestic situation. In addition to everything else, Aunt Amy gave me forward momentum and the means to overcome mental difficulties with physical effort.

After teaching myself how to ride the bicycle she gave me, I used it to venture into the Great Creek Locks Forest, an intimidating tree-lined hamlet with a long row of houses down the road. That's how I managed to establish a friendship with John, and a foothold for further penetrations into the wilderness.

John was a highly intelligent, confident and sensitive kid. For me, deficient in those qualities, he greatly aided my growth and maturity. For example, as I was riding to see him once, in front of Carlos' house I used my front tire to run over a caterpillar. When I proudly told John about it, instead of being impressed, he shamed me. He forced me to think twice about what I had done. I never again looked at nature the same way, and never again without respect.

When John was angered, however, he had a habit of expressing his emotions in a string of expletives that was shocking to young ears. He would say "god damned fucking piece of shit." It didn't bother me. They were just words after all. Despite the trust I placed in her, Aunt Amy wasn't perfect. When I told her about John's words, in code, she told me to stay away from that boy. For once, Aunt

Amy was wrong, and I knew it. Still, an important lesson lurked between her perspective, John's value to me, and my own instincts. Sometimes it's necessary to ignore the best advice from the best sources.

As sisters, Great Aunt Amy and my grandmother were extremely close. They wanted to spend their final years together. That's why Aunt Amy came to live with us after we moved. Almost as soon as she arrived, though, she left, saying she just couldn't take it, meaning with us and how we lived. She returned to Syracuse to live with her much younger sister, Great Aunt Bert. It was said that I had met Aunt Bert as a baby but she was a stranger to me.

Aunt Amy continued to visit from time to time but the trip on the bus was longer and less convenient. She often wrote letters to my grandmother, and in every letter she told Grandmother to tell me, to write her a letter. Grandmother reminded me countless times. It wasn't that I didn't want to write. I was young, full of energy, disinclined to sit still, and would spend as much time as possible out on the streets until after dark. Nevertheless, one evening I did sit down and I wrote Aunt Amy a long and sincere letter.

It wasn't long after the letter was mailed that we got a strange unexpected phone call from Aunt Bert. Stranger still, she wanted to speak to me. When we were connected, Aunt Bert told me that Aunt Amy had taken ill and died at the hospital. Aunt Bert wanted to let me know Aunt Amy died while holding my letter to her in her hand, which she kept reading over and over, and she wanted to let me know my letter gave Aunt Amy peace of mind in her final moments.

As an old man looking back, I'm ashamed that I didn't write her more often. It's unfathomable what my feelings would be today if I didn't write that one letter, or if it didn't reach her in time. For everything Aunt Amy did for me, I gave back scant and insufficient compensation.

When Aunt Amy took it upon herself, essentially to come to my rescue, she was not seeking personal credit. Good parents, conscientious adults, exceptional teachers, don't make sacrifices for their own interests but because in addition to their support of individual children they are serving a greater good. And if they are self-serving and not sincere, astute children, almost always smarter than adults realize, or are willing to acknowledge, see right through them. I was fortunate in the way Aunt Amy encouraged me without trying to smother me. She didn't try to transform me into a different person in her own image; she encouraged me to be a better version of myself.

If an adult such as Great Aunt Amy does succeed in steering a lost child onto a better life course, the good that is accomplished is bound to extend further than the individual child. However an adult treats a child is how they are ultimately treating that child's future children, and who knows how far through posterity.

All of this said, Aunt Amy's motivation was pure and not selfish, but it doesn't hurt for a child who benefits from largesse to provide positive feedback. And in some cases that feedback can do a world of good.

Worse Than Hell

March 27, 1964 was the day I was plucked from my place of origin and transplanted in another location. Everyone, mother, father, sisters, grandmother, two dogs, and myself, were piled into a car and a rental van Beverly Hillbillies-style, as we moved to another small town downstate called Rosendale. I was tugged into the van and placed next to Father at the steering wheel. It was a journey that lasted years and years. The date, March 27, 1964 was always easy for me to remember. That was the day an earthquake rearranged the topography of Alaska. And it was the day I personally became collateral damage.

The domicile in Esperance was a house. What we moved into didn't merit that designation. It was more appropriate to call it the abode. There was a front door and a door to the cellar, but if anyone lived there before us they didn't care much for doors. When we arrived, my younger sister and I ran inside and found a phone attached to a wall. Unlike the phone in Esperance, when you picked up the handle and heard, "Number please," the phone had a dial to spin. It was the only amenity and the only change that qualified as an improvement.

There was no running water. Yet. Father said he had to do some work and we would have to go without running water for a while. As always I was too young to know the details and no one made an effort to inform me as to what was going on.

The same as in Esperance, my room was a closet without a door, with access only by walking through my parents' bedroom. Their bedroom didn't have a door either. In lieu of a door, at the top of the stairs next to our parents' bedroom, a curtain was added to my sisters' shared bedroom. That at least gave them a pretext of privacy. My excuse for a bedroom, above the kitchen, had an open vent in the floor putting me on call for services on demand. All the rooms, upstairs and down, were tiny and bunched together in side-by-side mouse traps.

The abode was not comfortable, but throughout my life the comfort I sought was always of the mind unrelated to material values. I could have lived with conditions inside the abode. I was not able to live with what happened outside the abode.

On the first day of school, as soon as the door opened to my new second grade classroom, the teacher looked at me like I was something a cat dragged in. No sooner had I sat down when she said to a girl, take him to the back of the room and see if he can read anything. She was clearly disappointed when the girl had to tell her, I read better than she did.

It wasn't long after that, the class was given an arithmetic task in our workbooks. I only did two of the five addition problems because the instructions literally said to do any two of them. Apparently she didn't want us to pay attention to instructions. When the teacher walked up behind me, saw my workbook and accused me of laziness, I thought she was going to punish me. Self-preservation caused me to point to the instructions as, while shaking with fear, I loudly pled my case. She let me off the hook that time and said, in an angry voice, "Just make sure you do the others."

Years later one of my classmates, a great friend through twelfth grade and then again in junior college, told me he liked this teacher. All the kids seemed to like her. Later in life, in one of the rare occasions when a therapist said something relevant to me, when I told her about this teacher she said I was her scapegoat. That was true, of course. Still, I was never able to process or to understand how an adult, and a teacher, could hate me that much at age seven even if I did look like a sewer rat.

Many children have suffered horrendous abuse and endured worse hardships than myself. All my life it has infuriated me to read about them. If I hadn't already been lacking in self-identity and self-esteem, and therefore ill equipped to handle the teacher, her impact on me wouldn't have been so debilitating. For three months during which I could not escape her wrath, I felt only terror in her presence. I had no sense of security. There was nothing and no one to hold on to. No one to hear me if I screamed. I was alone in my misery. Getting on the school bus in the morning was like going off to hell. Looking back, the best I can describe my mental state at the time is to say it felt like my brain seized up.

Inside the classroom, the teacher threatened me. She told me, in front of the class, that if I didn't get my mother to clean me up she was going to take me over to the sink on the side of the room and give me a bath herself. In hindsight, it would have been better if she had actually done it once and gotten it over with. Her repeated threats increased my humiliation, and my terror, incrementally. What was worse, though, were the messages she was sending to the other kids. She encouraged them to disdain me the same as she did.

Outside the classroom, when spring arrived and we were sent out to the playground for recess, boys attacked me. Always the same five boys. They ganged up, punched, kicked, tripped, and flipped me over their backs with impunity. The teacher often watched as she stood by the swings. Even after I was on the ground she wouldn't intervene. Nor would she allow me safety.

When class was let out for recess, as the other kids ran off to play, I tried to get away with holding back; I sat on the ramp outside the door that led to the playground. As soon as she saw me she walked back, grabbed me, dragged me to the playground, then resumed her post by the swings. That was until one day, as we were let out and I sat on the ramp, a male teacher happened to be standing behind me. When the teacher came back to grab me he spoke up for me. He said to her, let him sit there if that's what he wants. Perhaps he shamed her. After that I stayed sitting on the ramp every day for recess. By then the school year was almost over, though, so it didn't matter anymore.

The damage was already done. The ordeal was more than my immaturity and weakened mental state could endure. On the first day, I stepped into the teacher's classroom as one person. On the last day, when the school year ended, I left her classroom as somebody else.

Starting Over

My younger sister introduced me to religion. I was four when she took me with her as we walked over the bridge and into the village for Sunday School. Our parents never influenced us one way or another. I genuinely liked Sunday School. The adults at the church were pleasant and made me feel welcome. My sister didn't always attend. After her introduction, I sometimes went by myself.

Additional exposure to religion came in the second grade. Kids at Duanesburg Elementary were allowed to leave school early in the afternoon for Religious Instruction. It was 1963 and women were permitted to pick us up in their cars and take us to a house in Delanson, for what amounted to bible studies. I asked my mother to sign a permission slip so I could go too. Halfway through second grade, I was both curious about and amenable to religion.

After being uprooted and transplanted downstate, and assigned to a teacher who hated me for reasons I couldn't understand, I was an Atheist. Before moving, my mental faculties were already compromised. I had been skating on thinner ice than what is healthy for a young child. After moving, every single day I was petrified with fear to attend school. I had no way to release the tension that built up. Something inside me broke. I stopped believing in adults, in myself, in life, and I stopped believing in god too.

After the school year ended, I often went down to the creek to sit by the water. It was the best place to be alone. A transformation was taking hold within me. I thought a lot about the people I knew, their relationships, about my parents, about a teacher who hated me, and I thought about god and religion. A question that had never crossed my mind, but which I then couldn't stop thinking about, was whether god in fact existed. If he did, where was he?

Feeling as low as it's possible for a seven-year-old boy to feel, trapped in desperate solitude, I tried again and again to answer that question. The only way the existence of god made sense was if god was testing me personally. That test of faith was mentioned at both Sunday School and at Religious Instruction. But I couldn't make myself believe that god had singled me out for such a test. That would have made me special in some way, when every indication was the opposite.

Once doubt crept into my thoughts, religious claims became hurdles I couldn't get over. That a god could always hear you, and how could he hear everyone at the same time?, that god was perfect, always existed, and that god loved everyone, me included, argued against his existence. By the end of summer I emerged from the creek a seven-year-old Atheist. It wasn't something I set out to be, or wanted to be. Struggling to find meaning in life, and in myself, I merely wanted to understand my place in the world. I no longer trusted any adults, religious or otherwise, to know what they were talking about. All burdens of proof had shifted.

The transformation within me, I believe now, was more than psychological. Although my theories are those of an amateur they were derived after many years of personal painstaking analysis. It's known that very young children, usually infants or toddlers, assume alternate personalities in response to stress or abuse that is too much to handle. The brain of a seven-year-old is still developing so that could have happened to me. Or, maybe, I suffered a nervous breakdown. A third possibility is that after the second-grade school year ended, with a chance finally to release built up stress, I suffered from post-traumatic stress. Stress that was never diagnosed, treated or remedied.

All of the above are clinical terms for clinical explanations. What happened to me might have been any one of them, a combination, or something else entirely. The prevailing theory that I ultimately developed is that brain waves inside my head were permanently altered. Among other changes, altered brain waves can explain a near total loss of external emotions and a compensatory reliance on the intellectual functions of the brain. Intelligence is innate, a different quality, that would stay the same. Altered brain waves might also explain a fractured facial appearance, and why throughout my life gay men have come on to me obsessively thinking that I was gay too. They are probably also why therapists were never able to tell me something I didn't already know, analyze, and consider.

In the early 1960's, no doubt more so in rural settings, there was not much emphasis on the mental health of young children. No one in my domestic unit questioned my state of mind. That meant it was incumbent on me to adapt, by myself, if I could.

Whether I even wanted to continue living was doubtful. I wasn't exactly suicidal. Looking back, though, it's clear that to my troubled soul at the time dying was no worse than living.

To my relief, there was no more bullying from boys or problems from a teacher after starting third grade. This may have stemmed from my outward demeanor that was obviously not that of a healthy boy. Cruelty tends to stop after a targeted victim stops resisting and I had already given up all hope. The previous second grade teacher was no longer there. She must have quit. I on the other hand was among the walking wounded.

As summer turned towards fall and raced towards winter, as it used to happen in upstate New York shortly after Labor Day, before anyone had heard of global warming, I neglected, refused, didn't bother to wear jackets or any protective clothing. My guess, in hindsight, is that I was so numb on the inside that any feeling at all was welcome, even if it brought on death. By December, with a fever of 106, adults were forced to send me to the hospital with pneumonia.

Eight months later, I was a dare devil. With my bike at the top of a steep hill, the equivalent of a mountain downgrade with a winding curve, as steep as a set of stairs, I started out pedaling down as fast as I could make the bike go. I lost control coming out of the curve, rolled over an embankment, smashed my head, and lost consciousness. A justice of the peace who lived at the bottom of the hill found me and drove me to the abode. I never talked to the man, can't say why he did that, or how he knew where we lived.

Someone told me later that my older sister answered the door, and that after seeing me she immediately threw up. I was so knocked out that only two direct memories of the aftermath remain. On the way to the hospital, somehow, I noticed my father passing another car despite a double yellow line, making me think he must have cared about me a little bit. My next memory is at the hospital. Probably because I had lost too much blood, masked people held me down as doctors stitched up my face without anesthesia.

Neither hospitalization was a suicide attempt. The common denominator in both of them, I believe, was my willingness to flirt with death because there was nothing to lose. However, it was during this time that a suicidal seed was planted inside me. Thereafter and throughout much of my adulthood, suicide was my escape plan, my fallback option, my trusty companion, a condition like an addiction that had to be managed. Many years later, after a long period of dormancy, the seed grew and broke the surface.

Between age seven and a half, and nine, is an unusual part of my past. More than at any other time my memories for that period are murky. Many changes, however, occurred then that are indicative of a time of transition and transformation. For example, it was shortly after second grade that I felt sorrow towards my parents. Even though they were older, my sisters didn't see, but I did, that our parents were alcoholics and chain smokers because they were addicted, which had to have had root causes.

As a result of second grade trauma, there are child-like traits manifested both on the surface, and into the depths of my personality. They include indecisiveness, naivety, relating to animals better than people, avoidance of hostility, a tendency to submit to authority - until realizing it's intolerable. I often see others, complete strangers and those who have known me for a long time, quickly pick up on these qualities.

On the other hand, below the surface where people can't see, lurks an analytical mind with a compulsion for intellectual stimulation that substitutes for human relationships. It was childhood trauma, I'm sure, that funneled me towards a life of independence, leading me, the older I get, to gravitate to the lifestyle of a recluse, due to distrust and discomfort around people; it's not a matter of liking them or not.

The passage of time always distorts perceptions. But there is one lingering truth to which I'm absolutely sure. After second grade, and the trauma it caused me, I was no longer the same me.

Like Father Not Like Son

Although he was easily unhinged my father was not an abuser, at least seldom overtly. It's more accurate to say he was manipulative and a master of exploitation. It was at the age of eight, after two hospitalizations, that I approached my father with an aim of being helpful to him. I offered to hand him tools as he worked and to do clean up tasks after one of his projects was finished. Hindsight tells me this was foolishness, because with my father, in for an inch meant in for a mile. But I'm able to understand now what I was thinking then. I was so desperate for crumbs of self-worth, there wasn't anything I wouldn't have done to acquire them.

Typical for men of his era, my father didn't pay attention to small children. Our paths seldom crossed before moving downstate. Afterwards, we didn't develop a normal father and son relationship, and it wasn't a love-hate relationship. Oil and water don't mix. We didn't either. Yet, whether it was due to circumstances or matters beyond my control, we spent countless hours of my childhood alongside one another.

It's incalculable how often I rode with my father in his pickup truck with the home-made camper, to get hay or oats for my sister's horse, parts from a junkyard, or something from a lumberyard.

He had a passion for automobiles and bought a lot of wrecks from an Honest John used car dealer. They broke down. He fixed them. Then when he was bored, he would trade them back in and get another. He also had big plans for our abode, even though they were exercises in futility. Real improvement never crept into the imagination of anyone else.

My father and I talked a lot but we didn't communicate directly. Our dialogue was in code with our respective vulnerabilities off limits. And we did a kind of dance whereby he demanded, when I was very young, requested, as I got older, and later tried to manipulate me into assisting him on one of his (in my opinion useless) projects. Eventually, I learned how to go along with his plans only after we hammered out an unwritten contract; I agreed to help him after extracting favors, usually in the form of a ride to somewhere which meant unrestricted freedom after the job was done.

If anyone could have turned the abode around and made it a livable dwelling that person was my father. He was a former Eagle Boy Scout who, I surmise, earned every merit badge, and he mastered many skills. He had no need for auto mechanics, masons, carpenters, electricians or plumbers. Father could pitch a tent in the wind, tie a fly on a fishing pole, discuss guns and ammo with experts, cane a chair, and he knew the difference between sham antiques and those that were valuable. He affixed an antenna on the roof and wired it to a rotor, so we could turn a dial and bring in TV reception on two channels, sometimes three in good weather. If Father was still around today, I would bet on him to out geek the geeks. He achieved small successes but he never made significant progress, and he was capable of so much more. My father was held back by his inner demons, which is why he drank too much and lacked the motivation to get out of bed in the morning.

His demons were always a factor in our relationship. When I was very young, too young to walk home, he sometimes took me on an errand, stopped somewhere along the way, then forgot about me out in the car for hours. He might agree to pick me up from a Little League game, then show up two hours after the game was over. His profanity, depending on his mood, was often offensive. He engaged in tricks and mind games designed to get under my skin. For example, he would scream and blame me because a tool was missing. After 15 minutes of demonstrative phony outrage, he would find the tool in his back pocket. If we had a different kind of relationship his tricks might have been funny. Instead, he only eroded trust which is a dangerous practice for an adult with a child.

Father never stepped out of his vaunted overseer's role. When we worked on one of his projects, he basically wanted a servant to do the grunge work he didn't want to do, often as he stepped inside for a cup of coffee and came back out when the hard part was done. He might give me a ride to a Little League game but he never stopped to watch me play; of course, none of the other abode members ever watched me play either. When I was old enough to do hard labor, but too young to outright refuse, my father forced me to surrender two summer vacations, and baseball aspirations, to help him build a barn for my sister's horse. Then when the barn was built, taking care of the horse became my responsibility too.

It wasn't just myself that Father unnerved. Inside the abode he was a volcano prone to eruptions. I often felt obligated to be a peacemaker. I didn't know it then but now I know why. As the youngest abode member, I was the one at greatest risk if the domestic arrangement fell apart. He also started feuds with neighbors that I felt compelled to smooth over.

There were many reasons for me to avoid being around my father. On the other hand, most of the time he was soft-spoken, thoughtful, even polite. He was witty and loved humor, and wasn't too proud to invoke self-deprecating humor. He was a Samaritan who often stopped to help people whose cars broke down, or if they were stuck in snow banks, as only he could. When one neighbor ran over another neighbor's dog, Father buried it for the owner. He was warm hearted towards animals and never flinched at paying vet bills. After I recovered from injuries following a bike accident, my father bought me a new and better bike that served as my car for the rest of my childhood. My father got along with, and respected, my friends and the friends of my sisters, no matter who they were or what they were like.

He was not a shy man. He wasn't especially sociable but he wasn't anti-social either. By dint of personality my father was withdrawn, but he could comport himself with poise in any social situation. And it's hard to fault him for wanting control in his own home. Away from the abode he was the poster boy for the Little Guy. At his job, for instance, despite his respectable clerical position for the New York State Department of Transportation, his personal office was a corner cubbyhole out in the garage with the trucks and the manual laborers.

Due to his unpredictability, and the nearly but not always tension between us, my only recourse was to learn how to negotiate with my father, and to make deals with him. Whatever contributions I made were given with ulterior motives. I was never interested in his tasks. In fact, what my father liked, I learned to hate. He was a terrible teacher. I was a terrible pupil. That's why in 8th grade I nearly did the unthinkable. I failed shop. Initially anyway. It wasn't rebellion as such. I just didn't care. However, Mr. K., the head of all three shops, plastics, metals, and wood, added points to my grade to cover up my shameful failure. Whatever. I didn't argue.

For my 13th birthday, Father gave me a 20-gauge shotgun. Nothing illustrated our respective differences more, as well as what he wanted from a son. No one brought it up but other abode members must have known that his arsenal, drinking, and susceptibility to anger-driven rages was an unhealthy mix. I grew up hating firearms and never wanted to own one. I never once shot with the shotgun he gave me. Yet it saddens me to think back on how much that must have hurt my father's feelings. He was never going to have the son he wanted. He got me instead.

Father wasn't philosophical by nature but I always was. I'm an unapologetic animal rights advocate, and at the same time remain an ardent supporter of the 2nd Amendment, believing it's the most important check on government power, that all the rights on paper mean nothing without the means to defend them, that people have the right to defend themselves against evil.

As long as we didn't violate each other's vulnerabilities, my father and I could discuss controversial subjects. He was a little-guy conservative who saw a lot of himself in the television character Archie Bunker. By his crass language an outsider might think he was a racist and a bigot, but he actually wasn't. Underneath his veneer my father was a fair-minded man who didn't grow up around different kinds of people. As he aged, the more time he spent around different types, if they were little people like himself, the more he learned to like them. So, when I was a senior in high school and I told him I smoked pot, he admitted to trying marijuana; with a black guy who was his new after work drinking buddy. His last friend on earth was a black woman who picked him up at his assisted living facility, and drove him around to do his shopping and to buy his cigarettes. My father evolved along with the times he lived in.

The Department of Transportation yard was located just down the hill from the junior high school. In November 1968, I walked down after intramural football practice to catch a ride back to the abode. When I met my father, I had never seen him in a better mood. It was because the early indications were Richard Nixon won the election and would be the next president. It was a rare triumph for the Little Guy. A few years later, after Nixon was forced to resign, I never again mentioned Nixon's name to my father. I knew how much it hurt and how vulnerable he was. Watergate ended my father's hopes for a better life.

Politically, like everything else, we were polar opposites. He was conservative. I was progressive. Sometimes he made off the cuff remarks on a subject in the news, and I challenged him. At least he was informed thanks to his subscription to *U.S. News and World Reports*, back when it was a prop for conservatives. I was ignorant. That meant I had to talk louder and cheat like a bastard, which ignited him. What started with sparks often led to full-fledged arguments. Then Grandmother would rush in from the kitchen and tell us to stop fighting, and we would tell her we were just discussing. Then as soon as she turned her back we got heated up again.

Believing deep down that I was always more right than he was, even if I couldn't prove it at the time, our arguments, no doubt, contributed to my pursuit of a political science degree and later law school. But life is full of contradictions. In a conversation I had with him shortly before he died, my father told me he was going to vote for democrat Andrew Cuomo for governor of New York. That really made me scratch my head and wonder: What was he thinking?

Maybe he thought he owed me something for my labor. After the barn was built for my sister's horse, he proposed a father and son fishing trip up to the Adirondacks. I didn't want to go. My escape plan was to fail 9th grade science forcing me to go to summer school instead. But then, my best friend told me, that when he went to get his grade, the science teacher told him that he added just enough points to my final exam to allow me to pass. Once again, a well-meaning teacher was only trying to help. After that, I was figuratively and literally on the hook.

The trip went okay. I caught fish. He didn't. However, before going and during the planning stage, I suggested a diversion to Montreal to see a baseball game, since it wasn't far from the campground. He must have felt guilty. When we got back he countered with a new proposal. He suggested going down to New York City to see a game. It must have been the lesser of evils.

He had me compose a letter requesting box seats for a game at Shea Stadium. Totally ignorant, as always, I wondered why we wanted to sit in a box. A short time later, tickets arrived in the mail along with a note that said they were the best seats available. That is how we ended up with nose bleed seats for a double header between the Mets and the Pirates in late September. We didn't anticipate a late season pennant race and the Pirates' many Hispanic fans in New York City. When we got to the game, the seats were so high up we only saw the players in miniature. Every ten minutes, a jet flew over us and the noise made us cup our ears. Still, Father was considerate enough to let me bring my friend John with us, and we had a thrill. I will always remember watching Roberto Clemente make one of his great sliding catches. That was one time, I have to admit, Father met me half way.

On the other hand, nothing was ever going to earn me respect from my father. As a young child, it was wolf whistles to get my attention. If anything went wrong on one of his projects, it was always my fault. Never his. One afternoon in my senior year of high school, Father walked out of the abode and met me in the driveway. Reflecting back, I still can't imagine what he was thinking. He told me he'd spent a lot of money helping my older sister get through college, and a lot of money on my younger sister's horse. Now, he said, there was nothing left for me. Was he rejecting me personally? Was he expressing his belief that boys needed to fend for themselves? He didn't know it yet but by then it didn't matter anyway. I knew the score. I was already talking with military recruiters.

The only decent feedback I ever received from him came as a backhand compliment after my mother died. He acknowledged that I'd been on my own a long time. Yes, I wanted to tell him, but didn't, since the age of 17.

Nevertheless, one must give credit where credit is due. Despite my efforts to keep a distance between us, at times Father was extraordinarily helpful. For three years, from ages 13 to 16, I worked at the local pharmacy on Sunday mornings. When I'd accumulated $450, I was ready to buy a car. Father insisted on helping me.

He vetoed the first three cars we looked at in response to ads in the paper. At first I thought he just didn't want me to have a car and was trying to stop me. But then we saw a car at a dealership in Kerhonkson and he said, "Get this one." He also had me wait outside, I'm sure, as he went inside and negotiated down the price. The 1964 Plymouth Valiant wasn't pretty but it had low mileage and ran like a top.

Occasionally, when he was in the right mood, Father could be a fountain of wisdom. For example, he told me, "Whenever you buy an expensive item, make sure you consider three possibilities before you part with your money." And, he said, "Never use your personal vehicle for an employer because it's a bad deal. They'll pay you gas money but in two years you will have a beat-up car and need to buy another." He was right about that too. There are many examples of his sage advice that have served me well over the years.

Beginning with military service, I needed separation from my parents, and afterwards estrangement from them. But I didn't blame them for anything, and I did not want them to feel guilty. So I maintained contact, mainly by calling them two or three times a year. I continued to call my father in the same way after my mother died. The phone calls continued after he sold the abode and moved to another town. Then he moved into a city apartment where he started the fire that drove him into the clutches of assisted living facilities.

Several times I called their offices only to be told he was transferred again. Each time, someone gave me a phone number, I wrote it down, and then reestablished contact by tracking him down at a new place. It often made me wonder why I bothered. He never initiated contact with me, or my child, his grandchild, and he never would have. However, I knew it bothered him to end up alone and that under his hard exterior he was a sad man.

At the beginning of every phone call with my father, he started by asking, "Have you heard anything from your sisters?" That was a vulnerability, so I always had to deflect the question. There was no way to tell him honestly that I was estranged from my sisters, never heard from them, and didn't expect to ever hear from them again.

The last time I called my father was in June of 2012. As always, he was outside smoking and I had to call back in an hour. When I did, and someone at the assisted living facility brought him to the phone, he launched into one of his old mind game tricks with an intent to belittle me. I don't know why it happened on this particular occasion, other than I was already well into my 50's. I suppose it was one insult too many. I hung up the phone in disgust. Eventually, I would have called him again, but for the longest time I couldn't motivate myself to pick up the phone and place the call. But time has its own agenda.

In September of the following year, I was sitting outside my Florida apartment reading a book and watching wildlife at the pond, my normal off duty pastime. I heard someone clearing their throat behind me. I turned around and saw a Hillsborough County Deputy. He asked who I was. I then said, "Let me guess, my father died?" He didn't need to say anything. As I stood up to walk inside, he put his hand on my shoulder to comfort me, no doubt thinking I was sad. But sadness is not what I felt.

My initial feeling was guilt for going more than a year without calling him. Guilt sticks to me like cat hair to Velcro. However, the guilt didn't last long. Within a week or two the guilt had dissipated and it was replaced by a realization. If you add up all the data on both sides of the ledger, which is an incredible amount of data, in the final analysis my father and I broke even. He was a fair-minded man. I'm sure he would agree.

Reaching First Base

Before moving into a different childhood home, I was a youngest child in a domestic arrangement that resembled a family, feeling like an outsider and lacking identity. After moving, and subjected to life changing trauma, my low self-esteem along with a lack of identity worsened. I had no sense of self-worth. It's not an exaggeration to say I was a dying child clinging to life. I was desperate for something, anything, to hold on to.

At our abode I fell in, or was drawn in, to the servile role of a gofer, doing favors and fetching objects for others when they didn't want to get up and get them themselves, and always on call due to an open vent, the hole in the floor of what sufficed as my bedroom over the kitchen. If I was ever going to find an identity, or acquire a shred of self-worth, it had to happen away from the death trap at the abode.

It's amazing how Great Aunt Amy intuitively knew I needed a bicycle, and gave me one without me even asking. It wasn't a new bike but as it turned out it was a great gift. A bicycle was a tool at my disposal and potentially a means of escape. To make use of her gift, though, I had to solve a few problems first. One of which was, I didn't know how to ride a bike. Also, although fearful and a nervous wreck at the abode, I was just as nervous and equally afraid to venture out into the outside world.

Because the bike Aunt Amy gave me was a boy's bike, it had a bar between the handlebars and the seat. I could pedal and make the bike go forward all right, but the bike was a size too big for me. Stopping was torture. Every time I stopped, I crushed my balls on that bar so hard, I started to question whether Aunt Amy loved me or not. Eventually, however, with raw determination I taught myself to slow down, lean left, and use the bottom of my sneaker for a brake pad.

The abode was advantageously located at the terminus of dead-end Webster Locks Road, a tenth of a mile long with virtually no traffic. It was the perfect training ground. Up and down, I rode until I mustered enough confidence to turn right onto Creek Locks Road, also rural with hardly any traffic. Progress came in baby steps but it was the beginning of the rest of my life.

Once a day, I explored Creek Locks Road. Dirt drives with mailboxes, power lines, curves in the road were landmarks. Each day I attempted to ride a little farther. Until, less than a quarter mile down, I reached a curve that bent to the left, saw an opening, and heard children's voices. The opening between trees was one end of a long row of houses that constituted the eponymous hamlet of Creek Locks. I stopped and stared for several minutes trying to figure out what to do, and was startled to suddenly see a kid I recognized from the school bus run into the road. Familiarity was enough to lure me closer. Slowly, cautiously, I approached his house.

He recognized me too. Minutes later we were playing together. I played with him two more days before realizing, he wasn't a playmate; he was a wild animal. Nonetheless, having made it that far, I was coaxed into taking more risks and making further penetrations into the Great Creek Locks Forest. Over time, with deeper penetrations, I found better mates, but not until after a rejection and a disaster that sent me back to square one to teach myself more skills. Knowing how to ride a bike was not enough to get me anywhere.

Half way through Creek Locks, a dozen or so houses down, there was a house of another boy that rode the school bus, who later became one of my best childhood friends. The first time I managed to ride that far, I peered through some trees and saw him playing baseball in his back yard with a few other boys. Back in Esperance I had played a version of baseball with my sisters and some kids that lived next door, using a broom stick for a bat and a taped wood block for a ball. So I overcame fear, took a chance, and asked if I could play too. They said sure.

There weren't more than a handful of boys playing an improvised game with make-do ground rules, typical and necessary in a rural setting without many kids. Someone pointed to a place for me to stand in the field, in the vicinity of first base. A few plays later a ground ball was hit towards me and I watched as it slowly rolled through my legs. A hot-headed kid, the "god damned fucking piece of shit" kid mentioned earlier, who also became one of my best childhood friends, was pitching. He was so mad he took off his glove and threw it in my face. In shame and disgrace I stormed off the field, got on my bike, and rode back to the abode. The outcome couldn't have been worse. I was back to being a fly in a spider's web.

It's hard to believe now, but before the proliferation of television, baseball in the 1960's was bigger than football and without rivals as America's number one sport. The significance of baseball filtered down to the world of kids, and I must have picked up on its popularity. Unable to establish self-worth inside the abode, or to that point outside the abode either, I was forced to find a solution to my entrapment, or else succumb to madness. That's what goaded me to teach myself how to play baseball, entirely alone.

It started with sticks and stones. Standing at an imaginary home plate, I tossed the stones in the air and swung as they fell. After countless frustrating strike outs, I learned to time my swing, hit the stones, and eventually to count my home runs. Honestly, I always swung for the fences. I threw balls that bounced, usually sponge balls, against steps and walls and taught myself to anticipate their hops to catch them on the rebound. After acquiring an actual bat and a soft ball, I walked to a nearby field and improved my hitting. I tossed the soft ball up, swung, hit it as far as possible, walked to where it stopped rolling, called that home plate and hit it back. I did that for hours on end. I also practiced by throwing balls straight up in the air as high as I possibly could so as to teach myself to catch like an outfielder.

There was little off time and no off season. If I rode my bike to Creek Locks Road and turned left, and rode up a short incline, there was an underpass for the New York State Thruway. That allowed me to practice on rainy days and in winter. Later in childhood I taught myself to play tennis under that underpass. It took about a year of autodidactic practice before I was ready to play baseball alongside other boys my age. Only then did I finally feel like somebody with self-worth, and I had the beginning of an identity.

Baseball was a key to a door that opened to a new world. As a result childhood was divided yet again. First it was divided chronologically between before and after moving. Then afterwards it was divided geographically between floundering at the abode and everywhere else that wasn't the abode - which also meant psychologically between despair and hopelessness as opposed to a vision with hope for a future. What started with baseball led to an interest in the entire realm of sports. Moreover, my father had no interest in sports, couldn't relate, and therefore they became a convenient wall of separation between us, as well as a way to elude him. "Can't help you today, Father. I have a game."

A toe dip into baseball became an immersion which became an obsession. I collected baseball cards, studied their statistics on the back, watched televised games on Saturday afternoon, read newspapers and magazines about baseball, listened to games on radio, and played baseball every chance I got. One of the biggest thrills in my life came after trying out for Little League, and then getting a call from a team manager telling me I was drafted.

Baseball meant far more to me than a sport to play, or an excuse to escape the abode on a regular basis. Late in life, I had a job that put me in contact with famous baseball players who made millions of dollars playing baseball, some of them household names. I would often see them and think to myself, they would never know it but baseball meant more to me than it did to them. After all, what's more important than a reason to live.

The Cruelty of Kindness

My analysis in regards to relationships inside our abode is theoretical. It follows from a great deal of afterthought. It's important to emphasize, I harbor no blame for anyone. And other abode members may have interpreted our shared history differently. Reflecting back after many years, every other abode member has left a favorable impression on me. The familial system was thinly constructed and problem-ridden, but the abode sheltered only good people. There were no bad apples.

The key abode member for me to understand in the maze of relationships was the least prominent member, the least likely to get involved, directly anyway, and the one with the purest intentions. That's why it took me a long time to focus in on Grandmother and the role that she played.

My father's mother who lived with us was one of the best people I have ever known personally. She was straight as an arrow, with impeccable morals, had a strong work ethic, and she was the one adult my sisters and I could count on to be sober at all times. On the rare occasion when she spoke up, what she said was important and made perfect sense.

Grandmother, like my grandfather, was born in the rural region of the North Country in upstate New York. She seldom expressed her feelings. She embodied more Yankee stoicism than the entire state of Vermont. She was so passive and unemotional, I often wondered if she suffered abuse in her upbringing, or at the hands of her husband, my grandfather. And, if so, how bad was it? Although maybe Grandfather was protective of her and never abused her. To guess is not the same as to know.

If given a box of chocolates for a present, Grandmother got most of her pleasure by walking around and offering them to other abode members one by one. She baked specialties of all kinds clearly with the enjoyment of others in mind, cookies, pies, homemade peanut brittle, many more surprise treats. Until the last year of her life she cultivated a large garden out back from which she produced a wide variety of fruits and vegetables. Inside the abode, she washed the dishes, swept floors, dusted, and fought a war of attrition against cobwebs. She did everything without drawing attention to herself. Nevertheless, with her fine qualities, kindness, and good intentions, I believe our relationship issues inside the abode can be traced back to Grandmother.

While I have no grounds to claim my grandfather abused her, I'm convinced he had abused my father when he was young. My theory then, is that Grandmother's sense of propriety, and feelings of guilt for not protecting her son and only child from her abusive husband, made her overly protective of our father as an adult. She seemed determined to make up for her weakness, back when it really mattered.

My grandparents were both born in the 1890's when standards between a husband and his wife were not the same as they are today. If Grandmother was subservient in the relationship with her husband, it's easy for me to understand, and to forgive her, even if my father never could. Although I never saw a hug or sign of affection between them, inside the abode, Grandmother doted on

Father as though she was his humble servant. She prepared most of his meals, served him hot cups of coffee on demand, ironed his shirts, defended him from criticism, and was always sensitive to his feelings.

Although Grandmother was passive and kind, she was self-assured in her correctness and subtly persistent. Problems developed despite her passivity because she had a stronger character than our mother. Grandmother and Mother didn't argue, or openly criticize one another, as might be expected between a mother-in-law and a wife. Mother acquiesced and conceded many domestic duties as Grandmother took on tasks that were rightfully hers. As a result, Mother was less of a wife to her husband and less of a mother to her children. That's how she became a martyr and why she retreated to her room to smoke and to drink in isolation.

Whether Mother was capable of being a normal wife and mother is an open question, one for which no jury will ever return a verdict. Because of Grandmother, and Father, she was never given the chance. She did more than she was given credit for, laundry, grocery shopping, pet care, chauffeuring children from place to place. Without proper standing, though, she became an outcast. However to our mother's credit, and my father's chagrin, she went outside the abode and got jobs; of all things as a drill press operator in machine shops, jobs she sometimes lost due to drinking issues. Uselessness is a terrible affliction. Mother fought hard to establish self-worth, to make a contribution and earn the respect that she never received inside the abode.

Grandmother never intended and never wanted to do harm to anyone. However, as a consequence of her heightened concern for our father, and supplanting our mother's domestic role, the relationships of everyone inside the abode were skewed and out of kilter. Relationship knots may have preexisted the move downstate (when I was too young to realize them), but after moving, when she and Father were reunited on a permanent basis, Grandmother was able to reestablish control and exercise responsibilities that were second nature to her. Then after Aunt Amy returned to Syracuse, almost as soon as she had arrived, Father claimed her bedroom as his own.

Aunt Amy's tiny bedroom was next to Grandmother's equally tiny bedroom behind the kitchen. Claiming that Aunt Amy's bed with its hard mattress was better for his bad back, which always struck me as a convenient excuse when he needed one, Father decided to sleep there instead of with Mother. Perhaps her bad habits were too much for him (she smoked and drank more than he did), or maybe it was too awkward in a bedroom with me passing through it to get to mine, or else their relationship had soured and become too burdensome for comfort. In any case, his moving downstairs to Amy's room eliminated any pretext to normalcy inside the abode.

Grandmother also had a strong bias in favor of my older sister. Exactly why was one more mystery. It might have stemmed from the fact, as a first-born older sister was the darling of our grandfather, and Grandmother continued to serve him posthumously through her. Or, maybe Grandmother saw in her the daughter she always wanted. Or, maybe older sister was also abused by Grandfather so that Grandmother was protecting her feelings too. In any case, there were ramifications. Because they both relied on her for favors and emotional support, Father and older sister became rivals of sorts in a tense relationship.

Father, with residual anger towards his mother, alienation from his wife, and tensions with his eldest daughter, was desperate for female approval within his domicile. In hindsight, I understand why he wanted to ingratiate himself with my younger sister, and why he pulled out all the stops to please her by buying her a horse. Then, of course, he needed my labor to help him build a barn for it, to go with him to buy the hay and oats, and to do other horse related chores.

My younger sister and I were close enough in age that in a better domestic setting free of relationship complications, we might have had a good sister and brother relationship. But due in large part to the requirements of the horse, and my unavoidable position between her and our father, and a father that cast a shadow over both of us, there was a wedge between my sister and myself. At times we tried to bridge the gap between us but we were never able to.

It's easy to fault my sister for not taking care of her own horse. There were good reasons though for her disinclination to do so. To have cared for the horse more would have brought her into the orbit of our father more often. She didn't want to be around him any more than I did. And his attentions toward her were excessive and likely inappropriate. Also, she too was a young child trying to survive a difficult childhood. Moreover, although it was never mentioned by anyone but tacitly understood, the reasons of which are entwined in the mysteries of my own life, keeping our father pacified was my responsibility. The horse was secondary.

My sisters shared a bedroom. Three years apart, they were also close in age. On rare occasions they fought physically. They were the only abode members that did. For the most part, from what I gathered, there was no apparent bond between them and they were neither rivals nor in an alliance. Only they would know the true nature of their relationship, and whether they ever made contact with one another post childhood, and after 1983 when we all met up again.

My mother and I had an affectionless relationship, but we also had a quasi-alliance. I always felt sorry for her, which was part of the equation. We also were likely the most emotionally wounded, although neither of us knew it or thought that way at the time. Certainly we were on the same page in not wanting to disturb the peace. Also, I had to walk by her every time I went to my room. Animosity was not in our interests.

Grandmother possessed the same stellar values and commitment to serve others as her sister, Great Aunt Amy. In her efforts to look after our father and safeguard his feelings, I believe, she was only trying to redress harm that had already been done to him in the past. Our grandfather may have rolled a bowling ball through time causing dysfunction in future generations, but if my theory is correct, Grandmother gave that bowling ball more momentum. She exacerbated relationship issues and disrupted the domestic lives of others, thereby causing still more damage. Although, I can never say and will never say that anything was her fault.

As for the relationship between Grandmother and myself, we generally got along well. There was occasional discomfort. For example, she pressured me into stepping on Mother's beer cans one by one so they would take up less space in a plastic bag, because she was embarrassed about what the garbage man might think. I hated that job. If I balked at having to take care of the horse, she would tell me to think about the poor horse. She was right, but her admonishment didn't help my feelings any. In the aggregate, though we didn't talk about it, throughout childhood Grandmother and I were partners in arms trying to maintain order.

One of the best memories of my youth was after my sisters moved on and moved out and my parents both had jobs. That was when Grandmother and I had an opportunity to talk, and to get to know one another without the static caused by relationship issues. I was a senior in high school. Before leaving for school each morning I would sit and have breakfast next to Grandmother. Together we listened to Earl Nightengale and his radio program, *Our Changing World*, which stimulated many interesting discussions and a refreshing exchange of ideas. We discovered that philosophically we had a lot in common.

In the summer after high school, I went to boot camp. Then barely a month after flying to California for training, Grandmother fell down stairs and died.

Grandmother and I didn't get to know one another well for long.

Addendum: Recently I bought a burial plot in Esperance, New York where I thought my grandfather and grandmother were buried. I did this for my own reasons unrelated to them. In 1993, after visiting my mother who was dying in a hospital, I drove to and walked through the Esperance cemetery. There were indications that my grandmother was buried in an unmarked grave, which disturbed me. When I mentioned it to my father he said a monument had been paid for. Knowing their relationship, however, I didn't trust him.

In 2021, when I went to the cemetery to meet with the director, we had a good-natured dispute. She insisted that my grandmother was buried next to my grandfather. I didn't believe her.

We came to a basic agreement about my plans to buy a plot, and we agreed to meet the following day to go over details. Before we met the second time, the director stopped to pick up an official document. It turned out we were both right. Yes my grandmother was buried next to my grandfather. But no, she wasn't there anymore. The document the director held up for me to see had a stamp in big bold letters across the page: DISINTERMENT. After her burial my grandmother disappeared.

One possibility is that a will provision caught up to her mandating reburial somewhere else. Did she not want to be buried next to her husband? Because he was abusive? My hope is that she was ultimately buried next to her loving sister Great Aunt Amy, somewhere near Syracuse. In any case Grandmother earned the right to rest in peace. Wherever that is.

Added Weight

Alcoholism is a difficult disease to understand in all its details and ramifications. I'm convinced that someone can study alcoholism for many years, become a genuine expert on the subject, and still be unable to tell an individual who has grown up in an alcoholic household something relevant. Just as no two individuals are exactly alike, no two alcoholics are the same. Since alcoholism is a progressive disease, timing by itself can form a filter from which it's difficult to see through.

Both of my parents were alcoholics, and heavy smokers. They were functional alcoholics, able to manage responsibilities (for the most part), including jobs, driving automobiles, contributing to the running of a household. They were not lazy, and despite their addictions they were conscientious.

The points in time when their diseases started, and when they became full-fledged alcoholics, are unknowable. By virtue of being older than I, by five and a half and two years respectively, my sisters experienced less of our parents' alcoholism than I did. How much difference that made is anybody's guess. To me it seemed as if there were multiple parents. The moods and personalities our mother and father exhibited at any given moment depended on their level of sobriety in conjunction with what stage of alcoholism they were in. Regardless, it was always incumbent on my sisters and myself to adjust to their habits, whether it meant dealing with their moods, or breathing through clouds of smoke.

Mother hated to drive, but out of a sense of duty she would drive anyone to anywhere if transportation was needed. As her alcoholism progressed, so too did her loss of eyesight, which made driving for her a burdensome chore. Still, I was never afraid to ride with her as she drove. It is significant that we lived in a rural area with sparse traffic. Mother was always a slow, careful, methodical driver.

Even if he had a beer in a little brown bag between his knees, I never felt safer with another driver than I did with my father. He was solid as a rock and always knew what he was doing. He didn't speed. He obeyed rules. He might criticize other drivers under his breath, but he was never flustered by them, even while driving in New York City.

Many of my school classmates perished young due to accidents caused by drinking and driving. The nation's highways were once a bloodbath, and often still are but not to the degree they were in the past. It was a positive development when Mothers Against Drunk Driving decided to do something about the problem, got involved, and forced governments to take action. I admire their work. Their influence was necessary. Yet reflecting back, it frightens me to consider what would have happened if our parents had been caught up in the modern era's consequences for drinking and driving.

They were never going to stop drinking. The abode operated on a shoestring budget, after subtracting what was spent on their addictions. Their incomes were essential. If they lost driving privileges, public transportation in our area didn't exist. Money for draconian fines, albeit fair, would have come out of household necessities. Abode members were already under enough stress as it was. We were fortunate our shared time together was during an earlier era.

The psychological problems our parents caused were a heavier burden than anything related to their driving. As hard as it may be to believe, and as humorous as it may sound, our mother and father each blamed the other for being an alcoholic. Children in the middle can't take sides. That was one more way they alienated their children.

It's common for children of alcoholics to develop a guilt complex. I can't say when it started, but years of reflection have shown me an obvious cause and effect. Oddly, perhaps, I didn't see signs of guilt in my sisters. They may have masked their guilt better or responded in healthier ways. The impact of alcoholism is often subtle, and like abuse and neglect, it can manifest itself in countless other negative feelings and defensive behaviors. Knowing firsthand, and from a vested interest, alcoholism can create clouds of mystery that children can wrestle with for the rest of their lives.

When my mother was near the end of her life, and confined to a hospital, I took my eleven-year-old child to New York so they could meet at least once before she died. My father tried to talk me out of it, arguing that to see her in that condition would be too traumatic for a child. Approximately fifteen years passed before I asked my child, then an adult, whether seeing the child's grandmother one time was worthwhile. The response I got was that it didn't make a difference because she was already too far gone. She was medicated and undergoing radiation treatments, but my mother dying in the hospital was not much different in appearance than the mother I grew up with. But for one exception.

She had a cousin who lived in Cape May, New Jersey, and she wanted to visit her. That was in March of 1979 after my service years, when I was living in the Catskills. She rode down on the bus. On the way to New Jersey, or shortly thereafter, she suffered a heart attack. It fell on me to drive down and bring her back to the abode.

When I met her at the hospital, she was unrecognizable. I was shocked. She hadn't had a beer or a cigarette for more than a week, and she looked like a normal person. Her mood was even chipper, which I had never seen before. Unfortunately her recovery was short lived. Once back in New York, she resumed the same smoking and drinking habits. That's how four years later, in 1983, a doctor was fooled into thinking she only had three more days to live.

Mother's daily practice was to start drinking almost as soon as she woke up in the morning. She continued drinking almost until she went to sleep at night. She was the type of alcoholic that had to have some alcohol in her system at all times. The changes to my mother's personality during the day, and over a period of years, was gradual and not likely to be noticed unless someone made an effort to think about her. I always did.

Our mother and fathers' habits were dissimilar. As I write this, it occurs to me I can't recall a single instance when they drank together. Nor did they borrow from each other's cigarettes. Father was usually sober at the abode. He drank with buddies after work, rarely a beer or two if he was driving around on a weekend excursion, or if he had an irresistible urge to tie one on. Mother drank alone in her room, only beer, always the cheapest available because quantity mattered, and to save money she rolled her own cigarettes.

Our parents' addictions were additional complications to our complicated childhoods. How much impact they had on my sisters and myself, separate from all the other issues, is impossible to measure. I only know we had to learn to live with both of them. And at the same time.

Imperfect Pair

When I was a child, I thought my parents had to marry each other because no one else would have tolerated either of them for a mate. Both dropped out of school at the age of sixteen. Both had self-esteem issues that must have had deep roots back to their respective childhoods. They had tendencies to withdraw and to isolate. Although my parents would socialize if an occasion required them to, and were well liked by outsiders, no one who saw them day-to-day would describe them as happy people. It's understandable, to me, why they relied on alcohol and nicotine for crutches to get through life.

They came from different backgrounds. My father was born in New York City, my mother in the rural center of New York State near Oneonta. My father's parents had jobs and disposable income even in the Great Depression. My mother's father was a farm worker who took jobs wherever he could find them, and dragged his family with him wherever they happened to be. My father's father had been an oil driller in the southwest and in Mexico. That's probably how he managed to save enough money to buy a chicken farm upstate, and how my mother and father happened to meet. Although how they met each other was never mentioned.

My parents didn't love one another. At least they didn't, or no longer did, by the time I was born. Their mutual disdain was never counterbalanced by an occasional acknowledgment of respect.

Neither hesitated to disparage the other behind the other's back. Although, to be fair and accurate, they would come together and cooperate if a situation demanded it; spending hours alongside one another repairing a broken-down automobile, for example. Clear necessity always trumped emotions.

The undercurrent of hostility between my parents was nearly constant, and barely subdued on holidays. The negative feelings between them often erupted into scenes like those in a dramatic play. Father was always the aggressor. It was common to see him chase my mother up the stairs spewing curse words and criticism. Father was easily unhinged and unable to keep his emotions in check (inside the abode), but he was not a violent man by nature. However, he had a habit of releasing his frustrations on Mother, verbally but demonstratively.

A case can be made that Mother was no prize for a wife, or a mother for that matter. Nothing justifies the threat of violence by one spouse against another. She was not in danger. If he had gone too far my mother had relatives who would have helped her get away from him. Father knew this and he would have been too ashamed to face them afterwards. Nor was he the type to pursue her if she had fled. He would have been devastated because, in the back of his mind, he knew she contributed more, and he relied on her more than he wanted to admit. For her part, Mother received security from a man who held down a job, who could be counted on to keep the lights lit, the home heated, and the water and automobiles running. And, to her credit, she was smart enough to know the difference between Father's bark and his bite.

My mother spent the last half year of her life dying in a hospital. I have wondered if my father visited her once in all that time. He was a master of excuses, so my guess is, probably not. My parents had no plans to be buried near one another, and weren't.

As I look back at my parents and their marriage from the perspective of old age, they were heroic. As is often the case in other facets of life, looking underneath the surface can yield a different fundamental truth. The dynamic between my parents, his frustrations and her willingness to stay with him to the bitter end, makes their marriage hard to understand and harder to appreciate. But they were not two losers stuck with each other. They were winners.

To understand my mother and father, and their unusual pact, a good place to start is with their old-fashioned values. I often find myself wondering if those values still exist. Consider that there were fewer years between the death of Abraham Lincoln and the year my parents were born (1926), than there are in my current age. Neither of them was born into a life of ease. They both knew from an early age, that they would have to forge their way in a difficult world. Theirs was a constant battle against the odds.

My father's parents had disposable income, but Father also had a regular route delivering eggs while driving a truck on public roads, when he was eleven years old. He endured physical abuse and who knows what else from his domineering father. When duty called, he enlisted and put his life on the line in WWII. My mother only talked about her childhood in snippets here and there. She was clear, though, about why she dropped out of school. She said she liked school, but her family moved too often and she was unable to keep up. After dropping out she, the same as her father, went to work and accepted jobs where she could find them. Separately, and together too, my mother and father were little engines that could.

In the country in which they were born, my parents were on their own to either make it, or not. They started out with virtually nothing. They bought and paid for a home (of sorts) and raised children. And it's the raising of children that highlights the incredible achievement of my mother and father.

One could make the argument that my mother and father were terrible parents. Certainly they were the worst role models. After reaching an age of maturity, their three children ran away from them like horses let out of a barn fire. So, it's necessary to look deeper still into the underbrush of my parents' marriage, to see the kernels of truth, and the equivalent of a pot of gold.

My parents couldn't get along with each other but they provided all the necessities, food, clothing, shelter, and transportation, which allowed their children to grow, and to prosper. They provided much more than that too, holiday celebrations, birthday recognitions, a household full of domestic pets, a set of encyclopedias, many extras. My parents were miserable together but they stayed together for the sake of their children, because that's what people with old fashioned values did.

My mother and father were believers in god but passive about their religious views. They allowed their children to form their own opinions, which, in my view, is another strong point in their favor. They may not have believed in each other (or did they?) but they believed in doing the best that they could for their children.

For more than forty years I have been estranged from my two sisters, and they with each other, most likely, as they remained estranged from our parents in their final years. However, they were both older, and I know to their amazing credit they earned college degrees and entered professional occupations. Like myself, they have had ample opportunities to live in more comfort than our parents ever did.

If one considers how burdened with emotion and struggle our parents' marriage was, and how they stuck it out through thick and thin for their children, and if one believes, as I believe, that the foremost purpose of parenthood is to provide the best opportunities for children, it leads to only one conclusion. Our parents hit the jackpot. What's sad is they ended their lives estranged from their adult children, and their grandchildren. They never knew they'd won. They never collected their winnings.

Pair of Aces

Both of my grandfathers died before I had a chance to know them. To understand who they were and what they meant to me, required patching together bits of information, along with a lot of guesswork. On the plus side, both grandfathers were WWI veterans. Both of them knew what it meant to work outdoors at physically demanding jobs. My information is insufficient to assess my grandfathers properly, but, from what I was able to gather, neither grandfather left a positive impression on me.

My assessment of them is tempered, also, knowing it's unjust to judge people of the past in modern times using modern standards; just as people in the distant future will probably look back at us and think we were all just primitive fools.

My paternal grandfather died when I was three and a half. If he had a direct influence on me it was pre-memory. However I suspect he had been an abusive father to my father, and I have reasons to suspect he was materialistic and a selfish man. Those are qualities that typically determine how much I can tolerate a person.

My maternal grandfather died halfway through my childhood. I knew him vaguely and occasionally interacted with him. My recollection is that he was a gentle soul with a pleasant disposition and not a bad man. However, there were indications derived from others who knew him better, that he was a heavy drinker whose drinking habits compromised his familial responsibilities.

In contrast to grandfathers, I knew my grandmothers very well and they always impressed me favorably. So, it mystified me why my mother maintained affection for her father that she apparently didn't share with her mother. It perplexed me because, from what I saw of her, Grandmother had an uncanny ability to make others around her feel better. She exuded good will and optimism. She had a wide range of interests and hobbies, playing pinochle, picking wild berries in the fields, making throw rugs out of old winter coats that she gave away as presents, and a passion for tossing a line in the water in hopes of catching a fish. She was always down-to-earth and responsible. For example, she might drink a beer on a hot summer day but not more than one.

Most significant, it seemed to me, I never saw an ounce of co-ercion or meanness in my grandmother. She possessed a power of self-assurance coupled with (apparent, at least on the surface) harmlessness that I've not seen equaled in another individual. She would announce by mail that she was coming over on the bus on a specific date to visit her daughter and grandchildren. When she arrived my father, the undisputed king of the abode, immediately turned into a meek puppy dog. He wouldn't hesitate to criticize anyone else on the planet but he never uttered a harsh or critical word about Grandmother. She also made friends easily, and never got off the bus without exchanging good wishes and a wave with the driver.

Above all else Grandmother cared about her grandchildren. That's why there wasn't a force on the planet capable of keeping her away from them. When her fourth and last child, much younger than Mother, left his wife and moved out west, despite the inconvenience Grandmother visited her ex-daughter-in-law, supported her with money, and thereby maintained a relationship with two additional grandchildren. All of her grandchildren were remembered on their birthdays.

She had a strong work ethic as well. She left our grandfather, it was said, because she could no longer tolerate his drinking. She didn't divorce him but instead obtained a legal separation. Then she accepted employment as a live-in maid for millionaires. After the separation, Grandmother continued to look after our grandfather. Then from his tiny hovel with an outhouse for a bathroom and a tiny kitchen that required you to hand pump running water, she slaved to put together family reunions.

Once when I was five and still living in Esperance, and the millionaires she worked for were away on vacation, Grandmother requested that someone bring me down to spend a weekend with her. Among other thrills, she took me to my first movies, a double feature of Disney films, *Big Red* and *Old Yeller*. What that weekend meant to me at the time can't be overstated. Before then, I thought my Great Aunt Amy was the only adult that cared about me. Over time, though, our relationship did not become particularly strong. She had many other grandchildren, and after moving away we no longer lived in proximity, and only met sporadically. However, I knew her well enough to believe she was amazing and special.

So, why did Mother show affection for her father but not her mother? What caused my mother's weak character, low self-esteem, and crippling despondency? One never knows what goes on behind closed doors, but it doesn't seem possible that Grandmother abused my mother when she was a child. Sometimes people who are overtly confident and upbeat make others feel worse, fearful that they can't measure up. However, Mother was her daughter and not just anyone. If Grandmother unintentionally made my mother feel small and inadequate beside her, that still doesn't seem to be enough to turn my mother into a martyr, a rag-wearing alcoholic, and a shell of a wife and mother.

It's important to point out that my mother had a work ethic too. She tried as best as she could to be valuable to others, and she was loyal to my father to the very end despite how much it hurt her.

She also got along well with her two older brothers. She apparently had been somewhat of a pseudo mother to her younger brother, fourteen years younger than she, and they remained fond of one another as well.

Nevertheless, for many years and until she died, Mother spent hours sitting hunched over on the side of her bed. On the wall eighteen inches in front of her, there were three photos, one for each of her three estranged children. Can anything on earth explain that much sadness in a mother? It was and still is impossible for me to connect that sadness to Grandmother. Despite the effort I made to understand her, whatever caused my mother to be the way she was remains, and will forever remain, unknowable.

It's revealing to recall the interactions between my two grandmothers. On the surface they were vastly different, but they were fundamentally very much alike. My mother's mother was a gregarious extrovert. My father's mother was taciturn and rarely had occasion to socialize with outsiders. My mother's mother lived in a millionaire's mansion that she kept clean and polished at all times. My father's mother never stopped trying to make our abode tidy and livable, even when the task was impossible. When mother's mother came to visit, she didn't utter a word about our living conditions. Of course she understood my other grandmother's Sisyphean burden, and she respected the feelings and boundaries of others.

When my grandmother from Oneonta came to visit, and both grandmothers were under our abode roof, it felt like there was a suspension of conflict and peace in time of war. My grandmothers did not criticize each other. They weren't contentious or competing mothers-in-law. Their mutual respect was plain to see. They understood one another because they possessed the same set of basic human values. That's why I admired them both. That's how I know some of their humanity rubbed off on me.

Footloose and Almost Free

To the extent I've had halcyon days those days were between adolescence and going off to boot camp. With minimal parental concern for my whereabouts, and no oversight, therefore with no control over me, I was in total command of my own life. With my father I drove harder bargains in our unwritten contracts, making it increasingly difficult, and eventually impossible for him to secure cooperation for his projects. Other than abode chores that I continued to do, automatically and unemotionally, so as to reduce background static, I enjoyed freedom in its purest form. I made my own decisions who to see, where to go, what activities to engage in, what organizations to join, what mattered and what didn't.

It was an active lifestyle full of athletic endeavors, jobs, and schemes to make money (raking leaves, shoveling snow, cutting grass), and running around aimlessly, that kept me agile, fit, and firing on all cylinders. I had no difficulty expressing myself: a gradual decline in the ability to think and speak clearly, and the onset of dyslexia, didn't occur until years later.

Polar opposite to the current lifestyle I've gravitated towards, I was sociable, even gregarious. I had a great compliment of like-minded friends to hang out with. At school, friends ran the gamut from brainiacs and greasers, to jocks and the Mennonites too. I liked everyone and everyone seemed to like me, as the underlying me was well hidden even from myself.

Scholastically, I went through motions, paying attention in classes just enough to pass without additional effort. That was the only option as it was impossible to study at the abode in a porous room without privacy. Out of necessity, academic interests and aspirations were stowed on a shelf for someday in the future. In the meantime, peace of mind was maintained by perpetual motion.

Most of those who I hung out with shared an interest in one sport or another. They came from good families, weren't rule breakers, and they were either college bound or had specific plans for their lives after high school. With a few other friends, however, I ran wild. We often flirted with mischief. We weren't destructive but we had no qualms about challenging authority. For example, for fun and the challenge of it, we snuck into high school football games to avoid paying admission. At 16, we went to over 21 X-rated movies. We knew which shops would sell us beer and wine despite being underage. And we smoked a few joints. It was the 1970's. Anti-establishment views were in vogue, so we did what we wanted to.

More than any other factor during those days, though, is that I was insulated with a false persona and a state of denial. That is what covered up my fears and fueled my social habits. It was years later that I saw how the abundance of confidence that had propelled me, and sustained me, was razor thin, and how bravado covered up insecurity. How I was able to fool people into thinking I was a more dynamic person than I actually was. A false persona and state of denial allowed me to enjoy the best period of my life, until years later when the phony scheme came crashing down on me. I had pretended to be normal without realizing I wasn't.

Although outwardly confident (but inwardly insecure), I didn't pursue girlfriends until the senior year of high school. I always lagged behind. Part of the reason was starting school at age 4. Most in my class were 18 and able to go dancing and bar hopping when I was still 17 and couldn't go. But it was more than that. Logistics and shame also hindered my ability to fit into the mainstream high school culture. And despite overwhelming and incurable ignorance, I was only attracted to girls who were intelligent and studious. So, when I finally got up the nerve to ask one girl out, picked her up to go to a movie and saw how she lived comfortably in a very nice house, it was unthinkable to ask her out a second time. The disparity in standards of living was too much to bridge.

At a dinner date before the senior prom, I had no idea what to do at a restaurant because I had never been in one. Then the cost of the meal shocked and embarrassed me when I wasn't able to pay for my date and myself. In so many ways I didn't fit in with normal teenagers my age. A false persona and state of denial masked ignorance and naivety that continued to lurk just below the surface. Nevertheless, they were the impetus that propelled me forward.

After Little League, I played Babe Ruth League baseball for three more years. My baseball skills were at best mediocre. Ridiculous naivety led me to hang on to hopes of becoming a professional baseball player long past the point of reasonableness. When the baseball mirage finally dissipated, it was, somehow, replaced with a different vision; more like a fuzzy idea that snuck into my head. I started to think about going to law school someday, and maybe becoming a lawyer, even though I hadn't a clue what that entailed or how one went about achieving such a lofty goal. My high school grades weren't even respectable. While I thought about many topics in a dreamy kind of way, I was incredibly ignorant.

What I see in hindsight, that I didn't see then, is that a pipe dream was necessary to ameliorate bleak prospects as a result of my childhood. Buried inside me, somehow, was a determination to live a decent life anyway, despite long odds against me; which in fact was all I wanted. What gave me a fighting chance was a mix of curiosity, objectivity, and physical energy. I was an open book trying to live while searching for solutions and better information.

Indicative, in 8th grade I again played intramural football after school. The new coach was a self-serving man, and a pompous ass. Contrary to the meaning of intramural, he managed to pull strings, and to secure permission to play two additional games against crosstown middle schools. Contrary to law, and the fact we were adolescents, after our school won both games - I barely played - he passed around champagne in the locker-room as if we'd won the Super Bowl. It's hard to learn anything meaningful from people with inflated egos. Nevertheless, although I despised him, the coach gave a demonstration one day that grabbed my attention.

At one practice, he showed us what to do if you're a ball carri-er and are grabbed by a tackler. He said, "Keep driving with the legs," and added: "You'll either break free or you'll gain the most forward progress possible before you're on the ground." It made so much sense that something in my head clicked. I seized upon it. The significance went beyond football. Mentally it meant not giving up until you're defeated. And the demonstration reaffirmed my lifestyle and what I sensed instinctively; that legs are the key to everything physical. I took the lesson to heart and have been driving with the legs ever since.

Not every lesson in those early years was serendipitous, but every realization that brought me closer to an always illusive reality was valuable. After a two-year hiatus, in 11th grade I wanted to play football again, so I tried out for the high school varsity team. Two-a-day practices began in the heat of August a few weeks before the school year started. Practices were exhausting, and for me grossly inconvenient.

When the second practice ended, around 5 p.m., my ordeal be-gan. Step one was to walk across town to the intersection of Route 32. Once, when trying a short cut along railroad tracks, a wino wanting money snuck up behind me and grabbed me by the collar. I only had four pennies. He scoffed and let me go with an insult that was worse than the grab.

Step two was to stand on the corner, put out my thumb, and wait for someone willing to give me a ride. Step three was getting dropped off at Maple Hill and walking half a mile to the abode. The walk-hitchhike-walk commute usually took an hour and a half. At the abode step four was to take two five-gallon buckets of water to the horse in his stall and hold them up for him to drink one at a time. Adding one more hurdle to the burden, in addition to the risk of encountering domestic turmoil, the abode bathroom had a sink, no shower, and a toilet that didn't flush without pouring in buckets of water.

One late afternoon, well into the routine, after two practices, walking to Route 32 and hitching a ride, a strange man picked me up. He immediately pulled out a magazine with photos of naked men, then began pointing to his favorites. It was one of the many times in my life, not even the first, when gay men have come on to me, or threatened me. Fortunately this old man was only creepy, so I made him drop me off in Bloomington and walked the long way back to the abode.

The scales tipped. Honestly I was not a good football player anyway and that was one factor. In any case playing football was not worth the effort to continue, so I never went back to practice and quit. As depressing as it was, however, the event brought me closer to a reality that has never changed. It was always me against the world. I could go through life forlorn and helpless, or learn to roll with the punches.

Meanwhile on the world stage, escalation of the war in Vietnam ran parallel with my journey through childhood. Despite all the controversy surrounding the war, I was too ignorant to form a political opinion. But I did watch the news. Especially after the Tet

Offensive, the escalation threatened me personally. I was forced to evaluate my standing in conjunction with the war, without money, connections, or a chance to go to college. Military enlistment was the only card I had to play, whether or not it included a tour in Vietnam.

Halfway through high school I started visiting recruiters in their offices, all of which were conveniently located next door to the local pool hall. After many visits with all the recruiters, for inexplicable reasons I decided to enlist in the U.S. Navy Seabees as an Engineering Aide. Looking back it amazes me how I managed to choose a branch to commit myself to for four years, and a professional line of work, that were acceptable if not inspiring. Despite their proud reputation the Seabees are not the U.S. Marines. Nor did I have any knowledge of, or a particular interest in civil engineering, which merely sounded good and matched an aptitude score on a pre-enlistment exam. In other words, I tossed a dart and got lucky.

As high school was winding down, with induction set for August, one sunny afternoon my younger sister drove down to the abode and met me near the barn. Her purpose, apparently, was to complain and lay a guilt trip on me. She was upset because without someone, meaning me, to care for her horse, she had to sell him. That saddened me too. Of course she was busy in her nursing program with little time to spare, but it hardly mattered once enlistment was official. So why the guilt trip? Except that's what other abode members did and she had learned by example.

My sister was already living elsewhere and was out of the abode permanently. Our older sister had earned her professional degree and was living in another state. Didn't I also have a right to a future? And a chance for a better life? Years later, in my darkest moments, I replayed this scene with my sister over and over again in my head.

By August of 1974, prior to induction and active duty, on and off Paris peace talks finally made progress and it appeared I would not have to go to Vietnam. The official end to hostilities, though, wasn't declared until the following year in 1975. Technically that has made me a "Vietnam War era veteran." Over the years since then, that designation has increased a few benefits here and there. Benefits I don't ask for because the designation is misleading and therefore shameful to mention.

It's unjust to associate my service with that of the intrepid men and women who did go to Vietnam during the war. Although I take pride in my work, and try to do the best job that I can whatever it happens to be, no one has ever accused me of having a gung-ho military attitude. Besides, I didn't enlist out of patriotic zeal. I enlisted because without any other cards in my hand there were no other options, and because I was desperate to end childhood and get on to something else. Anything else.

Odd Brother Out

For the most part growing up, my sisters seemed like normal sisters. They were older and they bullied me in the early years. When you're only three, two years older and five and a half years older is a lot.

On one occasion when I was still a toddler, they were behind me and one of them, I don't know which sister, shoved me in the back and down a flight of stairs. The tumble they caused me stuck in my mind not because of them, but due to how our parents reacted when I ran to them in the living room. They downplayed my pain and fear and instilled the message that my vulnerability didn't matter.

In essence, when we were very young, my sisters exercised typical sibling jealousy for an unwanted little brother. In their interactions with me as we got older, they replicated the attitudes and behaviors of our parents, which again was only natural. Then moving downstate was a challenge for all three of us, made worse since it happened in the latter half of a school year, and we had to adjust to living conditions inside a flimsy abode.

They were very young too, so my sisters can't be blamed for not noticing a change to my personality as a result of the trauma I experienced after moving. None of the adults at the abode questioned my state of mind either, not even after two stays in the hospital;

except when Aunt Amy visited and we played *Sorry* together, she kept insisting that I'd changed. At that time, I too was unaware of the changes occurring inside me, as I questioned the meaning of life, and, on a subconscious level whether I wanted to go on living.

Throughout our respective childhoods my sisters and I were trying to find our way forward under difficult circumstances. Reflecting back on our time together, I'm reminded of the Round Up (or Zero Gravity) ride at the fair. Riders stand in an upright cage along the perimeter of a circular platform. When they're strapped in and spinning rapidly, and the platform is tilted nearly perpendicular to the ground, riders are too distracted hanging on to their own life to think about other riders. As children, we focused on survival first, and only occasionally when there was no spinning or tilting, did we think about one another.

After moving my sisters and I tried to be normal, or at least pretended to be, although for us normal was at best an aspirational goal. None of us wanted to spend time at the abode but sometimes inclement weather confined us there. We played a few board games. We shared holidays, rode together on car trips, and knew each other's best friends. Emotional ties were thin but open hostility was rare. We had enough to worry about as it was without adding more aggravation.

Actually my oldest sister did show some concern for a younger brother. She'd volunteered as a candy striper at the hospital, which is how she got her start in her career as a pharmacist, an incredible success for someone from our blighted background. Because she knew the owners, she was able to get me my first job in the local pharmacy. Then too, the owners wanted someone willing to work for 50 cents an hour. I was only 13 and my unskilled labor matched the job requirements. One must start somewhere, however. I wanted the money and my sister's favor was a big one. Then on my 16th birthday the law mandated a hefty raise to $1.65 an hour.

Better still, when she was attending college, she invited me to ride up on the bus and spend a weekend with her and her collegiate friends. A big city was an anomaly for me, eye-opening, and educational. She made the weekend more memorable by taking me to a Harlem Globetrotters basketball game. All these years later, her invitation stands as the best unsolicited gift anyone has ever given me.

The relationship between my younger sister and myself, I believe, suffered the most from our domestic situation. Having to take care of her horse, which more accurately meant taking care of our father, was how he managed to cast a dark shadow over both of us. Also, underneath the surface, and admitting it would have increased our vulnerabilities, my sister and I were likely the most sensitive abode members. We were ill-equipped to handle the awkwardness forced upon us due to circumstances beyond our control. I felt tension with her that I never felt with our older sister.

While on active duty, I was assigned to a Seabee battalion based out of Mississippi. My younger sister, with her husband and in-laws, lived halfway between there and upstate New York. When I drove back to New York on leave, she and they graciously put me up for a night, which allowed me to divide the drive into two shorter halves. She and I had some good conversations. Without abode-driven pressure we seemed to get along fairly well.

My sisters, like myself, were caught up in the confusion in which we lived. They probably preferred to forget bad times and bad memories. When I placed a call to each of them, many years after our estrangements, and only minutes away from where they lived, I believe they were especially not interested in hearing from me. In fact, in the call with my younger sister she mentioned how she would like to see our older sister again. Apparently I was the odd brother they both preferred to remain estranged from. As I see it looking back, that makes perfect sense. I've spent a lifetime feeling odd and out of place.

My sisters probably recalled a phony brother, one full of bravado, one who was manipulative with a propensity to monopolize the television so as to watch his favorite sports. They didn't see, just as I didn't know, that unconsciously I was covering up for misery and the insecurity I felt inside.

Later in life, synonymous with recovery from depression, I discovered that I didn't have familial feelings. I can't speak for my sisters, of course, but from what I saw and remembered, all the relationships in our domicile were contrived and artificial. Except in the early years perhaps, and maybe not even then, my sisters were not normal sisters. In any case our sibling relationships were destroyed a long time ago. Unless one blames me for misery and insecurity, I didn't cause the destruction. They didn't either.

In hindsight there's no reason to blame my sisters for anything. I know the circumstances we lived under, and I'm impressed by what they were able to accomplish in spite of them. I hope they've found peace. If we ever did meet again that's one way we might find common ground. Starting from our childhoods in hell, we know how hard it can be for people like us to find peace.

Ashes to Ashes

After moving downstate from Esperance, outside Schenectady, to Rosendale, New York, south of Kingston, as a clan we moved into a dwelling I thought of as the abode. It wasn't a house of horrors per se; we experienced both good and bad times there. It actually wasn't a bad place to grow up. Everyone at least pretended to be comfortable and secure. Eruptions of all kinds could occur at any moment, but there were occasional long stretches between seismic events. The front door, atop a leftover towpath mound for the defunct Delaware and Hudson canal, never stopped opening and shutting. In addition to people, half a dozen domestic animals were let in and out at their whim. The seasons changed. The front door and the abode breathed laboriously while sheltering the skeleton of a family.

Christmas was celebrated with a live tree, presents, and a holiday meal. Birthdays were honored with cake and ice cream. The television could usually pull in two watchable channels. Pets also helped to keep dwellers distracted from reality. One summer, everyone except Grandmother went on a camping trip to the Adirondacks. The rare vacation seemed to go well. Back at the abode, however, there was no unity. Most had better places to go. The front door went back to doing hard labor.

If she finished her gardening and there wasn't a floor in need of sweeping, or a dish to wash, Grandmother sat on her stool in the kitchen smoking Pall Malls while listening to the radio, her link to the outside world. A highly intelligent and profoundly stoical woman, Grandmother listened attentively without offering opinions or comments.

Mother could usually be found upstairs in her room, sitting hunched over on the side of her bed, insulated with a lit cigarette in one hand, a beer at arm's length on the bedside stand, with her right hand propping up a Louis Lamour western in her lap. Except for her emphysema cough, a two-minute spasm every ten minutes, Mother made no more noise than a shadow.

If the kids had run off, if Father was at work, if the horse didn't escape from the field, there was no turmoil to speak of and no cause for concern. Serenity was broken only by an occasional dog bark, or the noon fire whistle.

Located two miles from the village and ten miles from town, the setting was rural and attractive. Behind the abode an acre of greenery was embellished with an assortment of pretty trees, catalpa, apple, sycamore, mulberry, weeping willow. Further back a strand of hard wood trees stood guard over a downward slope to the Rondout Creek. The creek offered recreational fishing and swimming, as well as a place to meditate, or to escape domestic turbulence. A hundred yards downstream the Rondout met up with the Wallkill River, then together they raced to the Hudson.

Two small cottages on tiny parcels abutted our abode property on one side. A small cottage, similarly on one acre, occupied the other. Across the road, two houses completed the cluster, one directly opposite hidden by a row of pine trees, the other positioned kitty-corner and half hidden horizontally behind a companion segment of the D & H towpath. It was an immaculate house that belonged to a stage actor who often drove up from the city, no doubt drawn to tranquility in a scenic neighborhood. At the terminus of the dead-end pavement, in front of the abode, a dirt road led to some more cottages off in the distance. They were components of a summer retreat and a haven for New Yorkers fleeing urban chaos. Everything askew was contained within our own four walls.

Appearances are often deceiving. In a rare instance when Father was willing to pay for outside contractors, asbestos siding was added to the abode. Then the abode at least looked like a normal house. In front it was a two-story structure. In back, without the towpath, it was three stories reduced to two after Father tore out the floor and never replaced it. He meant to but never got around to finishing the job. That was one home improvement project that never got off the ground, after which the ground remained in ugly display at the bottom of wooden stairs to nowhere. Dwellers inside didn't care. They had already learned to take subtractions in stride.

Peace of mind inside the abode was not disturbed so much by structural flaws but by something more sinister, something invisible, something with qualities resembling a contagious disease. Everyone inside showed signs of infection. Yet no one talked about the disease, if that's what it was, and instead merely endured this additional burden that applied only to us. A remedy was not foreseeable anyway. Abode members could either escape or submit to the inevitable and die there.

It's not possible to think philosophically when one is in a survival frame of mind, but the passage of time can heal wounds and lead to a better perspective. In hindsight, I have a lot of respect for other abode members. I can't say they were family. There weren't hugs or kisses because there wasn't any warmth or enduring emotional bonds. Not with me. Nor among any two other abode members.

Nevertheless, while we may have been diseased, there was a different element that balanced out the equation, a mysterious miracle from somewhere. Every abode member had a work ethic, tried to practice human decency, and fought through their difficulties with poise. Everyone contributed to the greater good of society and the country they lived in. Somehow, despite how loosely we were held together, everyone suffered and struggled but then ventured into the outside world with good intentions.

In August of 1974, I managed to escape the abode by going to boot camp. In November, Grandmother fell down stairs and soon afterwards died. Not long after she died, my other grandmother in Oneonta passed away. It was during my four years of active duty that my sisters and I drifted apart and became permanently estranged. One year after military service, I quit the state of New York and purposely established estrangement with my parents, keeping in contact I hoped, just enough so that they wouldn't feel guilty. There were cousins my sisters and I were once close to, but after moving downstate we almost never saw them again. In a handful of years everything that comprised my life up to the age of seventeen vanished. Afterwards, as the famous song goes, I was on my own. A complete unknown. With no direction home.

In 2007 my adult child was graduating from a nearby college, so I planned a trip to cover many bases from my past. I flew from Florida back to New York, rented a car, drove to and managed to find my mother's grave near Oneonta. It gave me solace to see she was buried alongside her mother and father and her older brother. Next I drove to see my father at one of his assisted living facilities and saw him for the last time. Then, since it was only a 40-minute drive from where my child was graduating, I wanted to re-walk my childhood. Specifically, I wanted to walk again through the Great Creek Locks Forest, the first foreign territory I was able to penetrate, and to conquer some of my paralyzing inner fears. That meant going back to the starting block at the abode.

After turning from Creek Locks Road onto dead end Webster Locks Road, and driving a tenth of a mile, a sight on my right immediately caught my eye. And it amazed me. Shortly after moving into the abode, my father built a stand to hold all the mail boxes in the cluster. Before then everyone had their own on a post and snow ploughs often destroyed them. My father went around to all the other residents, secured their permission, and built the stand to hold all the mailboxes in one convenient location. Forty years later his stand was still there performing the job it was designed for. Father should have itemized a bill and sent it to the national office at the U.S. Postal Service in Washington, DC.

Then I looked to my left and was amazed again. Struck senseless to be exact. At the top of the towpath there was no longer a front door working laboriously because there was no longer an abode. Instead, the space behind the towpath was empty and there was nothing between it and a new modular home down at the end of the field. Whoever my father sold the abode to must have concluded it was useless and had it torn down. While it might have been an eyesore, with structural flaws, and I wouldn't have said it was useless, there was no way for me to disagree with that decision.

The barn that my father and I built for my sister's horse was also still standing. The new woman owner told me it was where they kept their lawn and garden tools.

After my walk through the Great Creek Locks Forest, before driving away, I took another look at the empty space without an abode. Then I remembered the other place where I had lived. After moving the house in Esperance was rented out. Approximately a year later it somehow caught fire during an ice storm and was destroyed. The space where it once stood has been returned to nature. One childhood dwelling went up in smoke. The other, I assume, was reduced to a pile of rubble.

As I was studying the empty space that once held the abode, and for the last time, I had the strangest feeling. Suddenly I felt a wave of lightheadedness. Something akin to but not quite euphoria.

PART TWO

With No Direction Home

The Big Egress

L ate one evening, having had an eye out for just the right moment, I approached my mother and father in the kitchen. They were tired, well past sobriety, unlikely to put up an argument. I handed them papers to sign with an ambiguous description of what they were. Suspicious, they asked a couple questions, paused briefly but signed anyway. In February of 1974, at age seventeen plus four months, I thereby obtained parental permission to enlist in the U.S. Navy Seabees. I left the kitchen anticipating the end of childhood and life at the abode, while heading to a wide-open future come hell or high water.

Although woefully unprepared to do anything after childhood, still hopelessly naive and ignorant, I completed the paperwork, officially enlisted, and allowed the U.S. government to do with me what it wished. Due to a delayed enlistment, necessary to secure my slot as an engineering aide, active duty didn't start until August. However, the Navy already owned me. When my civilian time ran out the Navy recruiter made it clear. He drove out from town to pick me up, drove me to Albany himself (though I had no plans to escape), and put me up in a cheap hotel across the street from the induction center.

The hotel was one of many firsts. I was impressed. The room came with a nightstand, a lamp, and it even had a door. They thought of everything. The next day doctors stuck me with needles and inspected me thoroughly in places on my body I never thought about. I was forced to swear an oath to a god I didn't believe in, but I wasn't strong enough, or inclined just then to raise an objection. Before nightfall I was on a plane, another first, flying to boot camp near Chicago.

On the one hand, the reality of boot camp smacked me in the face due to ignorance and immaturity. On the other hand, boot camp was a walk in the park because I had advantages. From continuously driving with the legs on an escape treadmill, I was in great shape with exceptional stamina. Nothing physical was difficult. In addition, vulnerability was well ensconced inside a false persona and a state of denial. In other words, I still wasn't really me. The day before boot camp ended in October, I turned eighteen.

Leave was automatic after boot camp. That meant flying back to Albany for another first. In one of the biggest surprises of my entire life, my father was not only there to meet me, as I walked off the plane he walked up to me and proudly shook my hand. That was the first, last, and only time I saw that pride. Making me wonder what he was thinking.

The next stop on the Navy itinerary was Engineering Aide school in Port Hueneme (pronounced why me with a knee jerk in the middle), California. A big thrill was seeing an ocean for the first time. Although I came from New York and it was the Pacific Ocean, that didn't matter. Oceans are like ants and yellow cabs. They all look alike. Filling out Dream Sheets for where we wanted to go after training didn't matter either. They must have been for the amusement of office workers back at the Pentagon. Half of us were sent to Alaska. The other half, including myself, were sent to the Public Works Department at Guantanamo Bay, Cuba; which I thought had something to do with a famous Indian but apparently not. In four months at that school in California, I only learned a smidgen about civil engineering. As it turned out though that was plenty enough for doing government work.

Immediately after landing on the runway in Cuba, new arrivals began waiting to leave. It took a year. The naval base at Guantanamo was where I learned to drink, smoke, and swear like a sailor. Although if you call a Seabee a sailor, which he derisively calls a squid, he may hit you. By the time I left Guantanamo a year later, I had learned a lot of card games, only a little more about civil engineering, and virtually nothing about real life.

Next the Navy ordered me to report to a Naval Mobile Construction Battalion, NMCB-133, at Gulfport, Mississippi. Construction battalions were like yo-yos, either in homeport or out on deployment. A few months after my arrival in Mississippi, I was just another yo-yo on a plane, flying to an exotic location, an atoll in the Indian Ocean called Diego Garcia. For Seabees, Diego Garcia was a dreaded dead end and a place where they hated to go. I soon found out why.

Diego Garcia, at the time was in a primitive state of development. It was our job, along with other battalions on a rotation basis, to work it into shape. The only residents were a small contingent of British administrators, some donkeys left over from plantation days, and oversize nasty-looking but harmless bone-crushable coconut crabs. Women weren't allowed on Diego Garcia. Which explains why hundreds of young Seabees didn't want to go there. What merits further explanation, though, is what the Navy was thinking. This was 1976 and the Navy was already in a modernizing frame of mind. The Navy was worried about the reaction of young men to the sudden infusion of women. The Navy wasn't always stupid.

We lived and worked out of plywood huts with tin roofs. The atoll wasn't far south of the equator. Ocean breezes took the edge off of heat but there weren't any cloudy days and the sun was adversarial. We worked long hours six days a week, which made sense as there was little else to do, so no one whimpered about working too much. Still, we didn't work on Sundays and we had a few hours for leisure on other days. There was never a better time to initiate a change of lifestyle.

Before deploying to Diego Garcia I ran with the crowd, wanting to fit in, not yet realizing how futile the effort was. Camaraderie, alcohol, and (mild) drug use were distractions, and in some cases releases that helped to ease a troubled mind. Bored, stuck on an isolated atoll, I began to veer off in my own direction. I quit smoking, and drinking, at least temporarily, and stopped worrying about others' opinions of me. Instead I bought, traded, and borrowed an expanding library of books to try to finally do something about my ignorance.

The deployment to Diego was an opportunity to immerse myself in the wonderful wide world of books and ideas, that typically gave me more pleasure than hanging out with fellow Seabees. That, in turn, advanced the desire to go to law school someday. When I broached that desire with an older veteran Seabee, and tennis partner, asking him if it was possible in my case, he politely masked his doubts and skepticism and said there was a chance I could do it. His encouragement filled me with enthusiasm.

Part way through our deployment, there was a directive for enlisted personnel to report to the administration hut to fill out a form for new dog tags. We had flown half way around the world on the way to Diego Garcia without dog tags, making the timing of the directive a mystery. The form to be completed was brief. It only required us to fill in our name, rank, service number, and to choose a religion. There were three choices. Protestant, Catholic, or Jewish. None of them applied to me so I wrote down Atheist.

A few days later, I was called back to the administration hut. A clerk informed me my religious choice was unacceptable, but I could have No Preference on my dog tags as a substitute. I refused that option and calmly insisted that I was an Atheist and no other term described me.

A week or so went by before I was called back to the administration hut again. There was a new effort to get me to accept None, Buddhist, or Free Thinker for a religion. Anything except what I actually was. Although young, of low rank, and intimidated, again I refused to compromise. One clerk tried to persuade me saying the dog tags were only in case there was a plane crash on the flight back to the states, so authorities would know what type of service to provide. To which I replied, "That is precisely my point. If there's a plane crash and I die," I said, "I don't want any religious service at all."

Finally, the impasse was resolved. I was called back to the administration hut once again and someone handed me new dog tags appropriately stamped Atheist. A clerk told me what happened. Our Commanding Officer had to get up in the middle of the night to place a call to the office for the Secretary of the Navy, due to the difference in time zones, to ask what he should do about his Seabee who insisted on identifying as an Atheist. He was told to let the young man have anything he wanted on his dog tags. That's how I may have made history.

The following year on a different deployment, there was an article in the *Stars and Stripes* newspaper about a fleet sailor who'd been approved to have Atheist dog tags. Mine preceded his. Still, standing my ground and resisting the powers that be is my proudest life achievement. I'm proud to have been a barrier breaker making it easier for others after me. People have a right to identify as who they actually are and not what others want them to be.

On July 4th, 1976, as Americans were celebrating a bicentennial, I was walking the beach on patrol through the night making sure no sea monsters snuck up on us. In the final analysis, however, I left Diego Garcia with good memories of a bad place to spend a deployment.

A long period of confinement to a bubble of land on the northwest tip of an atoll, and a three-mile long, quarter-mile wide isthmus (beyond which was off limits and forbidden), just wide enough for a road that led to an airfield under construction, bottled up youthful energy. It's not an excuse, or justification, but it's a partial explanation for why I regressed to bad habits when NMCB-133 returned to homeport in Mississippi. I went back to smoking, drinking, socializing, and going to rock concerts all over again. That's how a highlight of my life, and one of the worst catastrophes of my life, occurred within a few hours of each other.

First, I hit a walk-off home run for the Engineering Aide softball team that launched us into base playoffs. Then, after celebrating, drinking, and hitting on a bong, and asininely trying to drive, my car did a 180 sideways. The car was upside down on its roof in the eastbound lanes of Highway 90. Two of my best Seabee friends were riding with me. They sustained serious injuries that only by pure luck weren't worse.

My ankle was broken and some damage was permanent. I could never again play softball, tennis, and other sports with proficiency, or enjoyment. It was a small price to pay though for the luck of survival, and especially the guilt I would have had to live with if I had done more harm to, or worse killed two of my best friends. At least a lesson was learned about drinking, drugs, and driving. The mistake was never repeated. And more luck, the lesson it taught me probably saved me from a worse accident at some point in the future.

A thigh-to-toe cast was removed from my left leg shortly before our next deployment to Rota, Spain. Rota was by far the best place and best time in my four-year enlistment. In fact, Rota vastly improved my view of the Navy and my four years of active duty. For the duration of our deployment, approximately nine months, I had disposable income, free time like normal people with a job, and a chance to see a foreign country. Rota also had watering holes that made the bulk of their profits when fleets pulled into port, staffed with bar maids that drifted there from around the globe.

Some bar maids, I know, made money on the side selling female services. Some were lonely and hoping to find a husband. And some, like me, were merely lost souls. With girlfriends from Finland and Ireland, I went to Portugal and Morocco. I went to European hot spots Torremolinos and Malaga. I saw a bullfight, and once was enough. On Sunday mornings, if the fleet wasn't in, I wandered off base and into town out of curiosity, so as to observe another way of life. Wanting to get the most out of opportunity, Spain exceeded expectations.

In addition to off base explorations, the deployment to Spain piggybacked on what had started on Diego Garcia. I continued to transition from a physically active person to an intellectually thoughtful person, at least by aspiration. Although, for the most part, I was still an opinionless blank page.

The majority of off duty time was spent in Silver City, the moniker for our small village of Quonset huts. It gave me ample time to read. On Diego Garcia I read what I could get my hands on. At Rota, a well provisioned bookshop at the Exchange turned me into a kid in a candy store. The bigger the books, the more controversial the subjects, the more they intrigued me. Hedrick Smith's *The Russians*, John Toland's *Adolf Hitler*, Susan Brownmiller's *Against Our Will*, Dee Brown's *Bury My Heart at Wounded Knee*, Eldridge Cleaver's *Soul on Ice*, among others, I recall, pushed me further into a brave new world.

The hardest part of the deployment to Rota, Spain was leaving, knowing that a pivotal point was approaching when I would have to make hard decisions, while expecting to encounter storms of uncertainty. Hindsight now helps me to understand feelings of alienation then, without a family to return to, or a compelling reason to go anywhere, despite knowing what it was that I wanted to do.

When NMCB-133 returned to Mississippi, most of my mates like me were short-timers nearing the end of their enlistments, marking time until discharged. Officers knew they couldn't expect much from us. We were allowed to muster and make it, which meant showing up to say here and then getting dismissed. With only five months to go, sharing an off-base apartment with Seabee friends didn't seem like a bad idea.

It wasn't a bad decision until I was woken up one night by a cop shining his flashlight in my eyes yelling, "Get up, birthday boy!" I was in my bedroom sleeping naked because it was summer and we didn't have air conditioning. A half ounce of weed was in plain view on the dresser. Although I didn't care anymore for smoking pot, incredulous as it may sound, I'd bought some from my roommates out of courtesy and to fit in, although it didn't make me any less to blame.

My two roommates occasionally sold marijuana, buying a pound and then selling it by the ounce, more for the thrill it seemed to me than for profit. Selling marijuana was a bridge too far that I refused to cross. My roommates were small time dealers and hardly abnormal. In the 1970s marijuana was everywhere and nearly as common as cigarettes. In fact, on arrival at Diego Garcia, NMCB-133 made it to a story in the *New York Times,* due to how many in our battalion were charged with illegal possession after British administrators searched our baggage.

The way the drug bust went down, I was told, my roommates and the guy that lived in the apartment below us were playing cards at the kitchen table. Without warning, a cop barged in, without a warrant, claiming he'd smelled marijuana through the open living room window. One roommate owned an incredibly expensive stereo system that attracted a steady stream of party guests. Apparently they were also customers. Local police were probably monitoring our apartment, but the cop's assertion that smelling marijuana gave him the right to enter without a warrant was dubious.

We were taken to the local police station and booked without being put into cells. After paying a bail bondsman, the four of us were released from custody. Not one harsh word was spoken and the entire procedure was amicable. The police even offered us a ride back to the apartment. The distance wasn't far though so we declined their offer and walked back.

We climbed the steps to the second floor, sat at the kitchen table, and discussed our options. Then the guy from downstairs said he still had weed and asked if he should go down and get it. The idea struck a chord; it was the right idea for the moment. So we grabbed four beers out of the fridge, passed a joint, and played cards. In stereo.

The guy from downstairs was also in divorce proceedings. The next day we made an appointment to see his lawyer, who shared an office with a young woman attorney, and they listened as we described what happened. The lawyer agreed to represent us if we paid his fee up front. The legal issues intrigued me, so days later, I went back to their office to ask follow up questions. Then the young woman attorney and I started dating and she became my girlfriend.

The night before our trial, my legally astute girlfriend gave me sage advice. She said our attorney was a really good attorney but he had a drinking problem, and he usually started every case by requesting a postponement. So, she said, if he arrives to court sober, make him try the case without any delays.

She was right. Our attorney did show up sober. Because we were all getting discharged in a few weeks, we expressed our wish to get the ordeal over with. Then as soon as the trial began, our attorney proceeded to embarrass the prosecutor. He ripped off so many objections so rapidly that trying to follow the legal arguments was futile. Although, the judge sustained every objection.

After three recesses, during which our attorney and the prosecutor went out to the hall to negotiate, we accepted a plea. We pled no contest, each paid a $100 fine, and in an essential element of the plea without which we would have continued to resist, a record of the case was immediately expunged. After the plea, our attorney assured us we could treat the case and charges against us as though they never happened. He also told us that in the last recess the prosecutor was begging for any face-saving settlement.

Once a radical, always a radical. The arrest for marijuana possession didn't change my political views one way or another. I had already started to drift away from the drug culture, seeing it as the antithesis of intellectual values. Nevertheless, antiestablishment views remain a part of my general philosophy. What people put in their bodies was not, and still is not a legitimate concern of government. On the other hand, if I steal or do harm to others, deliberately or with negligence, government is welcome to hold me accountable. In modern times, it nags me to see too much emphasis on substances and too little emphasis on consequences for bad criminal acts, and how incentives and disincentives are still out of alignment.

My roommates were discharged a few days before me. It fell on me to settle with the electric company and to close out the apartment. It was good experience to be repeated many times, but I didn't know that then. I still had discomfort in my ankle. It wasn't much but I worried it would persist or get worse, so I wanted to see a doctor at Keesler Air Force base in Biloxi one more time for advice. An NCO whose job it was to complete my discharge papers said to go ahead and get discharged first, then file a claim with the VA. The only thing I knew about the VA was that it wasn't tomato juice. So, I said, "Okay, I'll do that," and added the VA to other puzzles to be figured out later.

My girlfriend mocked me when I told her I was returning to New York. She was right again. It was a dumb decision. But that was one more thing I didn't know. My thinking was, I had no roots in Mississippi, no job, and the relationship with my girlfriend was too recent; not to mention she was far above my level of sophistication. And somehow I knew it was fairly easy to get into the community college back in New York if you graduated from the local high school.

Before leaving Mississippi, there was one more girl to disappoint. She was eight years old, lived in a neighboring apartment, and she had a little girl crush on me. I was her personal monkey bars. She used my knees, hips, and shoulders for steps. After climbing to the top of me she would do a backward flip to a perfect 10 landing.

The night before leaving, as it was already late August with no time to waste, she wanted me to take her to the store with her little girl pocketbook. I knew her mother and it would have been easy to get permission. But it was already past dark and I was worried about getting enough sleep to drive back to New York, 1,400 miles, in one stretch. It's a decision I've regretted ever since. Instead of making my gymnast angel happy, I left her too with a bad impression of me.

In a sweltering apartment, without electricity or air conditioning, I didn't get much sleep anyway. The drive to New York the next day in my tiny already beat up Dodge Colt did not go well. Due to sleep-deprivation-caused hallucinations, by the time I got to New Jersey I was seeing pink rabbits cross the road in front of me.

The box score for four years of active duty reads one damaged ankle, one arrest, and three bruised hearts; the two left behind in Mississippi and my own once I arrived back in upstate New York. And while I'd managed to acquire a smattering of book knowledge, I was still plagued by ignorance and woefully unprepared for living in the real world.

False Start

There was no time to fool around. I arrived back in upstate New York in late August. Fall semester at Ulster County Community College began right after Labor Day. I was unprepared to enlist in the Navy but military service provided all my basic needs without my having to think about them, food, clothing, housing, even a decent income. I hadn't a clue how to fend for myself on the outside.

The first puzzle to solve was figuring out where to live. That meant arguing with my parents and disappointing them. They had counted on me returning to my room, the one without a door and a hole in the floor, and they tried to talk me out of wasting money on rent. They were never going to understand my burning desire for academic achievement. Living with my parents and going to college at the same time was a ridiculous notion. I was naive and ignorant but not that stupid.

Right before a college semester begins is not an opportune time to look for a place to rent, but I had a stroke of luck. There was a classified ad in the paper for a cottage available way up in the hills. The location was perfect for my interests, eight miles from the community college and twice that much from the abode. It was close enough for me to visit my parents, if I chose to do so, and far enough away so that they couldn't call on me, especially since I did not get a phone. The cottage was atop a steep mountain grade surrounded by great scenic beauty. It was conducive to serious studying. Also to loneliness.

When I went to the college to ask questions, a pleasant woman behind a desk asked me if I wanted to matriculate. I stood there dumbfounded, until she broke it down into words I could understand. When she asked me if I wanted to take classes, I was able to shout, "Yes!" She made it easy. There was a well-established procedure for requesting that a high school transcript be forwarded to the college. In minutes my enrollment was assured. Even better, bad high school grades didn't matter. It was like opening day in baseball. I got to start out in first place.

So much for standings on opening day. Due to my ignorance, before the new season got underway I was already in last place. I knew nothing about going to college. I was intimidated, afraid of getting bad grades, and had a poor understanding of course credits and how to manage them. Therefore, I only signed up for two classes and six credit hours. Then I found out the hard way, my course load only made me eligible for part time G.I. Bill benefits, and they weren't nearly enough to live on. My cautious approach to attending college was incredibly stupid.

Fortunately, in anticipation of going to college, during four years of active duty I had accumulated a substantial amount in savings. As it turned out, though, that was also a stupid thing to do. Having too much money in a bank account made me ineligible for financial aid. Many of my Seabee friends bought new cars before they got out of the service. If they went to college afterwards, they probably got help with financial aid. But not me. I was stuck with a beat-up, road weary Dodge Colt that often broke down and needed costly repairs. Consequences for my ignorance however were just getting started.

My savings had to go somewhere. Trying to be smart, I had chosen the wrong high yield savings account at a bank in uptown

Kingston. Because G.I. Bill benefits weren't enough, the only way to live was to periodically drive into town and dip into those savings, and pay a penalty for early withdrawal, that was actually a gouge. One middle aged lady was always behind the counter. Every time I went to the bank, she berated me and lectured me for my foolishness. Gradually, relentlessly, my savings began to dwindle.

Sometimes on the way back from town, I swung back through Creek Locks to visit my parents. We talked for a while, or at least tried to. Both of them were in a late stage of alcoholism and struggling to take care of themselves. My father had progressed to drinking whiskey every night. My mother was losing her eyesight and could barely drive, though her ability to drive was their sole means of transportation. My parents needed me to do more for them then I could without sacrificing personal goals. I always drove away from the abode feeling helpless and depressed.

On one visit, my father and I got into an argument. He wanted me to cut classes for a day and drive him up to the VA hospital in Albany. I wanted to help, and would have, despite suspecting him of being manipulative, but cutting classes was my red line in the sand. He had other ride options, nor would he have leaned on my mother to drive him that far. I had no chances in childhood and had surrendered another four years to active duty just to give myself some hope for a decent life. Our argument was indicative of an ongoing struggle between my parents and myself.

On a later date, I drove up to the VA hospital for myself. My aim was the same as in Mississippi, to get information and advice about my bad ankle. After a thorough examination, plus a month or two, the VA sent me a letter approving me for a 10% service-connected disability. That wasn't my request or what I wanted. The money it amounted to wasn't enough to make a difference. What was done could not be undone.

The first semester of college went well enough. I at least learned the system. Thinking myself wiser, for the second semester I attempted to sign up for seven courses and twenty-two credit hours. An advisor had to sign off on the request. Reluctantly I let him talk me down to six classes and eighteen credits. It made me eligible finally for full time G.I. Bill benefits, but they still weren't quite enough to live on, largely due to costly car repairs. Periodically, I still had to drive to the bank for more lectures from my least favorite bank teller.

Sometimes on lonely weekends, if I had a few dollars in my wallet, I drove to New Paltz, a college town with a strip of bars along Main Street. I went in search of intelligent conversation, hopefully with women my age. A different kind of encounter occurred there one night.

In mid evening, I was sitting at a bar waiting for the night to get busy. A man walked in and sat right next to me. He was a gay man, who, like others before and since, read something in my demeanor or facial expressions that encouraged him to come on to me. He intruded on my space and made it impossible to avoid him. When he told me what he wanted to do to me sexually, my gut reaction was to stand up and walk out.

It wasn't long afterwards that I was at a different bar when the man walked in and sat down right next to me again. Other men might have reacted differently, with more anger, even violence. I never aspired to being a typical man, or a typical anybody for that matter. My passive demeanor is a trait I've learned to accept in myself; though it requires underlying strength that most people never see. The man gave me a small sample of what it must be like for women doggedly pursued by boorish men. Everyone has their limits though. Once more, I stood up and walked to another bar.

Once more he found me. Beyond embarrassment, he prevented me from talking with the opposite sex, which was my reason for being in New Paltz, and thereby ruined my evening. So when I suggested he get in his car and follow me home, he jumped at the offer, as I knew he would. What he didn't know was how well I knew the winding country roads in the area. Losing him was easy. After a mile or two, I rounded a curve, sped up, made a sharp right turn up a steep incline, then watched in the rearview mirror as he continued driving straight.

From time to time, I've looked back on this episode and wondered what happened to that man. Did he live? One thing he told me, ambiguously, was that he worked in the field of drama (a euphemism?) in New York City. The year of our encounter was 1979, a scant few years before newspapers reported that gay men who worked in drama in New York City were dying left and right from AIDS. I could relate to his frustration but not his aggression, and I hope he survived. In the aggregate, the episode was emblematic of my misguided return to New York. Nothing felt right.

Trying to succeed academically while fighting off depression was a balancing act that became increasingly more difficult. Observing my parents' gradual decline was wearing me down. Along with a dearth of good alternatives, feelings of guilt, of responsibility, and concern for my parents all contributed to my decision to go back to New York. Except for the community college, I had no strong reasons to be there other than them. As doubt crept into all my thinking I tried to come up with solutions, for them, and for myself.

One idea seemed to make sense. In every visit with my parents I broached the idea of going to AA meetings. My mother listened but never said a word. My hunch is, if she had gone to AA, she would have fit in and it might have made a difference. She had old fashioned values, though, and was beholden to my father's perspective. Then on one visit, out of the blue, my father surprised me and said he would go.

So I located an AA group and took him to a meeting. As soon as we arrived and were introduced, my father launched into a tirade, bragging about having been an alcoholic for thirty years. Was he mocking me for the audacity of taking him there? Some kind people saw my embarrassment and ushered me into an AL ANON meeting in another room, for dependents of alcoholics. From that room, I could still hear my father ranting.

It was a psychological blow. My effort to help blew up in my face. My father, and therefore my mother too, were not going to change. There was nothing I could do to prevent their downslide. A Rubicon was crossed and a hard lesson slapped me in the face. You can't help those who are unwilling to help themselves.

As the second semester of college was coming to an end, as I was writing papers and studying for final exams, I was seriously considering my future while wondering if life wouldn't be better somewhere else. But where can someone go when they don't belong anywhere? The dilemma with my parents was more than I could handle. That much was certain. A solution to their problems was beyond my level of ignorance. Depression steadily increased. I was grasping for straws trying to find a reason to stay in New York.

In Psychology 101, I always sat in the back of the room by the windows. An astonishingly beautiful girl always sat in the back on the other side. No students ever sat between us, and to my amazement, boys didn't approach her or try to talk with her. Beginning midway through the semester, not wanting to be too obvious, every so often I moved over one seat to my right. It was during the last two classes that we were sitting next to each other, conversing, finding common interests.

As often happens with me, my approach was too cautious. The plan was to ask her out after the final exam. I anticipated that the exam would be easy. What I didn't expect was that she would finish the final exam one minute before me, and I would find myself running after her with too many students between us for me to shout for her attention. When she went out the exit, my last good reason for staying in New York vanished along with her.

When the semester ended, somehow with five A's and a B, and not much money left in my savings account, it made sense to find a summer job. That's why I drove across the Mid-Hudson Bridge to Poughkeepsie to work as a rodman for a land surveying company. The first day, as soon as I drove up, two men walked out to meet me. The party chief said he needed the keys to my beat-up Dodge Colt so they could use it for a survey vehicle. Don't worry, he said, the company will pay you extra for gas. Lawyers would call this a material change to terms making a contract null and void. I stuck it out for the time being but I was never going to stay at that job. They didn't know that then.

It was a crazy idea but sanity was never my strong suit. The idea had roots in my life-long inability to distinguish between adventure and escape. On the way home, after the first day, I stopped at a bicycle shop just to ask questions. On Wednesday after work, I stopped at the bike shop to ask more questions. On Friday, I stopped again and bought the best most expensive French-made touring bike that money could buy. On Monday I treated my new employers with the same respect they showed me. I simply didn't show up for work and never went back.

There was a lot of risk involved, all of it worth taking it seemed to me, requiring a lot of calculation. That didn't necessarily mean good calculation. I didn't even have a clear destination in mind. A few letters and phone calls were exchanged with my girlfriend in Mississippi, so going there was one possibility. The thought of riding to Florida also intrigued me, although I had no connections to that state and didn't know anyone who lived there. My ambiguous plan was to ride south and figure out exactly where to go somewhere along the way. What I needed most, and it was a primordial emotional need, was a complete break from everything in my past.

It was a sink or swim moment. That meant leaving my parents behind, whatever happened to them come what may. I left the Dodge Colt behind for my parents too, which was a stupid thing to do. However, looking back, I understand my intentions much better. Leaving the car there was a ruse obscuring the reality of my escape, planting the notion that I would come back to get it, although that was not going to happen. That was because I had reached a point where I finally understood, a brand-new start somewhere far away was the only way I was ever going to have a life of my own.

The bike shop added a rack over the rear wheel for attaching saddle bags. That way I could carry a lot of gear and supplies. Maps were studied and the location of state parks, cheap places to spend a night, were highlighted. A minimum number of miles ridden per day was factored in, as well as an allowance for bad weather. I tried to prepare like a professional but I was flying by the seat of my pants.

An assessment was made for the risk of being a victim of crime or an accident. Nothing except a shortage of money remaining in my bank account gave me pause. That reality, however, tipped the scales. For very personal reasons I wanted to do everything for myself, and by myself, but monetary considerations forced me to listen to reason and common sense.

Therefore, when I mentioned the bike trip to a friend who never went anywhere, he surprised me when he said he would like to go somewhere too for once in his life. When he suggested we ride together in his car at least part of the way, I wanted to reject his proposal, but the truth was my money would have probably run out at some point. In fact, I anticipated finding work along the way, if necessary, before reaching a final destination. We haggled out the details and set a date to leave. Sharing a ride would pay dividends for us many years later but we didn't know that then.

A few days before leaving I was driving back to the cottage in the hills, through the local community of High Falls, where they were having a street festival. With nothing to do, I pulled over and stood on a small rise to watch the events. As I looked down on a small parade, right before my eyes, only a few yards in front of me, my astonishingly beautiful Psychology 101 angel was riding in the back of an old fashion hay wagon. Our eyes locked. No words were necessary. By the way she was looking at me, she was asking why I didn't ask her out. I was wondering the same thing. Although, at the same time, by then I also knew the answer.

Starting Over All Over

My bike and all my gear fit snugly in the trunk of my friend's Buick. We got an early start, and by nightfall we were able to check into a motel outside Raleigh, North Carolina. My friend couldn't relate to the seriousness and personal nature of my endeavor, severing ties to an ugly past, why I had wanted to make the entire ride by myself, but I was fortunate to start the bike ride free of congested northeast traffic. In the morning I bid my friend farewell and rode off on a diversion.

Although my undefined destination was somewhere south, my younger sister and I still had a relationship. We were on reasonably good terms. So I started by riding forty miles northwest to where she lived with my brother-in-law. He had once lived in New York also, and he had a job at a nearby boy's orphanage. After hours, when the boys were sleeping, I was allowed to shoot hoops in the gym. Sometimes we shot together. In North Carolina we spent two days bouncing around as he bought supplies and worked on his newest house for his nascent home-building business. When I woke up the following morning, and announced it was time to go, my brother-in-law insisted on driving me out of the heaviest tri-city traffic. With my bike and gear in the back of his pickup, he drove me to a country road and dropped me off. We waved goodbye. I never saw my brother-in-law again.

The first stretch of the bike trip took me through endless miles of tobacco fields in North and South Carolina. A hot summer sun scorched my exposed skin. Saddle bags, piles of gear, and an expensive touring bike made it obvious I was not out on a leisure ride. I attracted attention.

One hot afternoon a station wagon with four young men pulled up alongside me, slowed down, and matched my speed. The guy in the front seat on the passenger side asked where I was going. I wasn't sure yet but I told him Florida. Both of us in motion, he then handed me a joint through the window and said, here, you might need this. He paused, thought for a second, then handed me another saying, as a matter of fact take two.

Everywhere the bike stopped, even at a convenience store for a drink and a chance to cool off, people walked up and started asking questions. The impression was that a long bike ride to somewhere else was something they wished they were doing. Still, I had to pretend to be out on an adventure. They would have never understood the degree to which my ride was 99% escape and only 1% adventure. Nonetheless as adventures go it wasn't bad.

At the near end of a long hot day, I was riding through Myrtle Beach, South Carolina. I came across an outdoor round bar mere yards from the side of the road. The temptation was too great. Although it was part of a resort and probably expensive, I was tired and dying of thirst, unable to resist one beer to restore my body temperature. Shortly after sitting down, the beer as well as a complete steak and lobster dinner were set in front of me. I immediately began protesting that the order wasn't mine. A man in casual clothes, who minutes earlier had been sitting next to me, came back and sat next to me again. He was the owner of the posh resort. The meal was free. Even the tip was covered.

On most days, due to a shortage of disposable income, I didn't eat very well. Youthful energy and a lot of practice driving with the legs drove me onward. My bad ankle didn't pose a problem, since I had only lost lateral movement, and therefore could propel myself forward as far as my physical fitness permitted me. The pre-trip estimate for an average day of riding was conservative. Each day riding, my fitness improved.

Not every night was a lucky one, but on good nights I made it to campgrounds that offered the luxury of a cooling off shower. Indecisiveness added to my burden, and to the length of the trip. I was veering west towards Mississippi before settling on riding to Florida after all. A bit of news picked up from bystanders persuaded me to head in that direction.

When making convenience store pit stops, there was a lot of chatter about a monster hurricane bearing down on Florida. This made me want to go there. Yes, on a bicycle! I was at Guantanamo Bay, Cuba, in 1975 when Hurricane Eloise got everyone on the Naval base riled up. The storm was only teasing everyone, however, threatening mayhem before taking a sudden turn. Others breathed a sigh of relief, while I on the other hand, after all the hullabaloo, was sorely disappointed.

The power of nature always fascinates me. A general interest in natural disasters, floods, earthquakes, hurricanes, was originally stoked courtesy of a childhood subscription to *Life* magazine and its vivid photography. I don't want disasters to happen, but if they do happen I want to witness them. So, as Hurricane David got closer, I made a beeline for Jacksonville, splurged on a room at a Motel 6, back when the 6 stood for only $6, and waited for action.

History repeated itself. Once again nothing much happened and there was nothing to see. Hurricane David zipped eastward, stayed off the coast, and only produced gusty winds and sporadic downpours. On the plus side, a lesson was learned about the media and hurricane hysteria, why specific storm details matter, and about not letting oneself get bamboozled by all the hype. By the time the worst of the storm conditions had passed, I was already committed to Florida. It only made sense to continue riding south.

Although the motel room was paid up for a second night, I was anxious, too anxious as it turned out, to make progress, and I decided to leave early. I wasn't out of money yet, but my margin for error had gotten a lot thinner. Starting out in mid evening was not a wise decision. Worse, unlike other days, I had no plan for a stopping point. Darkness approached as occasional storm squalls sideswiped me. After a few hours I rode up to a patrol car stopped on the highway shoulder. Desperate for shelter of any kind, I asked the officer if he knew of a place where I could spend the night. He mentioned an underpass next to some railroad tracks a mile further south. So, I rode towards a sanctuary. Or so I thought.

Trains didn't disturb my sleep that night. Swarms of mosquitoes however were relentless. I slept on the bare ground in a sleeping bag with a teeny tiny hole in the zipper for air. Mosquitoes still found their way inside and feasted on me. A worse physical assault began in the middle of the night after I had finally managed to fall asleep. It was starting to really hurt when I unzipped the sleeping bag and had to squint because a cop was shining his flashlight directly in my eyes. He also initiated the assault by repeatedly kicking me as I slept. My voice cracking with nervousness, I quickly tried to explain how I was stranded by the hurricane, how a different officer had told me about the underpass. The cop immediately spoke in a pleasant voice and said, "that's quite alright son. I was just making sure you weren't already dead."

Although groggy from the lack of sleep, it was a relief to see the crack of dawn in the morning. The storm had passed. There were no more signs of Hurricane David, and no clouds in the sky. With a face that looked like sandpaper from all the mosquito bites, I rode off into the sunshine and palm trees of Florida. Every mile took me deeper into a strange new world. But at the same time it was easy to adjust to riding a bicycle on flat ground.

The thrill that occurred the next day more than compensated for the disappointment of Hurricane David. Also courtesy of a childhood subscription to *Life* magazine, and its amazing photography, and because once upon a time in this country the race to the moon was really important, the space program fascinated me as much if not more than the wrath of nature. As I biked southward and neared Cape Canaveral, it was impossible for me to ignore the billboard signs trying to lure tourists into taking a tour at the NASA Space Center. The cost in 1979 was reasonable. I was given VIP treatment by a polite woman who led me to a side room and a big locker for securing my bike and gear, telling me that about once a year they received a touring biker like me. The tour they gave me was great, and eye-opening. I rode away from Cape Canaveral a happy camper, but I was also running out of camp sites and into the jaws of urban madness.

In fact, there was only one more state park remaining while heading south. I rode to it, had one more shower and one more night of relative ease, then woke up and kept riding south, deeper into an urban unknown. I experienced another thrill when I stopped at a fast-food restaurant in Boca Raton. As I was walking to a table a girl in the back shouted, go ahead and ignore us foxy. I looked around but there was no one between her and me. Then she got up, left her friends, walked to my table and sat across from me. It turned out she was very pleasant, and very attractive, and we had a nice conversation. Foxy is a word I would have never associated with myself in a million years, but it did happen to me once in my lifetime. I rode away from the restaurant thinking to myself: Wow! These Florida girls are really aggressive.

That day's ride came to an end when, without rhyme or reason and long after dark, I came to a stop at Fort Lauderdale Beach. Most of the night was spent sitting up with a runaway girl from Poughkeepsie. Neither of us had a plan for the next day. I finally slept for an hour or two on a park bench. When I woke up she was gone.

My options like what remained of my money were limited. I was in an alien location, a big city, without a friend or acquaintance, and more than a little worried. A trash can caught my eye and an idea hit me. I walked over, looked inside, and found a newspaper from the day before. Combing through the classified ads, a local land surveying company was looking for a rodman. I got on my bike, found a store, bought a street map, and made my way to where the land surveying company was located.

Wearing my only pair of pants and a t-shirt, I went inside and filled out an application, the best that I could. Luck was on my side. The owner of the company was in his office. Someone must have told him I was there. I was invited in for an on-the-spot interview.

At first the owner was hesitant. He was studying my application and he asked me if working for one week in Poughkeepsie was my only land surveying experience. I then explained that I was a Seabee for four years and did some surveying off and on. That was true, but I didn't elaborate. I didn't tell him I still only knew a smidgen about civil engineering. He said, fine; and he added, if I could get there at 7 a.m. the next day he would put me to work.

I had a toehold in Florida.

Extra! Extra! Don't Read All About It

A toehold in Florida concluded a struggle to escape my childhood past, at least physically. What follows is a chronology of psychological struggles that may not be of interest to readers.

Also, significantly, it's necessary for me to discuss myself and my personal problems in great detail. I'm under no illusions. I know that individuals are not important except to themselves, if they have a sense of self-worth, and to their loved ones if they have them. In 1963 the president of the United States, also called the leader of the free world, was assassinated in broad daylight, the TV coverage of which I remember like it was yesterday. The world swallowed the tragedy and just got on with life. Beyond guess-work, the crime wasn't even solved. So, who am I to think that I am important?

Nevertheless, my life story will not be complete or have purpose without a discussion of my state of mind in all its ugly details. Unless a reader has known me personally, and maybe not even then, or they have struggled psychologically in much the same way, the remaining narrative might be too distasteful or boring. They are encouraged to stop reading here, or perhaps, if they still have some interest, to skip ahead to the end of Part Two and Part Three.

Steely Dan Man

There's a question that has been on my mind for years. Are thin men foxy? Having obtained employment, and expecting to have money coming in, I rode away from the land surveying company and rode down Federal Highway until I came to a Dennys. It was a posh restaurant by my standards, but I felt secure enough, and was hungry enough not to care about the cost. I sat at the counter. When I was done eating, the waitress slid my tip money back at me. She must have seen my bike leaning against the window outside and made a deduction. She said, "Honey, get settled in, then come back and tip me." Later I discovered my weight had shrunk to what I weighed back in the 8th grade. Here's another tip. If you find yourself in need of losing weight, try riding a bike to California. It's bound to work. In my case, I was never foxy more than once.

The next order of business was to move into my new Florida home. That meant riding further south to the friendly confines of a Motel 6 on State Road 84. Due to a budget shortfall, the meal at Dennys was my last supper for a few days, but the land surveying company didn't hold back paychecks, so I only had to make it to Friday. I survived. After that, weekly wages were enough to cover the cost of the room, to buy food, and ever so gradually to deposit a few savings in a local bank, in the right kind of savings account without having to listen to lectures from bank tellers.

Life was good at Motel 6. The room was affordable. It was comfortable, out of the elements, and within a 15-minute bike ride to work. My weekly paychecks also allowed me to indulge in refreshments. On the ride back in the afternoon, I stopped and bought a cold beer in a can. At the motel room I sat a few inches in front of the air conditioning unit, drank the beer, and basked in the relief as heat, absorbed while working outside in the sun, dissipated from my body. One could also call it a crash course in acclimation.

After adjusting to a new lifestyle, next on the agenda was taking college courses again. Despite setbacks, and that it was still a pipe dream, the flame hadn't gone out on the desire to go to law school, somehow, someday. So I did some reconnaissance. I rode out to Broward Community College (BCC) in Davie, Florida to see if I could take courses there. Luck was on my side again. An oddly scheduled course for Sociology 101 started in October. Any course would have sufficed. It meant riding an additional seven miles to class, and seven miles back twice a week, but by then I could commute through urban traffic nearly as fast as cars. I applied, and was accepted, contingent upon receipt of transcripts from previous colleges.

When stationed on the Navy base at Guantanamo Bay, Cuba, Old Dominion University offered a three-credit course to enlisted personal. I had taken the course out of boredom and for something to do. I had forgotten that it too was Sociology 101, which meant I was taking the same course twice. At BCC it didn't matter though. The course served its purpose. Once you're in a college system they never kick you out. My foot was planted firmly in the door.

As it turned out, taking a college class was valuable for more than academic momentum. A classmate from New York City, also escaping his past, told me about an apartment I could get into. He said the landlord let you buy your way in. You just had to pay a little extra each month until last month's rent and security were satisfied. On a monthly basis, the apartment cost less than the motel, and although the bike ride out to BCC stayed the same at seven miles west, the apartment was north of the Motel 6, closer to my job.

The apartment I rented was the lower left of four identical studio apartments stacked in a square. My classmate rented the one on the upper right. The other two, above and next to me, were also rented by young wayward sons from up north. We all became friends and hung out together. My apartment was slightly different, however, in that it was attached to a two-bedroom corner apartment also on the ground floor. A sealed off door with an inch crack underneath connected my apartment to it.

The two-bedroom apartment was rented by a young couple who I knew only by sight. In fact, out of disdain I tried to avoid them. They seemed to spend all their leisure time playing their only record album, *Steely Dan's Greatest Hits*, always at full volume, the same record and the same songs, over and over again. I never once heard any other record of theirs. And I heard *Steely Dan's Greatest Hits* so much, so often, and so loud blasting through the crack under the door, all these years later, I still can't stand to listen to *Steely Dan*.

Adding insult to injury, in the deal made with the landlord, I shared an electric bill with the young couple and had to pay for half of the electric bill, even though I used a fraction of the electricity. I only had a mini fridge and a hot plate for a stove. Nevertheless, life was improving and I was thrilled to experience a bit of upward mobility. That was until disaster struck.

One day while riding back from work, heading west on Davie Boulevard and tracing the right shoulder stripe with my front tire, a car passed me too close for comfort and almost hit me. Instinctively I slid to the right a couple inches. It was just enough for the skinny bike tire to sink into the slit of a storm drain. The force slightly buckled the frame and prevented the front wheel from turning. Instantly my sole means of transportation was a total loss.

The disaster didn't cost me my job, but instead of riding, I walked four miles to work in the morning and four miles back in the afternoon. It meant, however, I would have to drop my college course. So, I hitchhiked out to BCC. I was standing next to the professor at his desk, explaining why it was necessary to drop his class, when a student in the back of the room overheard me and spoke up. She asked where I lived. When I told her she said it was right on her way. She offered to pick me up on Tuesday and Thursday evenings and to bring me back after class.

Mary from Pennsylvania with her red VW bug averted further disaster. Looking back, she was one of the essential people many of us meet in the course of our lives, one who in my case managed to penetrate my stubborn independence, without whom we, and even stubborn me, would have never gotten anywhere. I was thankful then, and remain eternally grateful.

It seemed like such a small problem. In late afternoons, and on weekends, I awkwardly wheeled my expensive French touring bike around to local bike shops. At every shop it was the same story. There was nothing they could do; my bike couldn't be repaired. Then someone would launch into a sales pitch and try to sell me a new bike. Instinct, and stubbornness, which is sometimes a good quality to have, told me not to get suckered in. It was depressing, though, to see the bike in my apartment leaning against a wall serving only as a dirty clothes rack.

Then one morning I bumped into Steely Dan Man. The peculiar timing as we were both leaving and had opened our doors at the same time, made some greeting necessary. We nodded. Then one word led to another and we were soon asking about each other's line of work, which is how working men typically relate to other men and find common ground. When the subject of my damaged bike entered the conversation he had an idea. He worked in a machine shop and had to put in a few hours, even though it was a Saturday. So we loaded up my bike and headed there.

At the shop he placed the bike in a stand-up oversized vice, heated the frame with a torch, and bent the frame back to its original position. The front tire no longer pinched. The only differences were a tiny wrinkle and a small burn stain. Other than that, the bike was as good as new. I had my transportation and my freedom back. Florida skies were sunny again. Mary in her VW bug continued to pick me up on class nights. Nothing was ever going to make me like *Steely Dan* but I wasn't going to complain. Steely Dan Man was my new best friend.

1979 was a good year and it ended well too. The land surveying company gave out Christmas bonuses. I had never had one before and only started working there in September. It must have been a lean year. All the other employees were complaining about the paltry amount of their bonuses. But when I opened up an envelope and saw a check made out to me personally for $37.50, I couldn't believe it was all mine.

Extra money and being back in a college system went a long way towards improving my outlook. With an imaginary clock ticking inside my head, knowing how far I had fallen behind collegiately, wanting to make up for lost time yet again, for the spring semester I signed up for four courses and twelve credit hours. The classes were all in the evening, Monday through Thursday. It would mean a lot of bike riding, to work and back five times a week, and to college and back four times a week, but I was young and invincible.

Twelve credit hours also qualified me as a full-time student, making me eligible for full time G.I. Bill benefits. With wages from a full-time job, and the G.I. Bill, I could double dip. It was the perfect get rich scheme.

In New York, I was constantly depressed. Distractions caused me to lose focus and stifled hopes for a brighter future. 1979 began in an isolated mountain cottage in the dead of winter, and ended on flat ground in Florida sunshine with a new lease on life. The transition came with a lot of risk, as expected, but good luck outweighed bad luck and I had landed on my feet. I didn't stay there long.

One Fall After Another

1980 started out great despite the workload. Five times a week I rode a bike to work, worked outside for eight hours, then rode back to the apartment. Three times a week I rode out to BCC for a three-hour evening class, then rode home to sleep. Studying was crammed into weekends in tandem with *Steely Dan's Greatest Hits*. It was a demanding lifestyle that required a lot of energy, but I had had years of practice driving with the legs. Once a week, Mary, my angel in a VW bug, took an evening class. On those nights she again picked me up and took me out to BCC and back saving me time and energy.

The work day started at 7 a.m. College classes were from 7 p.m. to 10 p.m., unless a professor let students out early, which they usually did. The routine left little time for rest and relaxation. The routine also required approximately 100 miles a week riding a bicycle in urban traffic. Looking back through the prism of time, I can now see how my assessment of risk was off the mark.

For a little while anyway, with a weekly paycheck plus the G.I. Bill, I was turning a nifty profit. For the first time in a long time, maybe ever, life was on the right track: I was making forward progress. However, maybe it's a result of instability made worse by a lack of sanity. Or, perhaps I'm no different from anyone else, and maybe it's just a false perception. But it seems there were a number of occasions whereby the course of my life was radically altered by freak events. A few weeks into the new year, I encountered two freak events in rapid succession.

When I rode out to BCC one evening, I arrived to a complete power outage. Students were gathered around in small groups, in the parking lot, on sidewalks, in open spaces and near the buildings. It was blind chance that I was standing near the door to get inside, and a girl was standing next to me. It was too dark to see her except in silhouette. We exchanged a few words. As the power outage continued, words turned into a conversation. When it appeared that the power wasn't going to come back on, we agreed to talk somewhere else. She drove, I rode, and we met outside the campus at a Big Daddy's package store and lounge, which were once upon a time ubiquitous in Florida. The girl became my girlfriend. By the time 1980 ended, my girlfriend was my wife.

Shortly after our initial meeting, and after only one date, the process of getting to know one another was accelerated by a secondary freak event. At the conclusion of our creative writing class, I was riding home on a drive that went around the BCC campus. I was pedaling along at a rapid pace. A car driving towards me made a sudden left turn in front of me. We collided. For those who haven't experienced the thrill of a head-on collision with a car while riding a bicycle, my advice is to pass it up and find better forms of recreation.

Someone told me later that my head broke the windshield of the young woman's car. Whether that's true or not I can't say. Honestly I never saw the car, not even before it hit me. There was no recollection of seeing it anyway. Afterwards, I floated in and out of consciousness. I recall laying face up on the hood of the car while hearing background noises fade in and out. One of the noises came from the young woman crying to someone that she thought that I would stop. That made me wonder what she was thinking. There were no stop or yield signs and no reason for me to even slow down. Later her words brought me relief. She confirmed the accident was not my fault for not changing worn out batteries to my headlamp.

While on the hood of the young woman's car, it was like I was looking down at myself from above. My brain felt detached from my body. I was completely numb. Except for occasional background noises, I couldn't hear, see, or feel anything. The numbness was so complete I wondered if I was alive, or in the process of dying. What I remember clearly is the peace it gave me when I told myself, if I was going to die it was all right. It sounds like a contradiction but I'm a coward that doesn't fear death. When people say there are no Atheists in foxholes, they don't speak from personal experience.

People must have moved me from the hood of the car. My next memory is of me lying on the ground shaking like a leaf in the wind. People were yelling at me, apparently trying to figure out what was wrong, but it wasn't injuries that made me shake. A rogue cold front had marched down the peninsula bringing a dose of winter to south Florida. I was a live fish tossed in an ice chest. As told to me later, though I have no memory of it, somewhere between the ground and an ambulance I shouted for my girlfriend.

It must have been alienation, loneliness, vulnerability, or a combination that caused me to shout for her. Afterwards my girlfriend indicated it was inappropriate for me to ask for her then, as we still hardly knew one another. I surmise she was right. Appropriate or not, she was tracked down, and instead of driving home she drove to the hospital.

As it turned out my injuries weren't that bad. I had a broken clavicle, that hurt like hell, but doctors were mostly worried about a severe concussion. The concussion was so severe it could have caused me to go into a coma and killed me. They would not release me from the hospital, they said, unless my girlfriend was willing to sit up with me and make sure I stayed awake throughout the night. She agreed to do this.

She then drove me to my apartment where we both slept like logs. My girlfriend was an iconoclastic rebel, just like me. Also, nothing unites two people like a threat to life itself. Countless book and movie plots have exploited that theme. Whether my girlfriend would have become my wife without a power outage, and an accident, is an open question.

Figuratively my life was balancing precariously on the head of a pin. A freak power outage and a head-on collision, coupled with a drop of love that I wasn't prepared for, sent me on a head-first plunge. It was enough to knock me onto an entirely different track. Then I went back to doing what came naturally to me. I started to run again. Except this time, I dragged someone else with me.

My ex-wife may disagree, but I believe originally there was a great deal of love between us. Our love could not endure, in large part because of the manner in which I subconsciously lied to her. I projected the image of a young man full of energy, ambition, and confidence, one capable of achieving any lofty goal; but these were only the projections of a false persona with a state of denial. On the inside, I was still just a scared little boy, years away from discovering divisions within my fractured soul.

After the collision, I doggedly pursued my girlfriend. Then, once we were involved, in for an inch meant in for a mile, no matter how much it cost me: Or her. Therefore the truth is, if there were consequences to me later as a result of our relationship, and our marriage, I was the catalyst to everything that happened afterwards. It took me years to figure that out.

Split Decisions

A lifetime of drought was over. Like a dried-up shrub in the desert responding to rain, a drop of love was all that was needed to rearrange my priorities, and to transform my vision of what it meant to be living. In the aftermath of the bike accident, my girlfriend had indicated she might care about me as much as I cared about her. So out of character it seems to me, as I never acted that way before then, I pursued her, determined not to let her get away. It's not uncommon for young men attracted to young women to act that way. What distinguished me was the extent to which I could deceive her and also myself.

It's shameful to recall how much pressure I put on my girlfriend, to in turn put pressure on the owner of the house with whom she was living, to allow me to move in with them. I did not let up until resistance was overcome. Unbeknownst, even to myself, I was laying a trap.

The original idea was nothing elaborate. After graciously being allowed to move in with my girlfriend, and wanting to replace the touring bike that was destroyed, I persuaded my girlfriend that we should both buy new 10-speeds. Then we'd be able to take short trips, enjoy the outdoors, and get more exercise. That's what we did and at first it worked out as planned. One weekend we rode over to Key Biscayne on a Friday afternoon. We were too busy having fun to pay attention to the news. Sunday we saw plumes of smoke everywhere, because we didn't realize we'd be riding back through the McDuffy riots that rattled Miami. We were lucky to make it back without incident.

My girlfriend and I both dealt with the after effects of childhood adversity. We were vulnerable to mirages that promised greener grass somewhere else. So, when I mentioned riding a bicycle across country was something that always intrigued me, she provided a small amount of positive feedback. She said she would like to do something like that. Her lukewarm response was a red cape to my bullishness.

That was all I needed to explore, to plan, to scheme, and to make such a trip seem plausible. Truth be told, however, it was never more than a harebrained idea. Still, after gathering information and adding it to my amateur touring experience, I convinced my girlfriend it could be done. She agreed to go with me and we started to work out the details. Perhaps embarking on a cross-country bike tour wasn't a good idea. On the other hand, we were incredibly young. Young people look forward. It's when you're old that you look back.

What's particularly shameful for me is recalling how little thought I gave to the owner of the house where we were living. After she did me the favor of allowing me to move in, in a scant few months I took away her boarder and deprived her of income. She excused me, she said, because she didn't want to stand in the way of love. That's what I thought it was too, but it was more than that.

The spring semester at BCC ended. We set a date, quit our jobs, tied up loose ends. We started out biking westward on Tamiami Trail with an overly optimistic, and unrealistic, destination of Seattle, Washington. We knew some people along the way and were able to stop and visit with them, first in Lehigh Acres, then in Largo, Florida. That allowed us to break up the early part of the trip into small manageable segments.

We made it to Tallahassee and spent a couple nights in a motel there, resting and recharging our bodily batteries. We were impressed by how different that city looked compared to the Florida we were familiar with. In the back of my mind, it occurred to me that Tallahassee was still Florida, and not far distant from many of my girlfriend's relatives.

We made it across the Florida panhandle and to Mississippi, where we spent two pleasurable days with one of my Seabee friends and his wife. The bike trip had progressed well to that point. Nothing was too strenuous, or menacing. From Mississippi we rode a short distance to New Orleans, where my girlfriend's mother knew someone who could put us up for a night. Her friend did, but without enthusiasm, and indirectly through an acquaintance. Coincidently, this was where fun on the bike trip started to wane. Not helped by the fact we didn't know a soul between New Orleans and Seattle. Still, we kept going.

We were biking in June. It was a sizzling hot summer. We made it to Pine Bluff, Arkansas when my girlfriend suddenly announced she had had enough. Mine was a lone wolf voice arguing that we should finish what we started. She told me to go ahead, keep riding, but she wasn't going any farther. Her refusal was stronger than my argument. We boxed up the bikes and rode a Greyhound bus back to Miami. In hindsight she probably saved both of our lives.

Many years later, I was told, my girlfriend, then my ex-wife, enjoyed the bike trip and she was glad she did it. It was an impressive feat, after all, to ride bicycles from Miami to Arkansas. Old age is enriched if there are adventures and good memories to reflect back on. However for me, the bike trip is not one of my better memories. It's too disturbing to recall my boorish behaviors before the bike trip, my motivations that were hidden to myself, and remembering those times during the bike trip when I was a jerk. My ex-wife probably remembers what I mean. It's no excuse but there were occasions when the worst fragment of my divided soul reared its ugly head.

We arrived back in Miami jobless, homeless, and with no choice but to stay with my girlfriend's parents. Neither of us wanted to stay there longer than necessary. So I invoked a contingency plan. I reminded my girlfriend how attractive Tallahassee was, how it was still Florida, and not far from her relatives in the bay area. I emphasized how we could go there and establish new lives for ourselves. Selling her on the idea was easier after destroying the life she already had. Unlike many salesmen, it wasn't true that I cared nothing for the quality of the product once the sale was made. The problem was that half of me cared and cared a lot. The other half had ulterior motives.

While we were on the bike trip I asked my girlfriend to marry me, and she said yes. I found a life partner, I thought, and a wife. At the conclusion of the bike trip, also important to me I now know, and admit, was knowing that Tallahassee was a college town, not as densely populated as south Florida, with two universities, a community college, and a law school. After the bike trip was over and the dust had settled, we headed to a location that was better for me, and more comfortable for me, than the urban chaos of Miami.

Cracks in the Foundation

We started out as strangers in Tallahassee, aliens really, poor, jobless, with almost nothing in the way of possessions. We knew that we'd have to eke out a living, which is why we took out a lease at a cheap apartment. It was a crazy apartment that was once part of a big house carved up into odd rooms with odd features. Half the apartment had 16-foot ceilings. Because the landlord was useless for maintenance, I once changed a light bulb by standing tiptoe on a chair after the chair was placed on a table. The bedroom tilted downhill. The location was convenient, however, within walking distance of everything relevant in Tallahassee. The apartment was also one block over from a Chinese restaurant, where, if we had enough money, once a week we took advantage of an all-you-can-eat buffet.

It was a struggle at first, and even after we found jobs. We had to make car payments on a new car my wife had bought before we met. Prevailing wages were far below what they were in south Florida. We had to adjust to a reduction in disposable income, and adjust to Tallahassee's southern culture, which was easier for me with military service and having lived in Mississippi.

She went to work doing what she did in Miami, processing loan applications. I found another bottom-of-the-ladder job as a rodman for a local land surveying company. Despite a rough start, and financial difficulties, we made incremental but steady progress.

We decided to get married in Pennsylvania where she was originally from. That put the wedding within reach of most of our relatives. The wedding wouldn't have been possible without the expertise and extraordinary effort of my girlfriend's maternal grandparents, and their years of experience with weddings. Two of my school friends came but no family members. Her mother came but not her father. Our marriage began under poor auspices but I was too naive to notice.

Shortly before the wedding, I had quit my job and applied at the local community college. I was hell bent on academic achievement and only lacked eighteen more credits for an A.A. degree. The decision was justifiable because income as a full-time student with the G.I. Bill exceeded rodman wages. Although true, this was when disagreements about money crept into our marriage.

Initially though, we cruised along as a happy young couple. We went to movies and concerts, to the park on weekends, took short bike rides, saw famous guest lecturers at Florida State University, and from time to time we drove downstate to visit with her relatives and spent weekends with them.

Our values and opinions seemed well aligned. Once we went to a time share promotion on the beach. After seeing the presentation, we analyzed it together, came to the same conclusion, and rejected the deal because it wasn't worth the cost. We usually saw eye to eye politically as well. When passage of the ERA amendment nationally hinged on Florida's ratification, we walked over to the capitol where there was a last-ditch demonstration in support. We both wanted the amendment to pass. We lost. But we were on the same side and were both disappointed.

One afternoon, after classes, when I stepped into the apartment my wife was sitting on the sofa waiting for me. She told me she was pregnant and wanted to know what I thought. I said I wasn't ready to be a father. But she then said that she wanted to have the baby. I stood still for a moment in shock, then slowly turned left. I walked out of the long skinny living room and into the equally long skinny kitchen, paced back and said, "Okay. Let's do it." I was then and forever more all in.

Good communication between my wife and I was often a problem except for the best interests of our child. That was the one area where we discussed matters openly and effectively. When it concerned our child we were on the same page and virtually in sync. Neither of us wanted our child to face the adversities we had to deal with in our childhoods, and we were determined to give our child better opportunities than what we had had.

After we agreed to be parents, my wife suggested Lamaze classes. Once she explained what they were, and overcame my ignorance, I was eager to participate. When our child was born, nurses in the delivery room complimented me for having been a good coach. The minute we brought our newborn home from the hospital, I placed our sleeping child in the crib at the foot of our bed and took a photo. I wanted to document the contrast between a tiny beginning and a bright future. I was sure the most important time in a person's life, by far, is when an infant first begins to process existence in a brand-new world. Also, no way was my child going to suffer from the poor messages I received after I was born.

Every conscientious person knows that early child care is of critical importance. To that purpose, no greater contribution was made to our child than what my wife managed to accomplish. There wasn't a Family Leave Act at the time. She would have lost her job because her employer gave her hardly any time off after the birth of our child. I was finally a full-time student at the university. Somehow, miraculously, my wife found Mrs. Fuller, a middle age gentle as a lamb woman willing to care for an infant at her mobile home. She understood infants and their unique needs, and had the patience to care for them properly. My wife and I were able to breathe easily during the day, knowing that our child was safe and in good hands.

There's no way to know how much difference that may have made over the long run. Especially compared with the alternative, throwing an infant to the wolves potentially, putting a newborn in a day care center back when they received little public attention and had almost no quality control.

No doubt it was because of an upbringing with mixed messages and poor influences, that even as a child, I watched other children and their families and thought about child development. I observed, thought, and weighed what worked for other children and what didn't. As an adult my child rearing opinions were enhanced by additional research and study.

Before our child was born, I believed that it wasn't exactly the first three years or the first three months of a child's life that matters the most, although they are important. There's an inverted pyramid whereby the closer to birth the more significant are the early messages that a newborn infant receives.

And I believed, and it was confirmed, that newborn infants have greater cognitive abilities than are commonly recognized, which are too easily overlooked and underappreciated. Positive messages right after birth will aid an individual throughout their life, and it's why early (even subtle) negative messages are apt to cause lifelong damages, from which a person may struggle against for their entire life, and never know why. But that's not all that matters. It isn't only how much we love our newborn babies that counts. It's a two-way street. Equally important is what newborn babies, after opening their eyes and trying to make sense of where they are, think about us and their brand-new world.

Taking it a step further, I believe in treating babies and young children as individuals, free ultimately to form their own opinions about everything, politics and religion included. And, I suspect so much of what we see in the way of crime, violence, and war is a byproduct of poor childhood influences. Note that belief is not the same as fact and certainty. Doubt and humility are too much a part of my makeup for me to qualify as a know-it-all. Years later, as will be seen, doubts to my child rearing opinions and methods overwhelmed and agonized me.

In any case, nothing on earth was ever more important to me than child development. That was my attitude and motivation following the birth of our child.

When our newborn cried in the night, often with a nudge, always as a volunteer, it was usually myself that got up out of bed to see what the problem was. That's how I learned to distinguish between signs of hunger, fright, discomfort, and so on, which established an early meeting of the minds between myself and our child. I regularly read a three-page plastic bath book to our infant and then better books as our child matured. I safely tossed and caught our infant as an introduction to motion, crawled on the floor and played alongside our baby all through the toddler stage. I was committed to our child's development like nothing else in my life before or since, determined to give our child the best head start in life possible.

Almost every afternoon after classes, I took our infant for long walks in a stroller. My thinking was twofold. The more a baby sees the more it facilitates learning, and the wider the base the higher it's possible to construct a tree of knowledge. Second, words are an inadequate substitute for allowing babies to put pieces of a puzzle together by themselves, free of lectures.

From our crazy apartment we had moved to a trailer on the south side of town, conveniently next door to an elementary school.

Convinced that physical development is as important as mental development, and also easily overlooked, after hours and on weekends as our baby grew and was able, we went over to the school to use the playground equipment. Everything I did with our child was with the intent to encourage, never to force, or to suffocate, or to insist on a particular idea or lifestyle direction.

Maybe our child was exceptional and it may invoke disbelief, but I was learning from our infant and I saw what I saw. Once, when our infant was less than six months old, we were in the kitchen together, and our infant was in a car seat that was set on the table so we could see eye to eye. When my wife stepped inside the door I said to her, "Watch this." Our infant, practically a newborn, was able to raise an arm and point to objects around the room, the stove, window, overhead light, and whatever was asked. That confirmed my belief that baby cognitive abilities, even among infants, are too often underestimated.

My ex-wife may disagree, but I believe what I believe and it comes without criticism. We were barrier breakers. Relatively speaking, I was a humanist and she was a pragmatist, which made me better suited to play the maternal-like role for our child in early childhood, and for her to take over and play the paternal-like role in the latter half of childhood. In the era in which we were parents, and the southern environment in which we lived, it was necessary to pretend otherwise.

However, if I was a hands-on parent in a maternal-like role, when it concerned child care my wife and I were always partners. We openly discussed what helped and what hindered our child. We didn't baby talk to our infant. We talked to our baby the same as we did with other mature individuals. At age three, our toddler was so articulate a friend of mine commented, talking with our child was like talking with a very short adult.

We had purchased a kit designed to give infants a head start on reading by having them memorize words written in big letters on flash cards. It didn't take long for us to jointly decide the method was counterproductive. Years later, our child as an adult told me, since my wife and I were always reading, the child simply thought reading was normal, followed our example, and became a reader too.

Nonetheless, despite love and commitment, my parent qualifications were questionable. I had too many character flaws. My book knowledge was okay and improving, but my ability to function in everyday life was a work in progress. I lacked confidence, and perspective. I was too stubborn, too independent-minded. Naivety and a state of denial blinded me to realities. Everything seemed fine on the surface. I was enthusiastically taking political science courses at the university. Interacting with our child, and envisioning myself as a husband and a dad, gave me a great deal of pleasure, and they went a long way toward satisfying a weak ego. Contentment, however, was based on an artificial foundation. And the happier one is the more it hurts when happiness is lost.

My wife constantly pressured me to get a job in addition to going to college full time. I protested that my grades would suffer, which was important for getting into law school. I argued that the money I brought in, with student loans plus the G.I. Bill, was my fair share of income. I had been deprived of opportunities as a child, and put in four years of active duty just to give myself a chance. There was one more grievance that I didn't hesitate to raise, but for proprietary reasons I will not mention that grievance again. Suffice it to say our dispute was ongoing without resolution.

A chasm of miscommunication existed between my wife and I. We didn't discuss the nuts and bolts of income and expenditures. In my mind she was an expert, so I left money management to her. As a consequence for ignorance and a lack of attention, my ability to resist pressure underwent steady erosion.

The subject of money was not my only area of ignorance and ineptitude. Despite a 3.75 GPA and a pending undergraduate degree magna cum laude, I lacked confidence, and know-how, for going to law school directly after earning an undergraduate degree. The only positive step I took toward that ultimate goal was to sign up for and take the LSAT (law school aptitude test). I was too stubborn and independent-minded to ask for advice, and planned on figuring out how to get into law school by myself.

Full time course work was taken, and student loans were taken out in summer semesters, fast forwarding me through undergraduate studies, and earning me a bachelor's degree in December of 1982. As with other achievements, going back to elementary school, a graduation was just a feather in the cap. In lieu of a graduation ceremony surrounded by well-wishers, advancement gave me intensified arguments with my wife over money. Without me contributing to household income, she was not without justification.

After the last final exam, my wife demanded that I get a job immediately. As it was discovered later, below the surface something was weighing on her mind. I wanted a job too. Doing nothing is not in my DNA. Unfortunately, the timing of her demand coincided with an economic downturn. I tried to get a job at State of Florida offices in Tallahassee, with banks, box stores and grocery stores, everywhere I could think of. Nothing happened fast enough. There was no time to spare.

In desperation, my wife arranged a trip for me. She sent me downstate to spend a week with her paternal grandmother, to see if I could land a job down there. The story was the same though. Everywhere I tried to get a job I heard complaints about a bad economy. I even bit a bitter pill, humbled myself, and applied at local land surveying companies. However, most of them had already gone out of business. Ahead of time, I was warned about her grandmother's irascible personality. The only thing that went well that week was that the two of us got along like long lost friends.

Upon arriving back in Tallahassee, and not given any time to breathe, my wife was already packing up. She announced we were returning to Miami. I wanted to object but without college or a job I had no leverage. There was no choice but to leave one open-ended future and head towards another. At least we were still a team, I thought.

Before leaving, the owner of the trailer came by to tie up loose ends. Ours was a stand-alone trailer. He had others around town that he rented out for extra income. We didn't know that. He also told us he had been a civil servant for the state of Florida for many years, and we didn't know that either. He said he hated to see us go because he thought we were a nice young couple that always paid the rent on time. When he learned we were leaving because I couldn't find a job, he said he wished he'd known that because there were many state employees who owed him favors. He could have easily found me a job.

At the time this was a stake through the heart. It still hurts too much to think about it.

Bombs away

There was nothing wrong with Miami other than it was a place I didn't want to be. I am, after all, a small-town boy at heart; one who prefers quietude in the country to the hubbub of cities. Nevertheless, for those who don't have it handed to them, a living has to be made somewhere.

My wife soon found a new job as a retail manager in a mall, working for a corporation with retail stores from coast to coast. She landed a job that paid well with potential for advancement. Pressured to get a job ASAP, it didn't take me long to find a new job either, as a rodman for another small land surveying company - my fourth if you're scoring from home.

Land surveying jobs for me were like fly paper. Time and again, I was forced to take them for one reason or another. Time and again, they trapped me and prevented me from getting somewhere in life. Civil engineering had matched an aptitude on a military entrance exam, but it was impossible for me to disassociate that line of work with what I had to do to escape a hopeless childhood. To be stuck in a land surveying job, symbolically, meant to be stuck in an ugly past forever. The only future land surveying promised, as I saw it, was being a toady for the rich, while poorly paid, always being subject to layoffs in bad economic times, and in Miami the possibility of contracting skin cancer as happened to some of my coworkers after too many years in the sun.

On the other hand, life always has contradictions. I was born to work. The harder and nastier the work the greater is the satisfaction afterwards. For those not accustomed to hiking and sweating in the sun while swinging sledgehammers and machetes, getting bit up by bugs, wading in swamps with snakes and alligators, spending their workday on freeways among screeching tires and honking horns, or next to an earth-shaking pile driver, they may miss out on the satisfaction at the end of the week when picking up a paycheck, knowing how it was earned. Also contradictory, even as I hated being trapped in Miami, the surveying job there was the most fun I've ever had in employment. Our surveying tasks were so multifaceted, and stimulating, no one who didn't work with us could have imagined what it was that we did for a living.

The North Miami company that I worked for was one of the few that also did hydrographic surveying. One of our regular clients was the Army Corps of Engineers. In addition to different kinds of surveys on land, we surveyed lakes, canals, rivers, swathes of the ocean, as well as the Port of Miami and government cut, the dredged outlet for ships headed to sea. We also did work for a cruise ship company that twice sent us, by cruise ship, to do hydrographic surveying in Haiti.

Within Florida, our area of operations stretched from Key West to Fort Myers, including a centerline run across Lake Okeechobee, and up the east coast as far as the St. Johns River. We worked and breathed in a real world that encompassed every aspect of natural and human life. On any given day, a crew member didn't know if they'd be working in a subdivision, downtown, on a highway, at a landfill, a nuclear power plant, or on a lucky day sent to do a job on the beach. As it was Miami, it interested me personally to work with coworkers from all around the world. With our diverse cast of characters and unusual work requirements, and settings, some of us often ruminated on how our job would have made for a great TV sitcom.

If a crew member wanted to increase their paltry wages, and if they were willing to go out of town Monday through Friday on a Corps of Engineers job, their paycheck was sweetened with overtime pay plus a per diem supplement that exceeded living expenses. Despite the fun and satisfaction, however, the desire to go to law school never stopped burning inside me.

Between the two of us, my wife and I finally had income that elevated us to a decent middle-class standard of living. We were making headway and should have been able to improve on the lousy apartment where we were living. Then one day, I came home and discovered the bomb, that I surmise was placed where I couldn't help but find it. Looking back, it's depressing to recall how deep that bomb buried me, and for how many years after it went off. Nevertheless, I believe my reaction at the time was proper. I played the dutiful role of a family man trying to put out a fire.

The bomb was a letter written to my wife by the F.B.I. They were officially charging her with the crime of embezzlement. As a loan officer, she had made out a bogus loan application, approved it herself, and appropriated the funds to herself, which she expected to pay back if I had gotten a job in Tallahassee. Suddenly the reason for our emergency return to Miami was crystal clear, as well as what was behind all those arguments we had about money.

On the one hand, my wife had more material values and sought a higher standard of living than I did. On the other hand, as with so many other topics, I was naive about money. I had given my wife the latitude and the responsibility for managing our financial affairs. Differences in philosophies, values, and attention to details, resulted in a gulf of miscommunication. So, even though I knew nothing about the embezzlement beforehand, who was at fault was ambiguous.

It was certainly not in the best interests of our child if my wife went to prison. It made sense for me to do whatever I could to alleviate the difficulties we were facing.

Our first step was to repay the bank in Tallahassee for the amount of the loan. My wife and I cooperated and started doing this even before a public defender was assigned to represent her. Ultimately, this did make the right impression. After the public defender began working on her case, I volunteered to read a statement into the record at trial, in which I assumed responsibility for putting my wife in a precarious financial position.

The role I was willing to play by assuming responsibility also, and reading that statement into the record, would come back to haunt me years later. In hindsight, though, I would do it again anyway. Sometimes some things are more important than appearances.

Together my wife and I weathered the storm. As expected, the prosecutor at trial had no sympathy, and he argued for my wife to do time. An understanding judge, however, held him at bay. The sentence was relatively light. We were ordered to continue making restitution payments to the bank plus pay court costs. My wife was put on probation. A probation officer regularly checked up on her. Hers was probably the easiest case he ever had. After the final restitution payment was made the criminal record was expunged and the case was closed.

Many years later, our child as an adult, questioned why we had moved back to Miami. I tried to explain what happened, and why. Ironically, perhaps, I found myself in the position of defending my ex-wife against our child's skepticism. Not only was I not blameless, we were young, and young adults often make mistakes that they later regret. My mistakes as a young adult were more numerous and more shameful. At least she didn't almost kill people.

Besides it wasn't just the embezzlement bomb that did damage to the relationship between my wife and myself. Before we had a chance to recover from the first, a second bomb did extensive damage that, I believe, brought an end to what remained of our little family.

Circus Act

The North Miami apartment where my wife, our child, and I lived, was on a street with other complexes. Ours was the worst and the cheapest. The apartment was one-bedroom with a curved living room wall on the second floor, literally a pebble toss away from a side street intersection, giving us a scenic view of gray asphalt and sun-bleached sidewalks. Bits and pieces of greenery were so few as to be irrelevant. The other tenants were mostly lower-class working people. They were good people and not the criminal element, but it was not a good place to raise children

Arriving home from work one afternoon, I saw a fellow tenant loading half of his possessions into the back of his pickup truck. The other half was already stolen. In a case of mistaken identity, apartment management had cleared out his unit and put everything he owned out on the sidewalk. But they had the wrong apartment number, and it was someone else that didn't pay the rent. I helped him load up what was left. What sticks in my mind is the look and expression he gave me before driving away. When I suggested he try calling a lawyer, he looked back at me and said, "Yeah right."

It's never talked about but there are countless people among the poor and working classes for whom help from the legal system is either unimaginable or unaffordable. They endure all kinds of injustices and indignities, believing that laws and lawyers are only for the rich. That's exactly how I felt the following year at that apartment complex.

Like other tenants we rented month by month without a lease. We were responsible, always paid on time, and didn't cause problems. After living there for a year and a half, with a child that had just turned three, the apartment complex was sold to an attorney who bought it as an investment. It was patently obvious he was after money. He immediately and radically raised the rent on all the units, and demanded that someone from every apartment go to the complex office and sign a lease. He threatened to evict those who refused at the end of the month, right after Christmas, with just three weeks-notice.

To my surprise, and disappointment, almost all the other tenants capitulated and signed leases, despite the drastic increase in rent. Perhaps they were the smart ones. My wife and I were inherently stubborn, and inclined to resist. We were also paying restitution and court costs, with little financial leeway. We were already squeezed for money.

Walking over to the complex office one afternoon to make inquiries, I ended up talking to the new owner over the phone. We started out calmly enough, expressing our different perspectives. We finished the conversation a half hour later in a heated argument. He wasn't budging, not even to grant one more month and time for us to find another place to live. He held all the cards. That was the reality. We could either submit, call his bluff and dare him to evict us, or bolt and move out.

One other renter resisted. My wife knew her better than I did. Our child often played with her two toddlers at the complex pool, the only amenity, nothing special, standard fare for Miami, and the only place where kids could play away from the street. The woman had found a townhouse for rent a couple miles away in unincorporated Dade County. She insisted it was big enough for all of us, an upgrade, and with four incomes we could afford it. It was a preposterous idea that I initially opposed. I had never even met her husband. However the threat of eviction loomed, the clock was ticking, and with no better options in the week between Christmas and New Years Day, we took the plunge. Ill-advised or not, we moved in with them.

For the next twelve months we lived as two families, four adults and three preschool toddlers, under one roof. The townhouse was spacious all right, and materially comfortable by our standards, but psychological strains that started out small grew more pronounced over time. The move also occurred nearly simultaneous with my wife's transfer to a different store at a mall in the far southern part of Dade County. Whether it was the longer driving distance, because she worked more hours, she was bored and finding fault with me, or she just wanted to be anywhere except back at the circus, she was almost never home. We began drifting apart.

The woman we moved in with was Jewish but her husband wasn't. He and I had common interests and workingman values. We became good friends, though he, like my wife, wasn't entertained at the circus. He also had tendencies to be elsewhere. His wife had a stereotypical Jewish mother's protective instincts towards her children. Whether the stereotype is fair or not, that's a quality that warrants my admiration. In a platonic relationship, we spent a great deal of time together. She was the pseudo domestic mother of the household, and I the pseudo father; or perhaps more accurately a dad to my child and a big brother to her kids. It goes against everything I believe in to ignore young children.

That's why I spent most of my non-working hours with three preschool toddlers playing with them, trying to stimulate them into new ways of thinking, which I always do with kids, reading as many children's books to them as they wanted to hear before going to bed. The children were the reward that made it worthwhile, but on the heels of working at a physical job in the Florida sun all day, it was an exhausting and stressful lifestyle.

My wife had to come home sometimes. There was still a little glue holding our marriage together. She was also good with children when she chose to be around them. When we went on a small camping trip with our child, we took the other couple's children with us. We had occasional lighter moments that gave us both a reason to celebrate. That included getting monkeys off our backs by paying off the car loan, and making the last restitution payment to the court. There was a palpable strain between us now but together we had dodged a bullet, and we were finally in the clear.

Therefore, I didn't see any reason why I couldn't pursue law school again. I believed that in the long run, it would lead to a better future for all three of us. That said, in hindsight, it's understandable if my wife did not have confidence in me. To my way of thinking at the time, however, I'd been coerced into moving to an unwanted city and working an unwanted job. The pursuit of law school had helped me to close out childhood. It motivated me to put in four years of active duty, to ride a bicycle to Florida, and it fueled my efforts in college resulting in a high undergraduate GPA. Having survived criminal doomsday, I didn't see any more obstacles in my way.

One advantage I had on the second go-round was knowing how to go about getting into law school. Although, and perhaps more so for me, getting into law school was a project in and of itself. Since law schools required a current score, the first step was to take the LSAT a second time. It's commonly said that the LSAT is an aptitude test for which there's no reason to study. But everyone who isn't Einstein studies anyway. So, I applied, paid the fee, studied, and took the test again.

The next step was to study law schools separately. Fortunately, books were available that analyzed and compared virtually every law school in the country showing their requirements, costs, financial aid practices, and admission tendencies. The information was crucial for determining which law schools fit the best and were worth applying to. Every law school application required the submission of an accompanying fee. Law schools required transcripts from every college previously attended, for me that meant FSU, three community colleges, plus Old Dominion University, and every transcript request had a fee requirement too. Three letters of recommendation were required for every law school, and each provider given a stamped preaddressed envelope ensuring that an individual applicant could not interfere. Every law school required a personal statement from an applicant explaining their background and reasons for applying to law school. There were so many steps involved, in addition to a full-time job and watching preschool children until bedtime, getting into law school was a lot of work, and costly.

For me, the entire process was complicated by ongoing negotiations and struggles with my wife. I thought we were on the same page but we never were. I applied to fifteen law schools in fifteen locations, thinking it would give us the best chance for a match, a law school that admitted me, was affordable, in a city to where she could obtain a transfer to another store which she had indicated was possible.

To my relief, and pride before it became a bitter pill to swallow, all fifteen law schools I applied to accepted me. The chances were excellent that one of them would work out. Some didn't offer enough financial aid and therefore weren't viable. Several law schools, however, accepted me and offered complete financial aid packages with scholarships, loans, and fee waivers. All I had to do was accept an offer in writing and show up for the fall semester. Alas, it came to naught.

For years it troubled me to think about the life I might have had if I had gone to law school right then. There was never a better opportunity. I would have become an attorney, found my niche, and had a real career with a higher standard of living. In hindsight, though, I now know that I was destined for an emotional collapse at some point. How that would have unfolded, and what the consequences would have been, are impossible to know. Nevertheless, I'm comfortable knowing that my decision not to go then was the right decision for the right reason.

At every step, with every application sent, and every acceptance letter received, I questioned my wife about her prospects for obtaining a transfer to a law school's location. Her responses were always ambiguous, which gradually raised my stress level. I was suspicious, of course, but I didn't expect the final response that sealed my fate.

After a law school accepts an applicant, the applicant has a short window in which to provide an affirmative response and accept the offer. Otherwise, a law school will drop them from consideration so as to accept a different candidate. When the timing reached a climax, after all the law schools accepted me, as my windows of opportunity were closing, in desperation I finally demanded a definitive answer from my wife. That was when she said to me, you go ahead and go to law school. Maybe the child and I will join you later.

I was not so naive that I didn't recognize my wife was rejecting me. If she didn't love me there was no blame for that. It's the same theme. I never tell others what to think, what to believe, how to feel. However, it would have helped if she had been more up front about her feelings earlier. Anyway, that was not the problem that held me back.

There was a much bigger issue involved. Up to that point, I was the dominant parent that our child hung on to for support. I was the parent that got down on the floor to play with our child, spent the most time with our child, and frankly exercised the most care for our child. My wife was a better parent for the second half of childhood, I readily admit, but it wasn't possible for me to go to law school then, to walk out of our young child's life into an ocean of uncertainty. How could any parent do that to a child?

Mercifully, after a year, the lease at the townhouse ran its course. By the end, psychological strains were weighing heavily on everyone. My wife and I found another apartment but it was only temporary shelter. We didn't talk about it but by then we were only pretending to have a marriage. Approximately four months after the circus tent came down, it was over. My wife and I separated.

What started with an emergency escape back to Miami, ran through an embezzlement quagmire, and lured me into spending a year at the circus, ended in a broken marriage. Then everything started to unravel and I fell into a dark tunnel. But the descent had just begun and it was a long way down.

Down and Then Out

I t was apropos. The last apartment my wife and I lived in was directly behind a North Miami Beach funeral home. One day, without words, my wife gave me a clear and symbolic message that she wanted out of the marriage. It was a relief for me because I did too. The owner of the apartment returned our security deposit and last month's rent. We divided the money equally, and we agreed our child would live with her, and spend two nights a week and every other weekend with me. She quickly found another apartment on the water in North Bay Village.

It also didn't take me long to find another apartment. Or so I thought. With my share of the money, I paid my way in at another apartment down the road closer to work. It seemed to be a nice small apartment configured with others in a square around a grass courtyard. Two days later, ready to move in, carrying everything I owned in a bag of clothes, that landlord too returned my money. She said the apartment was no longer available. I surmised other renters saw me the first time and didn't like the looks of me. The refusal to rent to me at the last minute put me in a bind and in a mad scramble to find something else.

That's how I ended up living in the worst place I've ever rented. With no time to look around, I answered a classified ad, and rented a place through a real estate office acting as an agent for the owner. The owner lived in a different city. The apartment was also in

North Miami Beach, a city I lived in five times altogether. If you're scoring from home this was number three. I later learned the owner died while I was living there.

The apartment, if one could call it that, was a portion of a building in a bad neighborhood. There was no air conditioning, no lawn, one window bolted shut, and a stove that didn't work. Since no maintenance was available, for the duration of the lease I cooked on a Coleman camping stove. What I remember most, though, was inescapable heat along with air that didn't move. Trying to sleep at night was a chore. Most of my awake time was spent outside sitting on a utility box on asphalt. Very strange, and perhaps it's a reflection of my personality, in the year I was there I never met any neighbors.

The place where I lived was a hole, but the hole it ultimately put me in was tantamount to a dungeon tied to a ball and chain. The only furniture consisted of a bed, a chair, and a nightstand. My share of divided money was in a flimsy metal combination box. Having just moved in, coming home from work Monday afternoon, with plans to bike over to the real estate office and pay the balance of money owed, the combination box was no longer in the nightstand drawer. Probably someone who lived there before me kept a key and simply let themselves in. Nothing else in the next year was stolen. Then again, I didn't own anything else worth taking.

The theft was the start of monetary problems that buried me before I could even get started on my own. First I had to pay the real estate company extra each month until everything owed was satisfied, resulting in a monthly rent payment ridiculously out of proportion to what the apartment was worth. Then the IRS tracked me down.

Before we split up, my wife and I had filed for an extension for the previous year's taxes. The IRS, an agency I never ever, ever want problems with, convinced me I was equally liable, and it was better for me in the long run to just pay them off. In addition to catching up with the terms of a lease, I had to pay for a year of taxes on two incomes.

In addition to those difficulties, as often as possible, since she incurred additional child care costs, I gave my separated wife money orders in $50 increments. It wasn't much, but I didn't have much. By giving her money, I hoped to uphold my share of responsibilities, and establish my willingness to contribute. It was a normal state of affairs for me. Income, even occasional extra income from overtime and out of town work, belonged to others before it made it to my wallet. However, an even worse turn of events occurred after our separation. Monetary obligations, compounded by my profound ignorance, led to a gut-wrenching loss far more important to me than money.

Month after month I hoped to earn my way out of monetary difficulties, but I never made it. I felt helpless, and worried constantly, but I didn't send payments to the bank that handled my undergraduate student loans. I was ignorant about loans. I didn't know that a debtor could make nominal payments to keep a loan active, which I learned afterwards, too late to help me. Therefore, when the bank foreclosed on the loans, I learned the hard way; the only way to get the loans out of foreclosure was to pay them off in full. That, of course, was impossible in my case. A path to a better life that I had spent my entire life longing for, and striving for, so as to escape an abysmal childhood, no longer existed.

Only two factors held my sanity together. One was working outside in the sun. A man who works like a dog may feel defeated at times, but he knows he is not a bad man. The other factor was the relationship with my child. With a child seat mounted on the back of my bicycle, twice a week and every other weekend, I picked up my child from a sitter and we rode home up Old Dixie Highway. Somehow I managed to keep my child reasonably safe and stimulated despite a lousy apartment in a bad neighborhood.

But for the relationship with my child, I was stuck in a place where I didn't want to be, doing work I didn't want to do, earning peanuts for wages, while up to my eyeballs in debt. Depression was inevitable.

Then out of the blue my separated wife did me a favor that, at least temporarily lifted my spirits. She wanted another car. For a nominal charge she offered to sell me the Datsun 200SX that she owned, the car we both paid for originally. It meant buying the same car twice, but nevertheless I was thrilled. The Datsun was still in great condition. It made life easier and expanded my horizons.

After the lease at the worst apartment imaginable, finally, and mercifully ended, with a car I was able to rent a cottage on Miami Beach, the first of several times I would live over there. The cottage was comfortable, nicely furnished, and I could afford the rent. The ocean was a three-minute walk away.

Meanwhile, at the land surveying company, I made progress. I was promoted. First from a rodman to an instrumentman, then to the top of the ladder, a very short ladder since it was the end in a dead-end job, when I was promoted to party chief. The job title sounded prestigious but the result was deceptive. A party was only a three-man crew. A party chief worked exponentially harder, and took on enormous responsibilities, for a token increase in wages. Still, the work was stimulating despite my lack of interest, and it did increase my pay. Coupled with a decent residence, for a change life wasn't all that bad and almost good.

Until one afternoon when my separated wife brought our child over to Miami Beach to spend the weekend with me. She had an announcement to make. She was quitting her job, moving to the other side of Florida, and taking our child with her. After everything, moving to Miami, the embezzlement, the court case, the year at the circus, separation, and, though entirely my fault the loss of any chance to escape a childhood past, she was taking away our child and in effect severing our relationship.

Perhaps my reaction was to be expected from someone suffering from a passive-aggressive disease. I acted inappropriately. I made arrangements with my landlord, and we were both disappointed to part ways. I tossed my bag of clothes in the Datsun, drove over to 1-95, and headed north with an ambiguous destination of some-where else.

My thinking was, without a relationship with my child I had no reason to stay in Miami, or in Florida for that matter. If my separated wife was leaving, and taking our child with her, there was no reason for me to hang around in Florida any longer.

At the time it seemed like logical thinking. But it wasn't. Instead, I later found out, I dug myself into an even deeper hole.

Out and Then Down

Many land surveying crew members look forward to a promotion to party chief someday. Until they become one. Then in exchange for a slight increase in wages and a job title that sounds important, they learn that a party chief has to work a lot harder, bears all the responsibilities, gets barked at by contractors who are never pleased, must painstakingly document the crew's work in a field book, and justify their hours and productivity to the boss at the end of the day. A party chief also does all the driving. My average was 300 miles a week, most of it in thick urban traffic, shuffling my crew around from job site to job site. That's how I was sometimes teased into thinking, instead of driving to another job site, especially if it was a nasty construction job, how satisfying it would be to stay on I-95 and drive right out of Miami.

Always, though, there were other responsibilities that held me back. When my separated wife announced she was leaving Miami, and taking our child with her, those other responsibilities were no longer relevant. As a poor man, what could I do for my child 250 miles away that I couldn't do from any other location? The IRS was satisfied and paid off in full. My rent was paid up and was without a lease. I didn't owe anything to my employer other than an honest day's work for a day's wages, which I always provided. As cities go, Miami was all right but I had no reason to live there, especially after it felt like I was hoodwinked into returning there.

So, with steadfast determination I left Miami. A change of scenery was called for, and I thought necessary. Thwarted in my choice of a career track, stuck in a sweaty low paying job, having accumulated little more than a bag of clothes, about the same amount of possessions I rode in with on a bicycle years before, Florida just didn't work out. And I was still young. By leaving Florida it gave me another chance to start life over.

The day began early in darkness. After driving northward, more or less aimlessly, it ended in darkness on the outskirts of Louisville, Kentucky, which was as good a place as any to stop for a night of rest. The next day, the more I thought about it the more intrigued I became. As cities went Louisville seemed to fit well. The city was neither too big or too small. It was big enough to have jobs, probably, but small enough not to trap me inside a metropolis. Louisville had history, culture, a sense of character. Another city might have served my purposes equally well but I was encouraged to take the next step. A room at a Motel 6 became my base of operations.

With the aid of a street map and a phone book, back when the yellow pages were a rich source for local information, I spent several days driving to every listed land surveying company in Louisville, and across the river in Indiana. I filled out and submitted applications wherever they were accepted. It meant more land surveying, of course, but for people like me everything starts with a job.

In contrast to past practices, I had left Miami on a whim, in a huff really, without calculating risks in advance. With better planning the end result might have been different. It was late winter when I arrived in Louisville. The town was still shivering from a winter chill. At several places where I submitted applications interviewers invited me to sit down and share a cup of coffee with them. They weren't busy and seemed delighted to have someone to talk shop with. At several companies I was told they expected to be a lot busier as soon as the weather warmed up. If I had been offered a job on the spot, as had happened to me in the past, I might be living in

Louisville now. However, having visited every listed land surveying company, I couldn't afford to hang around spending money with no money coming in. So, I decided to make a diversion. I decided to go see my parents in New York, then drive back to Louisville.

The decision to visit my parents was fraught with trepidation. I had no idea what to expect. The last time I was there, five years before, was also the last time I saw my sisters, after we were told our mother only had three days to live. In a surprise, I discovered she was no longer drinking. Ultimately it was smoking and lung cancer that would kill my mother in another five years. My father also didn't drink anymore. Maybe he felt too much shame to continue drinking in her presence, after she was told continuing to drink was the equivalent of holding a gun to her head. I wondered how they both managed to stop drinking, as they were not the type to seek outside help, but I wasn't curious enough to ask questions. I had plenty of puzzles of my own to work on.

Thanks to my older sister who had made some contacts before leaving, never to be seen or heard from again, our parents received visits from a social worker that checked up on them from time to time and arranged for them to receive Meals on Wheels. The inside of the abode was still a disaster, while the outside was a jungle. A catalpa tree had fallen and landed next to the abode, and they just left it there, despite the fact it blocked the view from the kitchen window. My mother could no longer watch birds and animals out in the field, one of her few late in life pleasures. With time on my hands and nothing better to do, I decided to do something about the catalpa tree.

With a 55-gallon drum that my parents used to burn trash, a handsaw for branches, and my father's chainsaw for the trunk, I chopped up the fallen tree and fed pieces of it into a fire. I kept at it for four days, more or less, morning to night until there was nothing left but ashes. Looking back, it gives me some peace of mind knowing I did something for my mother in her final years of life.

Eliminating the catalpa tree also did something for me but it wasn't pleasure. Staring into the fire for hours on end was a catharsis that brought me clarity. The more I stared at the fire the clearer I saw the need to return to Florida. At least it was the same state as my child, who was still only six years old. If I could get a job near Orlando, a bustling town with an exploding population, and construction projects trying to keep pace, it would put me within a short drive to where my wife and child lived. So instead of returning to Louisville, I tossed my bag of clothes in the Datsun and drove back down to Florida.

It didn't take me long to find a job in Kissimmee, and a new home at a pay-by-the-week motel on Orlando's west side. The job was another surveying job (my fifth), but with an excavation company as opposed to a land surveying company. Officially my position was an instrumentman operating a transit and a level under the authority of a party chief. The excavation company only had one surveying crew. The excavation company's stock in trade was clearing huge parcels of land, as far as the eye could see in some cases, and turning them into dust in preparation for new housing projects, schools, and sometimes entire new communities. It meant doing the same boring work every day at the same boring places, not the stimulating kind of survey work with varied tasks that I was used to. That was one factor.

When needing a job, poor boys can't be choosy. That's how I found myself working for an outfit I didn't like, and alongside a man I couldn't stand. I didn't care if the party chief was in charge. I didn't mind showing him survey fundamentals that he didn't know. I didn't begrudge him his title or his wages. His unrestrained ambition was a different matter. Being around that much greed always unnerves me.

It weighed on me to hear him boast about marrying the daughter of the excavation company's owner, not because he loved her, for which I heard no signs, but for what it would do for his career.

Apparently his spouse was a piece on a chessboard and the marriage was a business decision. I wondered if he had any interests beyond his ambition. In actuality, and in the aggregate, the party chief was not a bad man, but for my purposes given that job, and thinking about my own future prospects, he was insufferable.

Unlike all the other party chiefs I had known, the party chief wouldn't stop at a convenience store on the way to a job in the morning, which gave crew members a last chance to get something for their lunch. It interfered with his production, and therefore his ambition. That was his right and I didn't fault him for that. One morning, though, after working at the job for a month, I pressed him into making a stop. I told him I had an urgent phone call to make, back when convenience stores always had a public phone. From a booth I called my boss in Miami. He said, yes, he would take me back. Then I walked back to the party chief waiting impatiently at the steering wheel and told him everything that was on my mind in just two words: I quit.

The following day I was back in Miami. The land surveying owner wasn't being generous by hiring me back. He knew, and I knew that he knew, that I was a valuable employee who would make him more money in the long run. It turned out to be a very short run but neither of us knew that then. With the security of a job as a crutch, I went back over to Miami Beach and rented a room at a pay-by-the-week motel.

It wasn't long after returning to Miami that my wife, then ex-wife, tracked me down. She sent me a letter announcing that she had finalized a divorce, and that I was now a divorced man. She added, if I cared or not. I didn't actually. Not about the divorce, but the grounds she claimed it was based on disturbed me greatly.

She claimed that I had abandoned our child. But I wasn't out of Miami for long and out of Florida even less, little more than two months total. Moreover, I only left because she said she was leaving and taking our child with her. In fact, she did move out shortly after I left. As long as our child was in Miami I would have stayed in Miami. She had to have known that. Claiming I had abandoned my child was a sucker punch.

Although maybe she had to put down something and couldn't think of anything else. It really didn't matter. Over is over. Or at least it should have been.

In any case, I was back to square one, a lot poorer, and still living apart from our child. The cost of the pay-by-the-week motel was nearly two-thirds of my weekly paycheck, making it a struggle to keep a roof over my head. I'd dug myself into a very big hole.

Weeks after returning to Miami I heard from my mother. She complained and wanted to know what to say to people. Their phone up in New York was ringing off the hook. Surveying companies from Louisville were calling. They wanted to hire me.

Banana Peel

A lesson was learned and there was no escaping the fact. To improve my standard of living, and to keep my head above water, my future depended on land surveying. Back in Miami, I applied myself more than I ever did before. It was no longer enough to do a good job. I wanted professional progress.

It started with an out-of-pocket expenditure for a calculator, advanced for its time but primitive by modern standards, with a special program designed for civil engineers and professional surveyors (the ones with professional licenses). In addition to the fact that better information always opens eyes and leads to deeper understanding, the calculator allowed a party chief in the field to decimalize angles (so as to add and subtract them), traverse with coordinates, work proficiently with triangles and irregular shapes, and do other mathematical functions without the time-consuming, mistake-prone burden of a pencil and paper. In the field surveyor's vernacular, I learned how to crunch numbers.

The boss then sent me to more diverse job sites involving more complex surveying tasks. He also increased my wages, although not proportional to more difficult work and greater responsibilities. Nevertheless, most significantly, it felt like I was achieving a measure of success.

The hole I'd dug myself into was deep but it improved some when I found a cheaper pay-by-the-week motel. The motel was older, a little run down, and the cost was still half of my weekly paycheck. What made it a bargain, though, was its location on Ocean Drive across the road from the Atlantic Ocean. It made for a great front yard. Despite how expensive it was, I liked living at that motel.

After earning one's living under the blazing sun of south Florida during the day, it was serendipitous to come home and jump in the water. The ocean also had medicinal value. In a treatment not recommended by doctors, twice I was able to take advantage of a resource and rid myself of poison ivy. After a few minutes of euphoric relief while scratching, and a few minutes of agony in the salt water, poison ivy disappeared without a trace. Unfortunately, for me, neither relief or comfort seldom last for very long.

Approximately five months after returning to Miami, my ex-wife sent me a letter. She wanted me to call her and indicated it was urgent. Worried that something was seriously wrong, I gathered a pocketful of quarters and walked to a pay phone in a public square. We talked for more than an hour. The gist of what we discussed was her invitation for me to join her, and our child again, on the other side of Florida where we could once more be a small family. At least that is what I heard, not realizing that we had talked a lot but communicated little. When we hung up I thought we had covered all the bases. So I made arrangements, quit my job, again, tossed my bag of clothes in the Datsun, again, and drove over to the bay area.

It was tantamount to stepping on a banana peel next to an open grave. In hindsight, however, I can't say it was a mistake. There are times in one's life when one needs a definitive answer to an open question, the absence of which will burn a hole in one's soul until the end of time. This was one such occasion. At the time, I believed that reconciliation was in the best interests of my ex-wife, our child, and myself, and that we had probably lost our way in the year we spent at the circus. But the result was that we took giant steps backwards and had to pay hefty penalties. We should have left well enough alone.

Local land surveying companies are a lot like fruit stands, active and vibrant in good times, boarded up with the doors locked in bad times. Absent a severe recession, in an urban area at any given time, there are bound to be surveying companies with golden egg contracts in need of more help, with a steady stream of field hands passing in and out of their doors. That's why it was usually easy for me to find another land surveying job, that was just another dead-end job. Within days of arriving in the bay area, I found another, my sixth, as an instrumentman - what we called running the guns - operating a transit and a level for other party chiefs. The survey company and the kind of work it did, and its personnel (typical wild characters among surveyors) were normal and okay, if uninspiring.

The apartment where my ex-wife had taken out a lease was an upgrade. At least for me. In fact, it was the swankiest place I've lived in. It also was affordable on two incomes. Starting on day one, though, my ex-wife and I could not establish domestic tranquility. I will not dispute my lion's share of the blame, having pushed the envelope too hard and too soon, without giving a resumption of our relationship a chance to develop at a normal pace. After clinging to existence back in Miami, I was worried, out on a limb, without a safety net, and with a sixth sense that told me to beware.

Suspicion as it turned out was justified. A few days after moving in, my ex-wife gave me important information. I didn't know if it was intentional or inadvertent, though I thought the latter. She left a letter out in plain view in the living room written to somebody else. By the contents of the letter, it was clear that it wasn't me she loved. That was her right. It wasn't jealousy that disturbed me.

Although I was the catalyst at the beginning of our relationship, and caused everything that happened afterwards, my conscience doesn't allow me to force love on another. Especially where it's obviously not welcome. What the letter did was to put into doubt my reasons for being there. Love to me (what little I know of it) can never be unilateral; it only works when two individuals are satisfied. Besides, I was in no position to blame anyone for not loving me.

It took me four months to paint the picture. Four months in a platonic relationship, exercising respect, always hopeful my ex-wife would come around to see our relationship differently. We didn't make progress. Nothing changed.

Eventually I came to the conclusion I was in the bay area on false pretenses. It seemed likely that my ex-wife only wanted a roommate, someone to share the lease so as to make the apartment affordable. Once the lease was completed, I had to suspect, she would move out and I would have to find a new place to live. But then I would be in the bay area tied to a job, a dad to our child again, with whom I still had a stronger relationship with than she did, while she would be free to live with someone else. If that wasn't her plan, we weren't discussing anything, or closing a gap in miscommunication. Some of the picture was attractive to me, especially restoring the relationship with our child, but it wasn't enough to hold me there.

For one, no one wants to be lured into living in another location by a trick. That's too big an insult. It's a feature of my personality, though, that I've seen played out many times. A passive demeanor, and facial expressions to match, encourages some to put words in my mouth and thoughts in my head that aren't mine. Some take the tendency a step further, thinking they can bend me to their will. They don't see the analytical person behind the mask.

On one side, people are wrong when they draw their conclusions about me. It's also true, as a byproduct of a fractured soul, that my demeanor makes me into a liar. I'll bend far into the wind before gathering my senses, and concluding, I'm not going to put up with what others are trying to get away with any longer. When it felt like I was lured out of Miami by a trick, and was being led around by the nose like a circus bear, it was time to leave. More so since the surveying job in Miami was a better opportunity for professional advancement.

The dynamics between my ex-wife and myself was analogous to what happened with my younger sister, when she laid a guilt trip on me for enlisting, forcing her to sell her horse. By coaxing me out of Miami for her purposes, not mine, my ex-wife was treating me as though I had no right to a life of my own. I'd spent too much blood, sweat, and years trying to disprove that reality.

When it was clear we'd reached a point of no return, despite all the negative emotions, including a lot of guilt, I called my boss in Miami and asked if he would take me back. He said he would. So, I made arrangements, gave my bay area boss a week's notice, and went back to land surveying job Number 5, Act III.

Everything was ventured. Nothing was gained. On the last day I tossed my bag of clothes in the Datsun and drove our child, now age seven, to school. I tried to explain the situation and my reasons for leaving the best that I could, but of course failed miserably. Five hours later I was back in Miami, a broken man in every possible way.

Sliding Down the Slippery Slope

Boomeranged back to Miami, I went back over to Miami Beach and rented a room at the motel with the Atlantic Ocean for a front yard. As much as I liked it there, when money got tight, that small amount of pleasure also went by the wayside. I moved to a cheaper pay-by-the-week motel down on 39th Street, close enough to walk to famous South Beach, but only on Sunday mornings. By then I didn't have a nickel to spare for entertainment, and I was never in a mood to face a crowd. Enthusiasm for living was approaching its nadir, though there was still a long way to go before reaching the bottom of the well.

Because she was unable to make rent payments with only one income, most likely, my ex-wife and our child moved in to the stylish home of her well-to-do aunt. Her aunt must have had good qualities, but the only side of herself she showed me was that of a proverbial battle axe. My ex-wife couldn't be blamed for doing what she had to do. In fact, it was a relief to me knowing she and our child had a place to go, a haven in a storm. Nor could she be blamed for petitioning the state for welfare benefits in my absence. What disturbed me, and burned a hole in my brain, was my ex-wife and her aunt taking our child to a psychologist and using the psychologist to drive a wedge between our child and myself.

The psychologist's written reports were in time, indirectly and un-intentionally, made available to me. The psychologist, apparently, lacked even run of the mill curiosity, and swallowed every false-hood and lie by omission. Not a word was mentioned about my devotion to our child starting before birth, about all the time I spent with our child, the embezzlement, escape to Miami, or my support of my ex-wife at trial. Most significantly, not a word was written about my ex-wife leaving Miami and taking our child with her while rendering me an impotent bystander. Like my mother before me, I was to blame for everything that was wrong, though it garnered me neither respect nor love.

It was a rude introduction to the psychological industry, one that left an impression that has only gotten worse in the years since then. A deeply flawed legal system has to at least pretend to listen to two sides. Psychologists, by contrast, can pass judgment without any standards for fairness. Or accuracy.

It's been my assumption the battle axe aunt was behind the vis-its to the psychologist, and probably for most of what was said during the sessions. Since my ex-wife with our child was living in her house, she probably had to go along with her aunt in order to appease her. In any case, whether it was because of the aunt, the psychologist, the emotional turmoil caused by the failure of reconciliation, or due to deficiencies in my character, something was lost during this period. The relationship with my child was never the same afterwards. Then for me, the change in our rela-tionship, magnified by separation, fed into the darkening clouds of depression.

Weeks after returning to Miami, a summons in the mail brought more dark clouds. It was a court order that demanded my appear-ance at a child support hearing. The summons forced me to take a day off from work and to drive back over to the bay area. A fair summons would have informed me of the right to have legal rep-resentation, even if I couldn't afford an attorney.

Upon arriving at the hearing, I was confronted by an attorney advocating on the behalf of the State of Florida, and a judge that seemed not the least bit concerned with impartiality, who acted like she was one half of a tag team. The outcome was preordained. Feeling like a bug in a spider's web, I proceeded to do what any vastly ignorant workingman, believing he was being railroaded, would have done. I challenged the system. I tried to argue my side. Nerves and emotions got the best of me and I made a total ass of myself.

The judge was not favorably impressed. She issued a ruling that garnished my wages, made me liable for arrears going back to the official date of our divorce, and charged me with court fees. All of that was fair, more or less, (although when he got the paperwork, my penny-pinching boss in Miami felt sorry for me and gave me a tiny raise to my $7 dollar an hour wage). When I pulled out an envelope at the hearing stuffed with money order receipts in $50 increments, given to my ex-wife starting with our separation, the judge disdainfully dismissed them as just gifts. They didn't reduce my liabilities one penny.

Note to men and women separated from their former partner and their children. Unless you're rich or a fool, beware of volunteering to help your ex with child care expenses. Make sure you get the court order first. Still, the law may not care about doing the right thing, but I always do. No one has ever accused me of being avaricious. My ex-wife and our child were welcome to every penny of mine beyond what was needed for sustenance and survival, which I found myself caring about less and less.

In the aftermath of the hearing, I wondered why the summons was even necessary. If results were a foregone conclusion, and the system was determined to railroad me, why couldn't that have been accomplished by mail? Why did I have to drive across state and attend? The hearing result also put into doubt my decision to return to Florida. Of course, the State of Florida with its long arm of the law would have caught up to me anywhere, but I might have been in a better place, in a better financial position, and maybe had the assistance of a lawyer while confronted with a system much more powerful than I was. Then, at least for a little while longer, I might have had hopes for a better future.

Nevertheless, despite the hammer blow from the child support hearing, looking back through the prism of time, I'm convinced returning to Florida and trying to reconcile with my ex-wife were good decisions for good reasons. In the short term, though, those decisions propelled me further down a rat hole of depression.

My emotional-laden and incoherent arguments at the child support hearing didn't win me sympathy from the state's attorney or the judge. They mistook my nervousness and feelings of outrage for anger. When the hearing ended and I was walking out the door, I overheard them advising my ex-wife to stay away from me, as they offered her the protection of security. My ex-wife knew me better than they did. She met me outside the courthouse. Together we went to lunch.

That did help to ease the misery I was feeling. After lunch, I drove back to Miami. Then I stayed miserable for a long time. It was the second period of my life, the first one after trauma as a child at age seven, in which life no longer seemed worth living. The labyrinth had no end. I could see no path to a decent life.

To the Hell That Exists Below Hell

Fair or not, the indebtedness imposed by the child support judge, combined with the high cost of pay-by-the-week motel rooms, put me in a choke hold. I was stuck with no chance to make progress, or a means of escape, when a friend and coworker asked me if I wanted to live with him at his house back on the mainland in North Miami Beach. His father was spending the summer in the mountains of North Carolina. Other than that, I had no idea why he made the offer, but he was in a select group, less than five people in my entire life, with whom I felt comfortable discussing any subject, politics and religion included. With a chance to save money, after paying him a nominal rent, the more important comfort I wanted was getting into an apartment that was less of a gouge on my paycheck. By summer's end, I'd saved enough to crawl into a studio apartment down the road in North Miami.

Emotional comfort remained out of reach. Day by day I was losing my grip on reality, as evidenced by my willingness to move into an apartment without furniture. Every morning I went to work, led a survey crew through swamps and urban chaos, followed blue prints, crunched numbers, and did whatever the job required, then I'd go home and sleep on the floor with a rolled-up shirt for a pil-low. The apartment had an L-shaped counter that stuck out from the wall separating the tiny kitchen from the tiny living room. The counter was my chair. I had no television, no radio, no phone, not even a toaster.

Every day I went to work and did my job. Then I would go home, sit on that counter, chain smoke, and wallow in depression while wrestling with the thoughts inside my head, always the same thoughts on the same themes. All I wanted was a decent life. Serving my father in childhood, taking care of my sister's horse, military service, riding a bicycle to Florida, earning good grades in college, supporting my wife and child during some bad times in Miami, the pursuit of law school, making my living outdoors in the sun, was for that one purpose. Yet everything I tried to do blew up in my face. At every juncture the path to a decent life was blocked. I tried to figure out why with an endless stream of questions that never gave me answers. Still, I asked the questions over and over again though they only led to throbbing headaches.

With nowhere else to turn, not knowing what else to do, I disregarded skepticism and delved deeper into therapy. I had dabbled in therapy a time or two before but wasn't impressed enough to take it seriously. In dire need for answers to the endless questions that tortured me, I made some inquiries and found out my employee health insurance plan would pay 80% of the cost for weekly therapy sessions.

That became a thorn in the side of the survey company owner who was disturbed at my use of his health insurance plan. He had no cause to get involved in my therapy - later he and the therapist would have phone conversations about me and they were both in violation of ethical considerations - but the de facto reality is, at small companies there are no secrets or rights to privacy. What the survey company owner didn't know, however, was that I basically agreed with him, that mental therapy shouldn't necessarily be covered by employee health insurance. But it was and I was so desperate I was willing to use any tool at my disposal. So I took a flying leap and tried what was called a process group for codependents, which as it was described sounded like it applied specifically to people like me.

As it turned out, though, therapy didn't stop my downward slide. The idea behind the therapy was to bring a handful of people together in a family, to replace the failed family they'd grown up in, and to provide the familial support that was sorely missing in their lives. I tried but could never buy into the concept. In my mind a replacement family was a phony family, and, particularly in my case, an obfuscation of underlying truths. I still didn't know what those underlying truths were; they were what caused the questions without answers. But group therapy was not giving me new information. Nothing I could use. Nothing that I hadn't already thought about.

For me, group therapy had another serious downside. Albeit without much emphasis, it was claimed that our therapy was a 12-step program in the same vein as Alcoholics and Gamblers Anonymous. That meant we were expected to come together at the end of every session to say the Lord's Prayer. Atheists don't pray. At first I tried to resist as group members tugged me into the center of the room to pray with them. Nice people that they were, they put me in the position of either demonstrably rejecting all of them, or going along. They didn't realize the agony they were causing me by denying me the right to be myself. So, in my mind, I stood next to them and supported them as they prayed, but the support only went one way.

The biggest problem with therapy, though, was that it just wasn't working. Therapy was in effect a last gasp effort to find answers, end suffering, and find a reason to go on living. If there were no answers in therapy, nothing to hang on to and turn my life around, it steadily weighed on me that there was no help available anywhere.

When therapy sessions ended, the same as after work, I went back to the apartment, sat on the counter, chain smoked, and wallowed in more depression until it was time to go to sleep on the floor. I started to project how much longer I could go on. But I not only wanted to die, I wanted to disappear never to be found, and was trying to think of ways to simultaneously commit suicide and bury myself.

Nearly to the end of my endurance, after months of trying to find a solution in therapy but having lost hope in its efficacy, at one of the sessions the therapist asked a question. She asked what each of us wanted most from other members of our family. When it was my turn, I said the only thought keeping me alive was knowing the psychological damage it would do to a young child to learn a father had committed suicide, but that a point had been reached whereby that was no longer enough. Therefore, I wanted the other members to say they understood and would support me. The therapist then interjected and said she was going to send me to a clinic of a therapist out in California who she was affiliated with.

The psychology clinic in California, apparently, was the brainchild of a nationally famous psychologist with a bestselling self-help book to his credit, as well as his own weekly television show. Our therapist had mentioned his name from time to time, but without owning a television, I had never heard of him other than from her. His undisputed reputation overrode my skepticism and persuaded me to give the clinic a try. I had nothing to lose at that point. At the very least I expected professionalism.

The night before departing on a plane from Miami to Los Angeles, final destination Van Nuys, California, a nagging concern pressured me to call the clinic on the phone. I asked a woman on the other end of the line, specifically, matter of fact, whether there was any issue with my being an Atheist, and whether they would be able to treat me despite that fact. The woman assured me it was not a problem. Did she lie? Was she deliberately deceptive? Or did she not know it mattered?

As I stepped off the plane at LAX, a pleasant young man from the clinic was there to meet me holding up a sign with my name on it, just like in the movies. He drove me up to Van Nuys and we conversed amiably along the way. The aura of pleasantness did not last long.

It was early evening and already dark, since it was late December, when the pleasant young man and I arrived at the clinic. The first order of business was a requirement for me to fill out a questionnaire. When it was completed, I was called into a meeting with three psychologists - that turned out to be a lecture. Based on a few honest answers to questionnaire questions, which gave them enough flimsy evidence to draw their own conclusions, the psychologists accused me of being an alcoholic. They had an agenda and were determined to shoehorn me on to their own set of beliefs. Their agenda, literally, was to make me a better Christian, assumably as a means to cure me of alcoholism though they never expressed their plans exactly. They assigned me a room and ordered me to read a chapter of the bible and be ready to discuss it in the morning. Obviously something was lost in the translation between the therapist in Miami and the Van Nuys clinic. The reason I was there, suicidal depression, apparently was premature and not broach-able yet.

The bible was on the nightstand next to the bed. I was more likely to pet rattlesnakes than to touch their bible. Despite a long day that started on eastern time and included a cross-country flight, I couldn't make use of the bed either. I spent the entire night doing a slow burn while walking the halls in circles. It's rare for me to feel the anger that was building up inside me. So much for my calling the clinic the night before to get reassurance for being an Atheist.

Early the next morning, I attended a mandatory meeting without their bible. The other half dozen inpatients, it was discovered, had been arrested numerous times for property crimes related to cocaine addictions. Essentially, they were predatory members of society polar opposite to myself. Clearly I did not fit in with them. Fortunately, and unfortunately, the group meeting wasn't underway for long when there was a knock on the door. My immediate presence was demanded at a different meeting with a licensed psychiatrist up on the second floor.

At least the psychiatrist was pleasant and a soft-spoken man. He listened as I gave him a complete and honest account of my drinking practices. The truth was I seldom consumed alcohol during the quagmire of my depression. Further, I told him how I had grown up with two alcoholic parents and knew more than most about the signs and ramifications of the disease. The psychiatrist then gave me his opinion that I was not an alcoholic. However, he confessed, he was powerless to counter the determination of the cabal of psychologists down on the floor below. That made me wonder why he was even there.

Nothing at that clinic seemed to make sense. No one there uttered the name of the famous psychologist whose clinic it was. Perhaps he was just a figurehead. My anger steadily increased as I was building up a wall of resistance.

It was a different era. Political correctness hadn't quite taken hold yet. Smoking at the clinic was allowed in designated areas. If you ran out of cigarettes, other inpatients told me, they were sometimes but not always available in the vending machine room. It was their belief the clinic didn't always allow the vendor to restock them. By then it didn't surprise me that the clinic could play mind games with troubled inpatients. When I went to the office and asked if it was true, I was told, "Whatever you do don't leave the premises; it's not allowed." I promptly marched out the door. A liquor store down on the corner sold me Marlboros.

The rest of the morning my insides did a slow boil. I walked more halls, stepped outside occasionally to smoke a cigarette, and shot a few hoops at a basket they had out there. At one point, the pleasant young man who drove me up from the airport came out and shot hoops with me. When I told him I was thinking about leaving, he tried to talk me out of going. By mid-afternoon, however, despite going without sleep for a day and a half, my mind was made up.

All the clinic had offered me was religion, and nothing related to suicidal depression. Moreover, the clinic I saw was a muddled scheme of smoke and mirrors without structure. When I went to the office a second time and informed people that I was leaving, not a word was said to deter me. No one asked why.

Although the psychology profession may help people, speaking for myself only, as always, I reserve serious doubts to its general usefulness, and believe it's greatly overrated. Ever since that day I have looked back at the burgeoning psychological industry with skepticism and disdain. Sometimes it takes hard work to ferret out underlying truths, and sometimes underlying truths aren't available anymore anyway. From what I saw among psychologists, there was too great a reluctance to say the three most honest words in the English language, which are, simply, "I don't know." They're difficult words to say, but psychologists, after all, are paid professionals. Also there's too great a tendency to cover up inadequacy with medication (usually an obfuscation of underlying truth), and with religion, as if troubled souls couldn't find their way to a church without the aid of psychologists.

However it's not from sour grapes that I decry psychologists, and I don't want to criticize anybody, in particular those with good intentions. But as for psychology as a profession, or an industry, I never saw any there, there. Ironically, though, attempting to find a solution for my troubled soul through group therapy, and then at the clinic in California, did help me, just not in the way they were supposed to. But before that could happen there was a more urgent problem to resolve. What to do with myself?

The first thought that occurred to me was, *why me?* It could only have happened to me that I would fly across country seeking a solution for suicidal madness, only to be disrespected and treated the way the clinic treated me, even after calling them the night before and being told it was going to be okay. Solitude is a normal state of affairs for me to which I'm well accustomed, and it typically doesn't bother me, but after the debacle in California I hurt like hell and I never felt more alone. That bled into my next line of thinking, which was, the sooner I ended life the better. That required making a decision where and how to end my life.

The idea of throwing myself in front of a train gave me a rush of twisted pleasure. It would have shown the cabal at the clinic how wrong it was, and maybe even made it legally liable for negligence. In hindsight, perhaps it's an important consideration for anyone contemplating suicide; if they don't care when we're alive they aren't going to care when we're dead. I didn't want to die in California. Nor, after running it through my mind, en route back to Florida, so hitchhiking back to Miami was tempting but also rejected.

The year before, in response to a junk mail offer that I normally would have thrown away, I acquired my first and still my only credit card. I needed an eye operation to correct strabismus, that would have been helpful and maybe necessary if I was going to go to law school. Despite raw emotions, a throbbing headache, and confusion, I came up with a plan. There was enough balance on the credit card to get a shuttle to LAX, and to pay for a flight to Miami on Eastern Airlines, right after it returned to work after a lengthy strike.

Even California can get cold in late December. In front of a window, in plain view of people inside the psychology clinic, I sat on a bus bench for five hours from late afternoon until mid-evening waiting for the shuttle. Not a soul from the clinic approached me. An offer of a cup of coffee would have been a nice gesture. Instead, in lieu of a modicum of consideration and an agreement to disagree, I spent five hours sitting on a bus bench in the dark feeling like a reject to the human race.

To the Bottom
of the Well

It was a few days before Christmas when the plane from Los Angeles brought me back to Miami. There was no holiday season though. Not for me. Instead of bright lights and cheerfulness, I couldn't escape darkness. Trapped in negative emotions, it was the worst I ever felt. Yet I made no physical efforts to end my life. I merely thought about dying every day. I was bogged down in confusion trying to understand what had happened in California, knowing it would have never happened to anyone that wasn't me.

So why me? Why was I so different? So that flying across country in desperate need of help for suicidal depression only resulted in disrespect, no relief, and no remedies for a troubled mind.

It was futile to seek answers from group therapy. I went back to the codependent process group a couple times, but communication there was stifled. I sensed that the therapist wasn't interested in exploring what happened to me at the clinic, or, frankly, in anything I had to say. Maybe the subject and me personally were too difficult for her to understand. Or the matter was too sensitive given her affiliation with the clinic in California. Or perhaps, my thinking went, I was so detached and outside mainstream society, I really didn't belong in the world. If anything, group therapy was counterproductive.

Meanwhile the previous pattern resumed. I went to work early in the morning and came home in mid-afternoon. Then I sat on the counter, smoked, and wrestled with thoughts inside my head. It wasn't a plan. I had no plans. For hours on end, just like before, random thoughts would trigger questions without answers that led to more questions, that brought on throbbing headaches.

In hindsight, it's amazing how much I was able to accomplish at work despite all the turmoil inside my head. I was productive, and maybe never more so. Sometimes in cameo roles, and sometimes making major contributions, projects I worked on are now fixtures in the South Florida landscape.

They include the Gratigny Parkway starting from scratch; the gigantic landfill on the way to Homestead known locally by some as Mount Trashmore; the I-595 spur from I-75 to the Fort Lauderdale airport; the placement of super-size power poles, that we called K-structures, along U.S.27 and Krome Avenue on the way to Turkey Point; the nuclear power plant where I would spend half a year doing construction surveys for the security upgrade project. I also worked on water surveys for the Army Corps of Engineers, including beach erosion surveys from South Beach up the east coast to Cape Canaveral.

Although contributing to the local economy, when not working I continued to contemplate my own self destruction. It must have been because going to work is ingrained in me and I wasn't dead yet. After work, at the apartment without furniture, I sat on the counter and nothing changed except for the tangential conundrum of what happened at the clinic in California, which was one more question without an answer. All the other questions related to childhood and familial relationships.

Why, for example, was it my job to serve and to pacify Father? Why did I spend two summer vacations alongside him building a barn for my sister's horse, only to make taking care of the horse my responsibility? Could I or should I have refused? Why did I give a damn about my parents despite feeling alienated from them? What distinguished me from my sisters who were older and able to walk away without looking back? Why did no one from my family care enough about me to watch me play organized baseball? Why did I skip out on ceremonies including high school graduation, knowing that no one would come? Why was everyone so quick to lay a guilt trip on me? Why was I vulnerable to guilt trips? What, if anything, did my grandfather burning in hell do to me? What was his influence on other members of the family before I was born? Why did my younger sister think I owed it to her not to enlist, to live at the abode forever, and never have a life of my own? How did I as a youngest child incur such a debt?

What kept my head above water was the anger I directed at the cabal of psychologists at the clinic, and to a lesser extent the therapist who sent me there; although it must be said at least she was trying to help. I was furious at the way the clinic mislabeled me and accused me of being an alcoholic to serve their purposes. More than that, I burned with anger at their depriving me of my atheistic belief. I always grant others the right to their beliefs. Why wouldn't the clinic reciprocate?

Atheism is my foundation for understanding life on this planet. Atheism is as much a part of me as my blood and bones. Surrendering a fundamental component of oneself for psychological relief is by definition no relief. Others can believe what they will but I was a cornered animal and no one outside of myself was going to take my life away from me.

In contrast to those who claim to be born again, perhaps, though I've no desire to discredit anyone, for me it was atheism that made me spurn the psychologists and walk out of the clinic in Van Nuys. Believing that I was right and others wrong, even if it was 95% of humanity, it was hanging on to atheism in anger that sustained me in the fight of my life. By invoking anger that put suicidal thoughts in abeyance, forcing me to answer unanswerable questions by my-self, and to find the way out of madness by myself, that is how mental therapy and the clinic in California helped me, but not in the way they were supposed to.

It was after January, then February, and almost April that I was sitting on the counter as usual, ad nauseam, when for no foresee-able reason I asked myself a question that I'd never asked before. There's no explanation for why it took me so long to ask it. I was thinking about my family, and the relationships within the family, when I suddenly said to myself, and asked myself: Wait a minute! What family?

There are qualities to families from which members draw strength and security that did not exist in my case. As far back as memo-ry took me, I was a lone wolf fighting for survival. Asking myself that fundamental question, *what family?*, allowed me to envision myself and separate myself free from family ties. Detaching from an imagined and artificial construct of family broke open the log jam of mental paralysis. Only then did I see that I'd spent my en-tire conscious existence trying to pound my square peg self into a round hole where I never did fit.

Without depression that disappeared like air let out of a balloon, with a freed-up mind, I was able to find the most important piece of the puzzle, what distinguished me from other members of a pseudo family, and for the most part from the rest of the human race. I saw how the trauma experienced at age seven, caused by a teacher who hated me for reasons I couldn't understand, radical-ly transformed me and made me a different person, which was, in fact, two persons. I was able to see how it was after the trau-ma nightmare ended that I felt alienated from everyone and ev-erything. And that it was right after moving that I lost what little self-esteem I still had, forcing me to reconstruct self-esteem some other way.

Significantly, and painfully, it became necessary to confront a harsh reality. Father and Grandmother weren't the only disruptive forces inside the abode. I was passive aggressive, manipulative, always acting with ulterior motives. I was a phony, so it was no wonder others felt as alienated from me as I felt alienated from them.

A false persona and a state of denial, I came to realize, were necessary to survive childhood and to go on living. They were also a cover for naivety, immaturity, ignorance, and an arrested development. They were why I'd allowed and unwittingly encouraged abode members (when I wasn't escaping from them), later employers, and an ex-wife, to take advantage of my weaknesses, often by laying on guilt trips as leverage. They were normal when I wasn't, acting in their own self-interests when I was willing to sacrifice mine.

Finally, understanding my underlying self was not a panacea; it didn't solve every problem. What it did was start, or restart, a maturation process. There are child-like traits that are forever part of my makeup; abhorrence of violence, easily frustrated, loathing of hostility, an underdeveloped ego, a shortage of genuine courage, curiosity in excess of intelligence. But knowing oneself and no longer fighting against oneself, is, I believe, a necessary and powerful tool for obtaining meaningful peace. I've been able to adapt and accept my character traits, even if they distinguish and separate me from large swathes of humanity.

With a better understanding of myself, and my origins, layers of mystery began to peel away. I started to find answers to questions that had agonized me. And I finally understood that some answers to questions, especially questions about a distant past, weren't always knowable. It was after the log jam in my head broke that I realized it wasn't possible to know what, if anything, my paternal grandfather did to me, directly, or indirectly through his influence on others. The solution was to substitute best guesses for truth and to stop thinking about him.

The more I thought about it the more it occurred to me, changes to my personality were probably not psychological, but physical in the form of altered brain waves. That explains an over reliance on the intellect at a compensatory loss of emotions. It explains why psychologists, regardless of motivation or level of proficiency, were never going to penetrate my inner self, tell me something I hadn't already thought about, or do me any good.

It was not necessary for me to blame my parents for anything. What distinguished me from them was a result of what happened away from and outside the abode. The reason I gave a damn about them, what made it hard to throw up my hands and walk away, was a child's innocence and sense of compassion. That, in turn, allowed me to see their many positive attributes. And I finally understood with clarity why I wanted to help them, but at the same time needed to escape from them.

Since a discovery of self, I've had to grow into myself, much like any child would if their development wasn't stunted at age seven. It meant learning to live with limitations but the knowledge was also liberating. With secrets to myself no longer hidden, and a phony scheme exposed, I was finally me.

Try Try Again

Roofers in Miami, working with hot tar under a blazing sun, and most of them seemed to be Haitians, were heroes of mine. Miami heat sometimes enticed me to sit with other party chiefs under a shade tree after work, to drink beer and talk shop, in what one party chief euphemistically called toolbox safety meetings. It would be a lie by omission not to mention this, as it was some, albeit scant and insufficient evidence for psychologists in California to call me an alcoholic. They probably didn't know much about working outdoors, let alone in Miami's sweltering heat. The get togethers after work were sporadic. They did not improve my outlook, or alter my sobriety (beer after a day in the sun ran through the body like hot water), and they were the sole extent of my entertainment and social life. When the meetings ended, I went back to stewing in my juices, back to sitting on the counter, in an apartment without furniture under dark clouds of depression.

Until the log jam in my head broke and depression vanished into thin air. Then everything changed. With curiosity reinvigorated and starved for nourishment, I ventured out and joined organizations, one of which was the Sierra Club. At just the right time I became a paying member at the Miami Metro Zoo, which is how I met Marjory Stoneman Douglas when she was more than 100 years old, and received an autographed copy of her book *The Everglades: River of Grass*. Per usual, seldom with ideas of my own to express, I mostly stayed in the background content to watch and listen. Clearly though, a thirst for knowledge was revived and I was back among the living.

No longer bogged down, I bought furniture and amenities that are part of everyday life for normal people. I bought a phone and got phone service, then drove across state and spent a weekend with my child at an Econo Lodge - the cost of which in normal times was three tiers above my pay grade - and told my child to call me collect anytime there was an urge.

Thinking it would help me understand people better and get more out of life, I bought a television. For several years it served its purpose and filled a void, before I came to the conclusion that television is actually anti life. Artificial life thought up by others and presented as real doesn't count.

When it rains it pours, and rain can bring good news as well as bad. When I met an attractive woman again, who I first met at an introductory therapy session, I asked her out. She proudly called herself a JAP (Jewish American Princess) and claimed she was among the 50% of Jewish people who are really Atheists. Although I question whether a successful relationship is possible between an Atheist and a person of faith, and more so the older I get, atheism was not the basis of our relationship. She was quirky and unusual in the way I was quirky and unusual, making us right for each other.

Soon more rain brought more good news. Well, it was good news initially. An agent for a collection agency with a contract with the bank that had administered my undergraduate student loans, and foreclosed on them, managed to track me down. On behalf of his agency, he demanded that I pay the loans back. I was delighted to hear from him. Knowing that student loan debt is permanent, here was a chance to do something about a headache, as well as to alleviate the burden of guilt. I willingly accepted his repayment plan, and with the aid of overtime work and out-of-town jobs, typically sent in more than the monthly minimum.

In little more than two years, the loan repayment obligation was satisfied, well ahead of schedule. Serendipitously, halfway through making the loan repayments, the agent informed me of something I didn't know and hadn't thought about. He told me that once the loans were paid off, all was forgiven. One could then apply for and receive more student loans. It was a light bulb moment.

My job was still okay most of the time. But I still hated it. Miami was okay but too urban for long term comfort. Together, the job and Miami, wore on me like a pair of ill-fitting shoes. Gradually, steadily, it crept up on me that I wasn't too old: Why not take one more spin on the big roulette wheel of life? Why not try going to law school one more time? There was no longer anything in my way, it seemed, and I had nothing to lose. As it turned out I was wrong on both counts. But I didn't know that then.

At least by then I was an expert at how to get into law school. The first step was to take the LSAT again; for me it was the third time with a nine-year spread between tests. After receiving a new score, that was somewhat better than the second, that was somewhat better than the first, though that's not supposed to happen since it's an aptitude test, I went to a bookstore and bought current guides to law schools. I sent away for catalogs that law schools sent back free of charge, along with applications. I again compared law schools on a number of factors, especially focusing on financial aid practices and admission tendencies. My child was older, settled in with my ex-wife, so I felt it was okay to attend law school in another state.

Applications were filled out and mailed back along with their fees. Requests for transcripts to be forwarded from previous colleges were made, five of them, and their fees paid. A new personal statement was written and included with each application submitted.

New letters of recommendation were required. That put me in the awkward position of asking for a new letter of recommendation from the survey company owner. He was peeved to the verge of anger because I was leaving again. He apparently thought that by hiring me back he owned me. He was a good man and a decent boss but our minds never met in a comfortable middle. I might be malleable, and I might be crazy, but nobody owns me. In any case the entire convoluted process for getting into law school was repeated. Then the waiting game began.

None of the law schools applied to previously were applied to a second time, and not nearly as many. I was more worried about money and financial aid than getting accepted. The first response I got back was in a thin envelope. Bad news. The law school at the University of Alabama rejected me. It wasn't high on my list but rejections always hurt. Fortunately, other law schools did accept me, including the one I most wanted to go to at the University of West Virginia. It was the best overall fit. And, a different state would give me a much desired change of scenery for opening a new chapter to my life.

The waiting game nearly ran its course. I was on the cusp of making a decision but wanted, in fact needed, to consider every possible financial aid offer. At almost the last minute, needing to make a decision before windows of opportunity closed, my ex-wife contacted me. That was when she told me I needed to take custody of our child or she was going to turn our child over to the state.

For crying out loud, I couldn't help thinking, why now? The timing couldn't have been worse. I didn't believe her and was tempted to call her bluff. However, our child's well-being and future were always more important than mine. No matter what was going on between the two of them, if my ex-wife didn't want custody, it meant our child was not in a good place. So of course our child could come and live with me.

Financial aid applications were already submitted, and financial aid offers were already established, based on me as an individual without dependents. My chance to go to law school was in jeopardy, though I remained hopeful it could still work out somehow.

Then, later than all the other law schools, so late I'd almost given up on it, my alma mater Florida State University sent me a fat envelope with an admission letter. It was mostly good news but it gave me a Hobson's choice. It wasn't exactly what I wanted, denying me the fresh start I was seeking. But with in-state tuition FSU's law school was the most affordable. Further, I thought, it was in our child's best interests to remain in the same state as the child's mother, only a five-hour drive down the road from Tallahassee.

The scales tipped. Instead of going to law school at the University of West Virginia, I accepted the offer for admission at FSU. How much this may have hurt me in the long run is yet one more unanswered question. One more for which no jury will ever return a verdict.

Mainly due to financial worries, it was a big risk to go to law school, but one I couldn't refrain from taking. After a lifetime of struggle to obtain it, there would never be a better chance to achieve a decent life for myself. I'd spent years calculating the variables, and the risks seemed worth taking. The acceptance letter from FSU arrived in the spring. The fall semester started in August. That gave me a few months to prepare, and to bask in the glow of an adrenaline high, knowing it was finally going to happen. I was going to law school!

Case Closed

Before my child came to live with me, with the pursuit of law school again underway, I walked out of the relationship with my JAP girlfriend. Of course I told her I was leaving her, but I wasn't able to say why. What I couldn't explain was that I was going to go to law school, that going to law school was a primordial need with roots stretching far back into my childhood past, and that I'd already been snake-bit by love once before, which prevented me from reaching that goal. My soul couldn't have taken it happening again. Therefore, I needed to go away without any holds on my future, and I would probably never return to Miami where she was settled and established in her line of work. Believing it was necessary, I walked out of her life, but I should have been more tactful and less clumsy in the way I brought an end to our relationship.

The sin was made worse when I spent more time with a soul mate from group therapy, who my JAP girlfriend also knew. My therapy soul mate and I were familiar with each other's histories and personal issues. She was in no way a hindrance to my going to Tallahassee as a free man. In fact, she was willing to help in whatever way she could, and she gave me furniture that she had kept in storage.

A few weeks before the start of the fall semester, I drove up to Tallahassee to find an apartment. From inquiries made beforehand,

I knew that Tallahassee had an elementary school with by far the best reputation. My most important purpose was to rent an apartment that would place my child in that elementary school, and I found one. An apartment owner assured me that if I rented his unit my child would attend that school; in fact, the school was within easy walking distance. So I took out a lease and returned to Miami.

Our child spent the last weeks of summer with my ex-wife. After tying up loose ends, on the way back to Tallahassee in a rental van, and to law school, finally, full of enthusiasm, I swung by the bay area and picked up our child. Together we drove the rest of the way to our new lives.

Immediately we were hit with a setback. I learned my child could not attend the desired elementary school because boundary lines had changed. The news was devastating. My protests were futile. Classes were about to start for every college student in Tallahassee. Either the landlord I rented from didn't know about the changes to school boundary lines, or he did know but refused to tell me. Now our apartment fell, just barely, within the boundaries of a different elementary school. Equality of education in Tallahassee at the time was still a mirage. I would soon find out how much that mattered.

Pressure on first year law students began immediately, before we heard from the dean at orientation. So much work, and so many reading assignments were thrown at students even before the first day of classes, it quickly became difficult to focus attention on anything other than law school. The stress was increased by the tacit but constant competition among law students.

Only the most gifted and confident law students, perhaps, didn't worry about where they stood before they received their first semester grades. For us, they were posted sporadically during the early part of the second semester in what was dubbed the Hall of Tears. In most cases, grades depended on how students performed on essay final exams with elaborate fact patterns to unravel, which exacerbated uncertainties. One of my fondest law school memories came after seeing the end of the final exam for Property Law. A wise and compassionate professor added a few words. He wrote: "Congratulations. The scary part of law school is over".

It was soul-comforting for me to receive my first grade. In Torts I earned an 84. That was a little above average, enough to ease my troubled mind, and it allowed me to believe that just maybe I belonged in law school. I didn't, however, but I didn't know that yet.

Grades were such a nerve-wracking underlying factor, and the competition for them so fraught with tension, at our law school they instituted a blind (BAGS) grading system. Towards the end of every semester, before final exams, students were given a new BAGS number. Professors graded a number, not names or students. Grades were scaled in such a way that the average for every course was an 80, with an equal number of grades both above and below that mark. If my theory is accurate, and I believe that it is, grades primarily reflected the intelligence of students commensurate to their respective IQs. A gifted student might put forth little effort but their grades wouldn't suffer much. A challenged student might try hard but only increase their grades a small amount.

Although I never inquired as to my final class standing, my grade point average at the end of law school was slightly above 80, earning me a JD degree with honors. Compared to other law schools around the country, FSU's law school was moderately difficult to get into. Roughly speaking then, I was an average law student in an average law school. In any case, the academic aspects of law school were burdensome, but manageable.

The biggest problem, and worst headache I had to deal with in the first semester was unrelated to law school. Instead, it was a direct result of the long history of racial discrimination in North

Florida's past. The elementary school where my child had to attend was primarily a black school in a black area of town. Of course measures were needed to improve integration and equality in education, justifying the redrawing of school boundary lines. My grievance had nothing to do with race, but with the fact my child's elementary school was sub-standard, stifling my child's growth and development.

Normally an avid reader, fast learner, curious and enthusiastic student, it was an ominous sign when my young child kept coming up with what appeared to me to be psychosomatic illnesses to avoid going to school. It didn't take long and but a few questions to discover my child was bored to tears, devoid of motivation, and in the wrong place. I often found myself arguing with my child in ways we never did before, afraid the child would exceed the permitted number of absences and get held back. In what was the start of a struggle that consumed time and energy, in addition to the challenges of law school, I contacted the school's principal. He was a good man willing to help.

The principal wondered if he knew my child. He asked if my child might be the one reading a book in the cafeteria while the other kids were having a food fight. "Yes," I said. "I'm sure that's my child." We discussed the possibility of having my child accelerated into a higher grade, or sent to advance classes at a different school. The principal informed me, however, these measures required approval from a higher authority. Apparently he was unsuccessful at securing that approval. A few weeks later he advised me to contact a particular administrator myself.

When I called Mrs. P on the phone, she had the audacity to tell me my child was "too white," and she would never grant her approval for advance classes. She even added that I would never be able to prove what she told me. I could point to a few instances in my life when I was discriminated against for being white. The instances were rare, fortunately, and I was able to shrug them off because I knew that for centuries the shoe was on the other foot; when those who were discriminated against had no access to remedies, and no options but to grin and bear indignities. In this case, though, there was a critical distinction. A bureaucrat was making my child bear the burden for past discrimination. That could not stand.

Out of frustration I went to work trying to find alternative solutions. In one possibility, I believed my child, with a little preparation, could have passed a GED exam but the child's teacher could not. What an injustice it was then that my child was trapped in her classroom. So I tried to find out who to ask, and what strings would need to be pulled, to obtain permission for an elementary school child to sit in and take the GED. More than likely, matters would not have gotten that far. Pressure applied to the educational system probably would have filtered down to Mrs. P and opened the closed door. Fortunately, though, while seeking alternative solutions, the issue became moot.

My ex-wife's timing before law school, coercing me into taking custody of our child, couldn't have been worse. She did it again at the end of the first semester, two weeks out from final exams. But her timing was apropos and this time I wholeheartedly approved her message. I was thoroughly fed up with fighting the Leon County school system when she told me she wanted our child to live with her again. She assured me that her aunt, for whom I had admiration, holding a high position in her county's school system, could get our child into an educational program designed to stimulate high achieving students. It was an offer that couldn't be refused.

My ex-wife and I struck a deal. Our child could not go back and forth, so this would be the last move. She also promised to provide stability that was sorely missing in our young child's life to that point, allowing for the formation of friendships and bonds that are essential to a young child's development. And my ex-wife did, in fact, adhere to the terms of our unwritten contract. As admitted previously, she was better suited to be a second half of childhood parent. It may not have been in my personal best interests, though, to allow our child to return to her. In a case of déjà vu, our deal came with a price to be paid later.

Throughout my time in law school, just as throughout my life, a shortage of money was an additional burden. A lifetime of learning to live cheap helped. So too did saving money in Miami in anticipation of going to law school. That got my child and myself started reasonably well. But despite those savings, and student loans, all the money was running out before the end of the semester.

That provoked me into doing something I wouldn't have done if it wasn't necessary. I applied for food stamps. My thinking and justification were twofold. I had spent years in the work force paying the taxes that made food stamps available to others. More importantly, my child was not going to go hungry. It unnerved me to stand in line to receive them, or to spend them. Others may have felt the same way. However, I stood out as a healthy-looking able-bodied man, a South Florida-tanned ex construction worker. By appearances, as well as psychologically, I did not fit in. Without criticism for those who needed them, and used them, I hated food stamps.

On a lighter and perhaps historical note, I attended law school from August of 1992 until December of 1994. PCs were just coming into vogue. Every other law student that I knew already had one, but their prices were beyond my ability to afford one. So I was among the last students, if not the very last, to make it through FSU's law school with only a typewriter.

At the beginning of the second semester, law students were encouraged to submit applications to the Florida Bar Association, a prerequisite for securing approval to take the bar exam upon graduation. The Bar Association's noble task was to review the applications, and assess the character of candidates, to determine whether they were qualified to practice law in Florida. There were events and aspects to my past, amounting to red flags, that were bound to raise suspicions.

They included an arrest for possession of marijuana, an auto wreck caused by driving while intoxicated, defaulting on student loans, child support issues, mental therapy that involved walking out of a clinic while rejecting its plan for improving my mental health. Not to mention its determination that I was an alcoholic. How could I possibly explain finding my own way out of madness without experts while living in an apartment without furniture?

Could stuffy lawyers in suits relate to, or understand, a childhood at the abode? I couldn't even provide addresses for my sisters as the bar application required. What about trying to explain how my life was derailed due to what happened to me in second grade? Then there was the biggest issue of all to explain, the crime of embezzlement that involved my ex-wife, and myself.

With information obtained through the law school grapevine, I was directed to go see one of FSU's professors. The Criminal Law professor then urged me to make an appointment with a lawyer who was a friend of his. The lawyer was a specialist in matters before the Florida Bar Association.

When I saw him, the specialist said he didn't think the arrest for marijuana was a serious obstacle, since the case was expunged as part of a plea deal, when the attorney for codefendants and myself said we could treat the case as though it never happened. He was skeptical when I told him, no legal actions were taken following the auto wreck I caused in Mississippi, and that there was never even an accident report made. But it was true. I'd sobered up instantly at the scene, and clearly overheard investigating officers say, in effect; they're all military boys so let the military take care of it. Then military authorities also took no disciplinary actions, much to my surprise, and relief.

The Bar specialist mildly mocked me for my lengthy explanations on the Bar application, saying I'd made it look as if I'd grown up in a log cabin. How else, though, was I going to explain an abode with a missing floor, a skeleton of a family, and the long winding road they propelled me down while trying to escape? No. Stuffy lawyers in suits were never going to understand, or believe me.

The specialist was mainly concerned with the embezzlement case. He wanted to know if my ex-wife would be willing to sign an affidavit stating that I had no prior knowledge before the embezzlement. I told him I thought so, but I wasn't sure. Even if she did sign such an affidavit, however, I had read a statement into the record at trial accepting my share of the responsibility. What freed me from a criminal accusation condemned me for being a naive idiot.

Particularly daunting to me was a clause in the Bar application that gave the Bar the right to charge extra, more than the standard application fee, that wasn't cheap, for their added costs to investigate a candidate's background. That meant, I had to agree in advance to pay lawyer fees, and to write the Florida Bar Association a blank check. Fair or not, for a poor troubled soul like me that was the same as slamming a door in my face.

One of the few endearing memories I have of my mother is from the first semester of law school. Twice, shortly before her cancer diagnosis, she sent me letters. In both of them she included a $20 bill without comment. My guess was that it was without my father's knowledge. The money was helpful but it was the gesture that mattered more. Most of the time she had a caring heart, that she kept well hidden, and she suffered greatly because of it.

It was during the second semester that my mother's cancer worsened. She was hospitalized for the last time and she would remain in the hospital until her passing. My mother and I didn't have a strong bond but I always felt compassion for her. Knowing she was dying was a weight on my mind, and it brought back feelings of helplessness I felt as a child.

Calls to my mother's doctor in New York disturbed me. The doctor was unable to tell me, or to guess, how much longer my mother had to live. Something in the doctor's tone of voice worried me that he was prolonging my mother's life, and thereby her suffering, for profit. I wondered about the purpose and reasoning for all the radiation treatments he prescribed. At the same time, however, it made me feel guilty because I wanted her to live longer. My child, age eleven, had never met my mother. I wanted the two of them to have a chance to meet at least once.

When the law school semester ended, in May, my ex-wife and child were in Pennsylvania on vacation visiting her grandparents. In the midst of uncertainty, I put together a plan. I flew to Pittsburgh, picked up my child after their vacation, and we drove to New York in a rented car. We managed to visit my mother in the hospital but the meeting between her and my child did not go particularly well. Maybe my father was right, that I should not have brought them together at that late stage. It was and still is impossible for me to know if I'd done the right thing.

She lived until August. My mother never complained about the obvious pain she was in. In her final months at the abode Father was impressed by how tough she was.

It was soon after the end of the second semester that my ex-wife applied again for public assistance. As a consequence, and not in any way her fault, the Department of Health and Rehabilitative

Services sued me again for child support. I was summoned to another hearing down in the bay area.

Law school typically requires three years of study. It's commonly said among lawyers, though, everything an attorney needs to know is covered in the first year; the last two years are superfluous. A more confident and competent law student might already have had enough skill to handle a child support hearing unassisted. The last thing I wanted was to go to another child support hearing feeling alone and unarmed.

Prior to the hearing, I had a grievance with the HRS bureaucracy. Because my child lived with me from January until December, I was eligible for earned income credit for the 1992 tax year. This was supposed to result in a refund of approximately $700 (worth in the neighborhood of $1,500 by the year 2025), money I desperately needed at the time. In what HRS agents admitted was a mistake, and even though I possessed an official letter from HRS stating that I had custody and no arrears existed, HRS intercepted the IRS refund. Presumably it was done with a key stroke on a computer. In separate phone calls, both the IRS and HRS claimed there was nothing they could do to help me recover what was in effect stolen money. A call to an attorney didn't help either. He assured me he could get my refund back, but his legal fees would exceed the amount of the refund. I never saw the money and eventually wrote it off as a loss.

It wasn't easy to find an attorney willing to help a man with a child support hearing, but the local attorney I eventually found was especially helpful. First she filed a preliminary motion and managed to have our hearing conducted over the phone. At least I didn't have to cut classes to drive downstate. Then she did a ton of research to arm herself with case law beforehand. Unfortunately, the judge at the hearing, a male judge this time, wasn't interested in or persuaded by anything she had to say. After the hearing she told me, because of the judge's blatant prejudices, if I had paid for a stenographer we would have had grounds to appeal and have him recused.

At one point the judge said he didn't care that I was a law student, because Florida already had too many lawyers. Nor did it matter that in the year I had custody I didn't receive a penny of support. Nor did it matter that HRS stole my IRS tax refund. Fair or not, arrears were established starting on the day our child returned to live with my ex-wife. That meant, only part way through law school, I was already a year behind in child support arrears. More important than that, though, the judge with his attitude destroyed my respect for the legal system. Afterwards, increasingly, I saw how often in legal disputes who is involved matters more than what happened.

Before she began her work, my attorney and I had negotiated a fee. When the case was over, I managed to pay her, with difficulty, and told her it was a ridiculously small payment for all the work she did. She then said my acknowledgment of that was her just compensation.

Maybe the judge did have an ounce of empathy. Or maybe he just felt guilty for his injustice. He tossed me a bone when he made it part of his ruling that arrears, separate from monthly child support payments, could be spread out and the lion's share paid upon completion of law school. The result was no favor. After law school, the arrears, plus all the student loans I had to repay, created a mountain of debt on the brink of an avalanche.

After the child support hearing, I considered dropping out of law school. But to do what? Or go where? It might have prevented, or at least reduced life-strangling indebtedness. However, having expended so much of my life's hopes and energy getting into law school, stubbornness kept me going. In hindsight, though, the child support hearing was when and where, after reaching for the sky, I had landed with a thud.

In each of my last three semesters I earned six credit hours working pro bono as an intern at the FSU College of Law's Children's Advocacy Center. Without taking the Florida Bar exam, as reflected in court documents, I officially became an attorney of record, perhaps qualifying me for having reached my law school goal. Under the supervision of a licensed attorney, I had a practice with clients and cases, and I experienced the law, minimally to be sure, as an insider. The clients were juveniles charged with criminal offenses.

Before law school, my vision of life afterwards wasn't elaborate. I was not after money, prestige, validation, or trying to assuage a bruised ego. If I could have made a decent living doing anything with a law degree, but especially if it helped disadvantaged children, that would have made going to law school a success. After all, the measuring stick for improvement on one end started with a childhood spent at the abode.

Unfortunately, as an intern, a chance to help disadvantaged children is not what I saw. In fact, it was just the opposite and it was further discouragement for pursuing a career in the law.

My apprenticeship began with a rude introduction. My first client had been represented by a different intern in the previous semester. It was stunning to see how that intern had my client's file for months but never lifted a finger on the case. There were no notes for the next intern, no preliminary investigation, nor any legal research done, not even an attempt to contact and interview the accused juvenile. The entire contents of the case file consisted of charging documents from the prosecutor's office. Prosecutors routinely provided police reports. All a defense attorney had to do was ask for them, but not even this basic initial task was taken. In short, the previous intern had taken the course credits without doing the work. It's not hard then to imagine my dismay, and incipient distrust of the legal system, upon learning the previous intern had graduated, found employment, and was now working in the prosecutor's office, while I was saddled with a naked case file and a trial on all counts and charges scheduled for the following week.

The juveniles I represented were often charged with crimes they didn't do. Resources necessary to adequately investigate charges against them, and represent them properly, weren't available. At the same time, juveniles usually committed more crimes than what they were charged for, and those crimes typically fell through the cracks and went unsolved, presumably due to expediency and limited state resources. Neither the juveniles or the general public appeared to be well served by the juvenile justice system. Or maybe it evened out. Or based on economic criteria, the system worked as well as it could. Or else it was a charade. Final dispensations of justice always seemed to come down to what bureaucrats wanted anyway.

At sentencing, serious and repeat offenders were sent to out-of-town and in-house rehabilitation programs, or else, if bureaucratic resistance was overcome and prosecutors prevailed, to a just started boot camp for juveniles. From my perspective they were all black holes lacking accountability. No one was able to give me information indicating that treatment programs made a long-term and positive difference in the lives of young juveniles. Once a juvenile was in a treatment program, a case was closed: The system was satisfied.

As an intern I saw no way around an entrenched bureaucracy, no way to use the law to help children. Then too, I was probably too naive to expect that in the first place. Then too, a deteriorating attitude towards the law did not help with objective analysis.

Stubbornness, like all human qualities, is both a sword and a shield. In my case, stubbornness was always coupled with dogged independence. Together, they've allowed me to do things others would have trouble doing. Together, they prevented me from taking advantage of resources, getting more out of the law school experience, and making law school work in my favor.

In classes I listened attentively and took a lot of notes, but I did not raise my hand to participate in legal arguments, no matter how hypothetical and stimulating they were. I never tried out for mock court, or wrote an article for the law review publication, feathers in the caps and pads to the resume for many law students. In my defense, efforts at self-aggrandizement struck me as a form of brownnosing, which I refused to do. Stubbornness and independence prevented me.

The law school had a placement office to help students find employment and get started in the legal profession. I never consulted with the experts there. Although perhaps I would have but for feeling stifled.

Many of my classmates found part time jobs as law clerks. As a state capitol Tallahassee was rich in law clerk opportunities, at state agencies, with interest groups, and busy law firms. Due to problems with the Bar Association, I couldn't answer a question on most law clerk applications, which was whether I expected to take and pass the Florida bar exam after law school. Not able to provide an honest answer, I felt stifled and shamed, and unable to explain the obstacle posed by my sordid past.

Feeling stifled, and a soul-robbing child support hearing, plus observations of the juvenile justice system resulting in disenchantment with the law, all played a role. So too did weak self-confidence which is not a good quality in an attorney. Of course it dawned on me that my personality was not a good fit for a career in the legal profession. In the back of my mind, though, there's still a sense that I could have found my niche. I will never know now and can only wonder about what might have been.

It's always harder to blame oneself for bad outcomes. If law school didn't work out for me, I blame no one but myself. Although it took a few years to admit it, in hindsight I am thankful to those at the FSU College of Law that approved my admission and gave me the opportunity of a lifetime.

At the start of the second semester, after our child returned to live with my ex-wife, a nice woman at the food stamp office called me on the phone. She wanted to let me know that as an individual without dependents my income still qualified me to receive food stamps. I politely told her, no thank you.

It was also in the second semester that the elementary school principal sent me a letter. He had finally managed to obtain permission for my child to take advance classes. He was a good man, but his help came too late to make a difference. Our child was already in a better place.

In the last semester, with law school almost over, the Florida Bar specialist sent me a letter. In it he expressed his belief that he could get me through the bar application process, that would allow me to take the bar exam along with my classmates. However, the second time I went to see him, when he said his meter wasn't running yet, he told me his fee was $180 an hour. But he couldn't give me an estimate how many hours a case like mine might require. At the conclusion of law school, I couldn't have afforded even one of his hours. The only money I had to live on came from selling my furniture, half of it given to me by my therapy soul mate in Miami.

As law school was winding down, a new licensed attorney arrived to supervise at the Children's Advocacy Center. When he learned what I was going to do after law school, he said to me, "You don't know how many of us are sick of the law and wish we were doing what you're going to do."

Because I took classes and had earned credits in summer semesters, which kept loans and income coming in, I had enough credits to graduate (without ceremony) in December of 1994 for the class of 1995. Student loan payments were automatically deferred for six months following law school. Having defaulted on student loans once before, I was determined to never let that happen again. The shame alone would have killed me. Student loan debt plus a mountain of child support arrears were a loaded gun pointed at my head. They put me in the position of running for my life all over again. I've rolled with a lot of punches in my life, but the end of law school was a punch to the gut and the hardest punch of all.

Concluding that I would never be a lawyer, or make a living with a law degree, but the bills still had to be paid, it was during the last semester that I came up with a new plan. I decided to do something that may have never been done before in America. Having achieved only indebtedness, I got in my Dodge pickup, headed east on I-10, and put law school and Tallahassee and everything they meant to me in the rearview mirror.

Another man might have been angry. Another man might have fought harder. Another man wouldn't have let it go. I decided to go back to work.

Return to Hell
Address Unknown

The first time I may have made history was in the military. I resisted pressure to conform and managed to obtain official permission to have Atheist dog tags, perhaps becoming the first enlisted man in the Navy allowed to have them. The second time I may have made history was when I went directly from law school to truck driving school. Unlike the first time, there was no pride in the achievement; I was not striking a blow for freedom. On the contrary, I was running scared trying to get out from underneath an avalanche of debt.

The truck driving school was located at Green Cove Springs, Florida, south of Jacksonville. It was a short drive east on I-10 to get there. The truck driving school's tuition, one more debt, was deferred until after a student obtained a CDL (commercial driver's license). The assumption was, a driver with a CDL would have no trouble paying back the tuition as truck drivers were in high demand. In stark contrast to law school, graduates didn't go looking for employers. Employers from trucking companies from all around the country came looking for truck school graduates.

The truck driving school also paid for a motel room for students needing a place to stay during the week. All the other students lived close enough to go home either every day or for the weekend.

I was homeless and had nowhere else to go. With my money running out and little to spare, I paid for weekends myself, then stayed in the motel alone until the following Monday. It was a strange time but times were about to get a lot stranger.

Driving a big rig did not fit any aptitude of mine. It was totally out of my purview and I was a fish out of water in the truck driving profession. Nevertheless, I couldn't afford to fail but nearly did so anyway. Only one other student failed the first road test at the end of the course. The school granted a student two tries. The second road tester asked why I failed the first time. I told him it was because I was nervous. He encouragingly asked, "You aren't going to be nervous with me, are you?" I wasn't. I passed the second time and dodged a bullet. Life went on. For a little while longer.

The next hurdle was to select a trucking company to drive for. Several recruiters came to the driving school to deliver their spiels, to promise the moon while tossing out statistics, and to hand out glossy brochures and business cards. The difficulty in choosing the right trucking company was like pinning a tail on a donkey while blindfolded. Most of the new CDL holders were just as confused as I was.

In addition to deciding on a trucking company, and the location of its terminal, though for over-the-road drivers that hardly mattered, a new CDL driver also had to decide whether to haul a van (commonly called a dry box), temperature-controlled freight (a refer), a car carrier, tanker, or flat bed. Some students already had plans to drive locally after they graduated. They were the smart ones. I was not one of those. For no particular reason other than it was a wild guess, I chose to drive for a trucking company that pulled vans.

It was late winter when I relocated by driving my Dodge pickup and everything I owned, basically a bag of clothes, to the terminal of a trucking company outside Atlanta. A six-month deferment, before student loan payments were due, started to cast a dark shadow, as a debt-fused time bomb ticked inside my head. The trucking company had an oversize lot. I parked the Dodge out in back and walked inside to join the other new hires in the lobby.

After reporting in and completing preliminary paperwork, I was told to wait. Nothing happened the first day. On the second day, I sat in the lobby all day from morning to evening. One by one, names were called as trainees were directed to walk out to a truck with a trainer, who presumably was a seasoned driver and a good instructor. A trainer's incentive was getting paid for his own miles plus whatever miles that a trainee drove. The trainee was paid a minimal base pay while gaining experience. When a trainer determined a trainee was ready, within a few weeks in most cases, he or she was taken back to the terminal and given their own truck to drive and take care of.

The longer I sat in the lobby on that second day, waiting for my name to be called, the more I worried and grew uneasy. My name was the last one called, when it was almost dark. In hindsight, the trainer I was directed to start off with was probably not a bad man. For my purposes though he was insufferable. We immediately had a clash of personalities. We were never going to establish a meeting of the minds, or to communicate effectively.

The first red flag was raised as soon as we drove out of the terminal. He began lecturing me on his method of child rearing. He proudly went to see all of his young son's teachers, he said, and ordered them to drive his son hard, with a heavy emphasis on the word hard. Getting rough was his modus operandi, and, it appeared, his preferred method of teaching. The way law school ended, and everything it meant to me including a life-long commitment, the last thing I needed was a man like him barking in my ear while learning to drive a truck. It was obvious to me that I was not going to learn under his tutelage. Philosophically, we were on different planets. I couldn't stand the man, and couldn't see a way out of the predicament I'd gotten myself into. I did a deep dive into depression.

He drove the first stretch. Then I drove. Then he drove again until we pulled into a truck stop at Altoona, Iowa. For me, it was the end of the road. When the trainer went to sleep, I grabbed my bag and walked a dozen miles to the Greyhound bus station in downtown Des Moines. I wasn't flat out broke. Yet. I had enough money for a bus ticket and everything else I would need.

Previously, when I thought about suicide, before and during group therapy, and following the debacle in California, I was on the brink but never crossed the line that said do it now. After the end of law school, walking away from the trainer, and truck driving too, ending life was the only thing that mattered to me. My justification to myself was that I wasn't qualified to live on the planet. That was why nothing ever worked out for me.

The Greyhound bus took me to Schenectady, New York. From there I walked to Esperance, about fifteen miles, and bought a mix of sleeping pills and poison along the way. It was almost dark when I got there and I wanted one more look around in daylight. I spent the night under the U.S. 20 bridge over the Schoharie Creek.

My plan was thwarted. I didn't think anyone could see me under the bridge but a woman had. She was suspicious and called law enforcement. Early the next morning, a cop managed to creep up behind me. He looked over my shoulder, read my suicide note, and Baker Acted me on the spot. He made me get in a car with him and his partner and drove me to a place in Albany that housed a lot of strange people. I fit right in.

Still, I wanted to get out of that place in the worst way. After the minimum 24 hours an impasse was reached. The facility couldn't release me, it was said, unless I could provide a plan and a destination. My plan was to finish what I started but I couldn't tell them that. The stalemate continued until I got frustrated enough to tell them I had a father that lived down by Kingston. It was no help to my depression when they put me on a bus and sent me there. No one bothered to check the contents of my gym bag.

Throughout childhood, and afterwards too, without blaming him, and even respecting him, I never wanted to be near my father. What a mistake it was to show up at the abode. If there was any hope of understanding, or compassion, it never existed there, or with him.

He didn't welcome me and I couldn't blame him. He was in his own home. I was an intruder on his domicile. We soon had heated arguments, although he brought almost all the heat; I was too mentally incapacitated to resist. That's how I quickly fell into old habits, doing favors and running errands as he easily manipulated me. It didn't take long for our mutual antagonism to reach a boiling point. I managed to hold on for two days before concluding nothing was worthwhile, or worth living for. During a hostile exchange of words between us, I grabbed my gym bag, certain that the moment to stop living had arrived, knowing from childhood explorations a good place to die. Then, literally as I was walking towards the door, a freak event stopped me. The phone rang.

My therapy soul mate in Miami was calling. She hadn't heard from me in a long time and wanted to know my whereabouts. The shock of her call and its timing snapped me out of a stupor. Months later, when I told her about the difference her call made, she didn't want to talk about it. She said it made her feel creepy.

That evening, after her call, I went out to a bar with an old friend. The same friend who drove me to North Carolina, on my way south on a bicycle. When I told him I didn't even have transportation, because my Dodge pickup was stranded in a trucking company lot down by Atlanta, he asked. "Why don't we go down and get it?" That was as freaky as the phone call. My friend almost never left his childhood home, the big exception being when we drove south together years before. That way, he added, he could revisit places and the one time in his life when he really did go somewhere. If he was willing it made sense to me. We worked out the details and put together a plan.

We rode a bus down to New York City, took a cab to La Guardia, and walked up to the counter of a rental car agency, where I had reserved a vehicle. Immediately there was a snag. I had to call my credit card company, and over the phone beg a woman agent to raise my credit limit, temporarily, with a solemn promise it was for one time only because I was in a serious jam. She was reluctant, but acquiesced (giving me more indebtedness). What is unknown, until now, is that her favor made me a loyal customer, and it's why I've only had that one credit card for more than 35 years.

With money from the credit card, my friend and I were able to rent a car and drive to Raleigh, North Carolina, which was where my friend most wanted to go. For two days I drove him around to see all the old sights he wanted to see. Then we drove down to Georgia to the trucking company. I was able to retrieve the Dodge from the back of the lot, and we returned the rental car at the Atlanta airport. Then we drove back to upstate New York.

As someone who has owned personal automobiles on and off, and probably more off than on, I can attest to one fact. Having a set of wheels does make a difference. And, sometimes, an automobile is serviceable as an alternate dwelling.

Hanging around with my father longer than necessary was not an option. So, when we got back to New York, I drove the Dodge down through the Great Creek Locks Forest, past all the houses to a long-wooded stretch on the way to Kingston. At a popular summer fishing hole, I backed the Dodge up at an angle under cover of trees, to the edge of water, which consisted of the combined force of the Rondout Creek and the Wallkill River, seasonally fattened up with melting snow. The scenery was great. Amenities were lacking.

It wasn't perfect but my new residence, sans mailbox, even had historical significance. On the other side of Creek Locks Road, deep in the woods, there were the remnants of an abandoned community that once belonged to Father Divine and his inspired followers.

After exhausting the extra credit card money, my body, and the Dodge were running on fumes. My friend might have loaned me money, but stubbornness prevented me from asking him. Truth be told, if I had had money to spare, I would have bought cigarettes before food. Fortunately, gas was still cheap enough that a dollar bought wiggle room.

For me everything starts with a job. The wiggle room was enough to drive to a temp agency in Lake Katrine that had an ad in the paper. I hoped it would have something I could do. Ironically, it seemed to me, people at the temp agency were mainly impressed by the fact I had a law degree, and it was the only time when law school and a law degree were of any use to me. As it turned out, though, the value was more than can be measured in dollars and cents.

The temp agency sent me to uptown Kingston, across the street from the Old Dutch Church, where once upon a time I had attended Boy Scout meetings. For a week, I was a two-finger typist and phone receptionist at the Kingston Public Defenders Office, filling in for a woman on vacation. At the end of the week, I had earned enough money to put gas in the tank, to buy cigarettes, and food, and to breathe new life into hopelessness.

It's rare to hit on the slots twice in a row. When the week was over, the temp agency found me another position. What irony however! The temp agency sent me down to the plaza (the Kingston equivalent of a mall for many years) to another secretarial job as a receptionist and two-finger typist. The irony? The job was at an office building for the New York State Child Support Agency, and it was my job to type threatening letters to be sent out to people who weren't paying their court ordered child support.

Meanwhile, back at my abode, living in the Dodge was not comfortable. Every day after work, I backed my dwelling up to the water's edge. Then I bathed in the creek, which in early spring was like diving into a tub of ice water. One night, while curled up on the front seat trying to sleep, in the dead of night I was rudely awakened by a cop shining his flashlight in my eyes. I really hate it when cops do that! He demanded to see my driver's license. When I handed it to him he was instantly impressed. He snapped it with his fingers and said, "That's a CDL!" I got the impression he wouldn't have been nearly as impressed if I'd told him I just graduated from law school.

With a CDL in his hand, though, he was interested enough to listen to me. I explained how I was employed, couldn't get along with my father, and was trying to gain enough traction to keep my head above water and get back on my feet. He asked how many nights I intended to park there. I said not much longer. He handed the CDL back to me and said, "It better not be."

Looking back, I can see it was a relapse and a double bounce at the bottom of the well. The six months following law school matched my nadir. The worst was over. But I didn't know that yet. If managed properly, a shred of hope can help an individual overcome long odds. That is what I had at the time, why I could tell the cop I expected to soon be out of there for good.

In slack time at the Child Support Agency, between typing letters and answering phones, I continually tried to call a number on a business card. The card was handed out at the truck driving school in Green Cove Springs. It was my last chance. After numerous attempts, when the recruiter was always out driving around, visiting other truck driving schools around the country, and I could only leave messages, I finally got a hold of him one afternoon. Impressed by my persistence, he said that if I could get myself to Yankton, South Dakota, and to a company that ran flat beds, he would put me with a trainer and put me to work.

The job at the Child Support Agency was an open position. I might have been able to apply for a job as a permanent employee. The man in charge at the temp agency told me the people there liked me, and I liked working with them. The wage the job paid was probably enough for me to live on, and a law degree might have helped me establish a career there (working for a cause I believed in) after catching up with my own child support payments of course. However, the location was in the same county and the same state where my father lived. There are some discomforts that money can't fix.

So, I collected my last paycheck from the temp agency. On the last night I spoiled myself, staying in a motel and basking in luxury with a hot shower and a bed. It was already May when I filled up the Dodge with gas and drove off west into the sunset. The debt-fused time bomb ticking in my head was about to explode. In addition to student loan deferments that were near expiration, I was way behind on child support, still had to pay the truck driving school tuition, and had a tapped-out credit card. I didn't know where the road would lead, or anything about where I was going. I only knew it was necessary to go.

Get Out on the Highway

The trainer assigned to me at the flat bed trucking company in South Dakota was a good man with common sense. I could tell instantly. At least he was reasonable and a driver trainee can't ask for more. He wouldn't allow me to smoke in his truck, but I was willing to grin and bear the torture long enough to make the transition from trainee to driver.

We picked up and delivered freight in many places from California to Rhode Island, giving me my first taste of life on the road, as well as the first ground level view of my country from coast to coast. The trainer taught me how to secure flatbed freight with straps, binders, chains, and tarpaulins. After five weeks he brought me back to the yard in South Dakota and said I was ready. The trucking company then gave me a truck and a load to deliver. I was on my own, accepting but not necessarily ready for adventure and whatever came my way.

In my time as a trucker, I started out as a rookie. When it ended, I was still a rookie. Learning happened every day and never stopped. It was incumbent on me to learn how to drive a big truck, but also how to live out on the road, as well as the ins and outs, nuts and bolts of the trucking industry. Everything that follows here, as with the other parts of this narrative, is either opinionated theory based on my - arguably peculiar - perceptions, or questionable if presented as fact. I was figuring things out as I went along and never obtained the status of a know-it-all. Although, I did make efforts to talk to, and glean knowledge from old timers who had lived the trucker's lifestyle for years and years.

The flatbed company was an irregular carrier that hauled freight everywhere within the lower 48 states, and Canada, even to Alaska once a year. It was somewhat between a small and a mid-size company with a unique business model. Instead of competing with big trucking outfits, always trying to haul more freight while trying to grow into a bigger company, the flat bed company searched for and tried to siphon the highest paying loads. How much a load paid per mile was its most important factor. It would pay a driver layover pay (compensation for being idle) rather than to bother with cheap freight. It was constantly on the look-out for oversize loads because they paid a better per mile rate.

What it meant for me was complete randomness. After delivering a load, I never knew where the next load would take me, how much difficulty it would pose, whether the next run would be long or short. Before it was given to me, every load was a surprise. My purpose for driving a truck was money, but the erratic adventure side of the business, I must admit, appealed to me.

In the nick of time debt wolves were warded off. Then, ever so gradually, I began to climb out of the debt hole I'd fallen into. I managed to make the first student loan payments on time. The trucking school tuition bill was soon paid as well. I began chipping away at child support arrears and paring down my credit card obligation. Forever, it seemed, all my work was for everyone but me. However, the cab of my truck with its sleeping compartment was my home. I didn't need anything for myself except food. And cigarettes.

Truck driving schools and trainers are just introductions to the world of trucking. They barely scratch the surface. The bulk of a rookie driver's education is on the job training.

For example, it's one thing to know, when you're loaded to the gills you need to take downgrades slow and cautiously. It's quite another to descend one alone the first time, and it may require a few of those experiences before a driver learns to relax, and can take steep downgrades while continuing to breathe normally. Knowing how to handle a truck in traffic, when to drive in cities and when not to, when to change lanes for exits, especially left lane exits, what to do at weigh stations (and every state is different), and knowing where and when to stop a truck to go to sleep are part of the learning curve for rookie drivers.

As an illustration, consider this imaginary but true to life example. A rookie driver spends the night at a truck stop in Indiana. He has a delivery appointment in Milwaukee for 9:00 a.m. the next morning. Worried about making it on time, he leaves the truck stop at 7:00 a.m. the next day. He fights all the stop and go traffic through downtown Chicago and makes it to his delivery by 9:30, only a half hour late. The experienced driver also spends the night at that truck stop in Indiana and he too has a 9:00 a.m. delivery appointment in Milwaukee. He gets up in the morning, has a shower, shaves, eats his breakfast, reads the newspaper and downs his coffee. He leaves the truck stop at 8:30 and makes it to his delivery at 9:30, also a half hour late but with the knowledge the receivers will understand he had to drive through Chicago to get there.

The longer a driver drives the clearer he may see the distinction between the image of driving over-the-road, and its reality. He or she may learn the hard way about waiting while shippers and receivers, unlike drivers paid by the hour, can take their time loading or unloading freight. Time wasted can increase a driver's stress, add to their fatigue, and put them in the position of either cheating on log books or surrendering time on the job for which they'll never be compensated. There was, and I'd be surprised if it's changed, a wide range in diligence. Many shippers and receivers did understand driver concerns and were helpful. Many others did not. On multiple occasions I waited ten hours, and more, for people to load or unload a trailer, time stolen right out of my life.

Trucking companies launched advertising campaigns with glossy brochures and slick ads in trucking magazines. They typically depicted drivers out on the open road surrounded by lush scenery, promising them they could be their own boss enjoying a life of freedom. The longer company drivers drive, however, the more they will find themselves stuck in urban traffic, with a lot of responsibility and very little control, and they're apt to see themselves as someone's monkey in a cage.

There are important distinctions among drivers that the general public is not always privy to, which seldom make it into discussions about policies and regulations. By virtue of owning the truck he drives, an owner operator is, in fact, his own boss. He may have a contract with and accept loads from a trucking company, but normally he can refuse loads, or quit and go home any time he wants, though he can't expect help from his company if his truck breaks down. By contrast, a company driver goes where he or she is told to go, and is but a game piece on a game board. There are local drivers, regional drivers (often out on the road Monday to Friday), and drivers with designated runs (out for a few days and then back).

The flatbed company I drove for had one and only one van. It must have been to fulfill a lucrative contract. The van was driven by a husband-and-wife team that drove continually back and forth between two airports with air freight, JFK in New York City and LAX in Los Angeles. I met them once in a truck stop in Missouri. They were happy with what they were doing. I wouldn't have been. It would have driven me crazy, if I wasn't already crazy.

There was a lot of uphill to my learning curve. An over the road driver, I found out, is actually a hybrid between a wage employee and an independent contractor. Most company drivers do not have benefits such as sick pay or vacations. There was no overtime compensation, although there was certainly overtime. As an old timer described it to me, a truck driver worked 100 hours a week to get paid for 50. It's amazing how accurate he was. It was a scheme that gave rise to the irresistible incentive to cheat on log books with a claim that said, "That didn't count."

For me personally there was a plus side. It came from saving receipts for every little expense remotely related to my work, giving me, thanks to a professional tax preparer, some sweet tax returns at the end of every year. Nevertheless, whether an owner operator or a company driver, or a local driver paid by the hour, no one made money unless the wheels were rolling. And, despite a few boasts to the contrary, no drivers that I knew, owner operators included, got rich by driving a truck.

At the same time, there were some unique rewards to driving a truck for a living. Before driving, I did not spend a lot of time thinking about factories, industrial plants, farms, warehouses, ports, railroad yards and the like. By driving a truck I got to see the underlying fabric of America and how it all fit together. For the most part, I was favorably impressed. I saw people working hard, hustling a living in various ways, parents getting their children off to school, and, though far from perfect, how the country in the aggregate ran fairly well. I went to all kinds of places, inner cities, mountain communities, small towns, mushrooming suburbs, rural outposts. I didn't see a lot of hopeless poverty or sights that alarmed me, though maybe conditions have changed in the last three decades. In any case, I saw myself, as some others did, not as a driver so much but as a professional tourist getting an education not available in books. Or from watching television.

Learning about the value of freight, and of loads, was another lesson. Before picking up a printing press in Whittier, California, going to Maine, a shipper refused to load my trailer until the trucking company in South Dakota faxed proof that they had at least $1,000,000 in liability insurance. Loads themselves were commodities, often sold, resold, or traded. Some regions of the country were rich in valuable freight, and others only had poorly paying loads. Once, after making a delivery, while talking over the phone with a freight coordinator in South Dakota I was friendly with, he told me he was having trouble finding me a new load. I got him to laugh when I said, let me guess. I'm at the Mediterranean and Baltic Avenue part of the board. On the other side of the spectrum a driver had to get familiar with Chicago. The trucking company had a persistent habit of sending drivers into that city. For valuable freight and high paying loads, Chicago was the undisputed freight capitol of America. And a bear to drive in even in the best weather.

It was standard practice in the industry that a driver earned one day of home time for every week spent on the road. It often happened, though, that a driver drove over the road for a few weeks, earned home time, and a day after arriving home they received a call from an overzealous dispatcher wanting them to pick up a hot load. Real hot loads were scarcer than two-headed fish. If a driver found him or herself angry a lot while driving, it was a sure sign they'd been out too long and needed rest. As I was homeless and drowning in debt, I often drove for two months or more before requesting home time.

The flatbed company hated to send me to Florida because the freight rates coming back out of there were too cheap. Unless it was peak tomato hauling season, in which case due to competition and the upward pressure it created across the board, the per mile shipping rates for all freight increased. After home time was over, to get my next load, the flat bed company might send me empty and pay me dead head miles as far away as Atlanta. Then I would again drive for weeks on end until the cycle was repeated.

I drove until I found myself getting too angry while driving, then begged, or demanded a load back to Florida. Home time was never enough though to fully recharge batteries. When the company applied pressure to get back out on the highway, I was always in need of more money to pay debts, so out I went.

Depending on where in Florida a load went, I would either take my home time in Miami and visit my therapy soul mate, or in the bay area to spend it with my child. When out over the road, I spent a small fortune on pre-paid phone cards to keep in touch with them. I can hardly express my desire that cell phones have driven those rip-off phone card companies out of business.

If I could take home time in the bay area, I would either stay at a truck stop in Lakeland next door to a motel, or go to what was once a Tampa institution with its own in-house motel, called the Cigar City Truck Stop. Either way, Lakeland or Tampa, I would call my ex-wife and she would dutifully, and obligingly, bring our child to me so we could spend time together.

After a load was completed, a trip envelope with a signed bill of lading was sent back to the terminal in South Dakota. When the company processed the paperwork, and it was very good at doing so without delay, it made out a check that was directly deposited in a bank account. Pay raises generally did not exist for drivers unless there was upward pressure across the trucking industry, caused by one of the nation's biggest carriers after it raised its driver compensation rates. Then all the smaller companies, including the teeny tiny companies, had to follow suit and raise their drivers' pay also. The demand for drivers was constant, and intense, and it was too easy for drivers to walk out of the doors of one company and into the revolving doors of another.

When I first started driving my compensation was 19 cents a mile. Roughly speaking, multiplied by highway speed limits, it amounted to approximately $12 an hour. Oversized loads paid a little more, usually 8 cents a mile more, but it varied somewhat depending on the dimensions of the load. If a load required a tarp the driver was paid an additional $30. I, probably like most flatbed drivers, would have preferred to forego those thirty dollars to get out of the thankless chore. If a load had more than one pickup or delivery point, each additional stop earned another $10. Empty dead head miles paid at the same rate as loaded miles.

No one ever said it out loud, but I believe there was an industry-wide state of denial that worked against drivers' interests. Since laws limited the number of hours a driver could drive, and therefore their pay, paying drivers for tarping and extra stops was in effect compensation for driving time lost. Whether or not the extra pay was equitable, trucking companies covered their legal liabilities (backsides). Then if those tasks took more hours than what was covered by the extra compensation, drivers had an incentive, and often were expected, to fudge or outright cheat on log books to get in the miles to make the deliveries that generated the revenue.

For example, an extra stop was worth $10, but I never made an extra pickup or delivery in less than an hour, and one that took half a day, or more, was common. Often I spent a lot of time tying down and securing difficult loads, especially tarps so they didn't rip to shreds going down the highway; although that burden was made easier after an old timer told me to buy disposable diapers and use them to buffer sharp edges. Afterwards I never left a truck stop or home without them. But every extra hour spent securing a load properly before hauling it, put me in a bind, forcing me to fudge on the log book or to cut my own pay. I hated the bind and I hated to cheat, but felt that realities left me no choice.

It made me cringe while driving to see lawyer-sponsored billboards that were popping up along the nation's highways like untended weeds, promising justice for victims of accidents with trucks. My experience with the legal profession informed me that the exceptional skills of cross-examining attorneys would easily overwhelm drivers on a witness stand. An inability to stay honest in their employment created huge openings for attorneys. As a result, truck drivers involved in accidents, regardless of innocence or degree of culpability, were extremely vulnerable to injustice. That was one more way the pressures of the freight hauling industry were placed squarely on truck drivers doing the work, and not on those making big money off of their labor.

There was one ongoing discrepancy in particular that irked a lot of drivers. Per mile compensation was based on what was called household movers guide miles, which from maps were the shortest possible routes between two locations, including back roads, roads forbidden to heavy trucks, and a few goat trails. As a result, a driver's compensation on average was around 10% less than actual miles driven. While I understood the grievance, and the perception of getting cheated, personally I didn't think that mattered. That's because of the massive number of truck drivers in America, and tacit but omnipresent competition among them, in conjunction with the law of supply and demand. Regardless of method, mileage pay ultimately would have worked out the same.

In other ways, however, drivers were definitely cheated which gave just cause to their feelings of distrust. It varied by jurisdiction but there were law enforcement officers in some states, with their own states of denial, masquerading as safety officers when what they were really after were contrived ways to steal truck driver paychecks by fining them for nitpick offenses. I surmised the money they stole fed bloated bureaucracies.

Here's food for thought. By the time I stopped driving over-the-road, I was convinced that company drivers, as distinguished from owner operators and local drivers paid by the hour, were in dire need of a union to provide push back against the powers that be, to prevent them from taking advantage of those drivers. Note that my support for unions in general is not across the board. It depends on the industry. Coal miners, for example, obviously need a union backing them.

A union representing over-the-road company drivers, if it could be organized for such a large segment of the work force, and the nation's economy, would have enough leverage to establish fairness and better working conditions for those drivers, both in regards to governments ripping them off, and their own companies. On the other hand, could the country as a whole afford to pay those drivers properly, and allow them to make a decent and honest living? More than likely we will never know the answer to that question.

To estimate paychecks and manage my indebtedness, after making deliveries I recorded a few details in a notebook that I've kept as a memento. What follows is a rough snapshot of what it was like for me. The miles shown are conservative estimates for what I expected to be paid for. The number of loads between home times is a little above average but not atypical.

After delivering a load of railroad ties going from Florence, South Carolina to Riviera Beach, Florida, and spending time with my child in Lakeland, I made the following runs:

- Winter Haven, FL to Levittown, PA / plastic pipe / 1,250 loaded miles / 40 dead head miles / tarp required

- E. Monongahela, PA to St. Paul, MN / steel ducts / 850 loaded miles / 300 dead head miles / tarp required

- Lake Crystal, MN to Knoxville, TN and Birmingham, AL (extra stop) /dump truck bodies / 850 loaded miles / 90 dead head miles

- Muscle Shoals, AL to Webster City, IA / lumber / 750 loaded miles / 125 dead head miles / tarp required

- Davenport, IA to San Antonio, TX / excavator / 1,100 loaded miles / 225 dead head miles / oversize load

- La Porte, TX to Crowley, LA and Plaquemine, LA (extra stop) / farm tractors / 250 loaded miles / 200 dead head miles

- Madison, MS to Pender, NE / steel tubing / 850 loaded miles / 200 dead head miles / tarp required

- Yankton, SD to Elkridge, MD and Richmond, VA (extra stop) and Roanoke, VA (extra stop) and Simpsonville, SC (extra stop) / machinery / 1,900 loaded miles / 100 dead head miles

- Charleston, SC to Lead, SD / gold mine drill / 1,800 loaded miles / 200 dead head miles

- Spearfish, SD to Sylmar, CA / clay land fill liners / 1,300 loaded miles / 20 dead head miles / tarp required

- City of Industry, CA to Humble, TX and Houston, TX (extra stop) and Asheville, NC (extra stop) and Raleigh, NC (extra stop) / electrical transformer, conveyor belt, fabricated guard shack, lathe / 2,800 loaded miles / 40 dead head miles / tarp required / oversize load

- Apex, NC to Jefferson City, M0 / powdered glass (used for painting stripes on highways) / 925 loaded miles / 15 dead head miles / tarp required

- Columbia, MO to Denver, CO and Cheyenne, WY (extra stop) / plastic pipe / 830 loaded miles I 30 dead head miles / tarp required

- Denver, CO to McMinnville, OR / conveyor parts / 1,250 loaded miles / 100 dead head miles

- Philomath, OR to Phoenix, AZ / lumber / 1,250 loaded miles / 100 dead head miles / very unusual no tarp required because it was pressurized lumber

- Phoenix, AZ to Houston, TX / structural steel / 1,175 loaded miles / 0 dead head miles / oversize load

- Waco, TX to Cicero, IL / lift truck / 1,000 loaded miles / 200 dead head miles

- Rockford, IL to Romulus, MI / machine parts / 375 loaded miles / 100 dead head miles / tarp required / oversize load

- Toledo, OH to Hialeah, FL and Miami, FL (extra stop) / 1,290 loaded miles / 60 dead head miles / railroad machinery, forklift

After 19 trips, four oversize loads, 10 extra stops, seven times wrestling with tarps, 22,000 loaded miles and 2,000 dead head miles making approximately 24,000 miles driven, a break from the road was earned, and necessary. Then there was little rest for the weary. Or debtors. After a few days off, it was time to head back out and do it again, and keep the wheels rolling. That was until a dispatcher assigned me a load I really wanted. But I caught an unlucky break.

From a small town in Oklahoma, I was sent to pick up a load of gypsum going to Salinas, California, the hometown of John Steinbeck. An admirer, I had read every book of his I could get my hands on. There probably wouldn't have been much to see related to Mr. Steinbeck, but the trip was enough to stir the imagination in the mind of a professional tourist. Instead of a desired run to Salinas, CA, however, all 18 wheels and my truck driving job came to a screeching halt. Something happened on the way to the office.

Katie and Oprah

Flatbed freight varies considerably. Many loads, approximately half, lumber, steel I-beams, plastic pipe, are reasonably square. They don't present a puzzle that has to be figured out before securing them, and transporting them safely on public highways. Some loads are inherently dangerous. Coils, sheeted steel wrapped tightly in circles and shaped like doughnuts, can weigh more than 40,000 pounds. There are two ways to secure them. They can be chained down so that if chains broke they would fall forward and into the truck cab, called, hauling them suicide. Or they can be chained so that if the chains broke the coil would fall off the side of the trailer, towards traffic, called hauling them shotgun.

For me, mixed loads of machinery, lathes, drills, scissor lifts, table saws, were the worst, and time consuming. I often had to stand back and study them before deciding where to use two-inch straps, or four-inch straps, and where it was necessary to use chains and their binders. After all the pieces were secured to the trailer bed, and sharp edges padded with disposable diapers and duct tape, it was another job to roll up tarps over everything, and then secure the tarps using a rat's nest of bungee cords.

Flat-bed freight can come in all kinds of shapes, dimensions, and odd characteristics. I once commented to the maintenance manager at the yard in South Dakota, "I bet you've seen some strange freight go in and out of your shop over the years." He said, "Yes, and a lot of things they never could figure out what they were."

Except for unusually heavy pallets, the gypsum loaded on my trailer at Medicine Lodge, KS, shouldn't have been difficult to secure. Because the pallets were so heavy, they were placed on the trailer in a 2+1+2 pattern to keep the weight evenly distributed, and the pallets were only waist high. The empty spaces between the pallets, however, created an awkward problem. The best way to handle the tarps, I thought, was to hop up on some of the pallets and unroll them. So, I climbed, unrolled, climbed, unrolled, and jumped down again. It's still a mystery how so much damage happened after jumping from a height of, at most, three feet. A jump like all the others. Suddenly I felt a jolting pain. I knew immediately that something was seriously wrong.

My ankle was broken, for the second time, and the damage was extensive. I was taken to the local hospital in an ambulance, which in trucker parlance is called a meat wagon. A doctor at the Medicine Lodge emergency room struggled to reset the ankle. As he was working on it, I asked him what kind of break it was. He paused before telling me he would describe it as a jagged spiral fracture. I had no idea what that meant, and still don't, but since then, I've learned to live with residual pain.

After breaking my left ankle the first time, twenty years earlier, pain wasn't constant. After the second break, if the case was pressed, I would probably qualify for a handicapped sticker that allowed me to park at the front of parking lots. But I still prefer to park in the back and walk more, and to drive with the legs as much as possible. Besides, I retain up and down movement, the discomfort isn't severe, while age has limited physical activities anyway making for only minor lifestyle adjustments.

At the hospital in Kansas, there was a recurring problem to deal with first. With a hard cast on my leg from toe to thigh, the hospital wouldn't release me unless I could provide a destination. Without a truck and its sleeping compartment I was homeless, and per usual didn't belong anywhere. My therapy soul mate in Miami was my only chance for release. She was engaged to be married, however, and justifiably worried about appearances. Nonetheless, she agreed to put me up, but for one night only. That was enough to get me out of the hospital, and to get me on a plane from Kansas City back to Miami.

With my soul mate's help, the next day I found an apartment to rent up in North Miami Beach, the fifth time that city became my place of residence. Then I settled in for the strangest six months of my life. Without the stress and grind of truck driving, away from the rat race, it wasn't a bad time at all. Courtesy of Workman's Comp, checks arrived in the mail every week while student loan payments were deferred. Strangely, although temporary, life without driving was even profitable.

The man that managed the apartment building promptly knocked on the door the first day of every month, demanding the rent in cash. There was no lease, no receipts, and no paperwork. I was always prepared to pay him. Peace was only disrupted one time. Late one evening a young girl, stoned out of her mind, barged into the apartment, collapsed, and a few minutes later got up and ran out, then zig-zagged while running down a busy street. I had to get on the crutches and chase down the manager and beg him to call the police, because I was worried about the girl's safety.

My soul mate improved my standard of living immeasurably when she loaned me a chair, and, best of all, a tiny palm-size black and white television. Normally I hate television but I looked forward to watching Katie Couric every morning and Oprah Winfrey every afternoon. And I didn't even particularly like Katie and Oprah, or *The Price is Right*, or anything else on TV. But something to do is better than nothing to do. I was almost totally immobilized and could do little else. Despite all the time on my hands, bowling was out of the question.

At the start it was a challenge to get groceries. Having prior experience using crutches helped. After trial and error, I figured out that I only needed to hobble down the sidewalk to the Winn Dixie two days out of three: because I could carry back enough groceries in two plastic bags, one wrapped around each wrist, while gripping the crutches. Also, for someone with sticks for legs, sunny south Florida was the perfect place to ride out the winter.

When my ankle healed enough to have the hard cast removed, but it was far too weak for employment, Workman's Comp had a requirement. In order to continue receiving weekly checks, I had to go to a clinic for physical therapy. To get there, twice a week I crutched to a bus stop and hopped on a city bus. It too became something to look forward to because it was something to do.

One session, towards the end of physical therapy appointments, with my ankle dipped in a whirlpool, the doctor whose clinic it was walked up behind me. He'd been watching me from a window in his office and wanted to share his thoughts. He said he had studied my x-rays and he'd been keeping an eye on me. He wanted me to know that he'd seen people come through his clinic over the years with far less serious injuries than mine, and it ruined their life. "But with you," he said, he could tell, "this won't bother you and you'll just get on with your life."

That was a high compliment and music to my ears that someone noticed and actually said it. At the same time, the doctor's words stung. They brought to consciousness the reality of a life without alternatives. No one in their right mind, not even me, aspires to be just another worker bee without a meaningful purpose to their labor.

An injured truck driver out of action can almost get spoiled doing nothing for a living. Alas, nothing in life that's too good to be true lasts forever. A future of some kind was beckoning me. And my debt burden was still immense.

On the way to physical therapy one morning, I got into a friendly argument with a city bus driver. We argued while discussing the merits of having a CDL, compared our respective jobs, and argued over whose job was harder. Off and on, I had considered getting a passenger endorsement that would have allowed me to drive a bus instead. That was until the bus driver won the argument. He said to me, "But your freight never talks back to you." He was right, and driving a truck never sounded better.

Still up to my eyeballs in debt, I had to do something with the rest of my life. My left ankle hurt and gave me a peg leg to make a pirate proud. Wrestling with flatbed freight didn't seem possible. So, I called up the Iowa trucking company, that bought out the South Dakota flatbed company a scant few weeks before I broke my ankle. That's why the state of Iowa sent the Workman's Comp checks. Since the Iowa company pulled both vans and flat beds, I inquired what it was like to haul vans.

Ask a stupid question and you can expect a stupid answer. The man I spoke with on the phone said it was simple. With vans, after you're loaded, you just close the doors and go. You can't attract drivers with straight forward honesty. But that was enough information for me. I told him to take down my name. If he could put me in a truck, somehow I'd get to Iowa.

Time out from trucking ended on a bitter-sweet note. Without a cast, still using crutches, I was making my way down the sidewalk from physical therapy to reach a bus stop. I was headed south along Federal Highway, the same as U.S.1, what locals also call Useless 1. Suddenly I heard my name called repeatedly. I stopped for a second before concluding it was either a mistake or for someone with the same first name. But the call was persistent, so I raised my head, looked forward, and saw my JAP angel standing in front of me.

Despite the passage of years, crutches, and busy highway traffic, as she was driving she saw me, recognized me, turned around and stopped to meet me. I was shocked, and thrilled. For a fleeting moment time stood still as I was transported back to the past. She was busy and in a rush. She wrote her number on a piece of paper and said to call her. I told her I would. But then I didn't.

By then it might have been possible to tell her the truth, why I was such a clod and rudely walked out of her life. But by then there was another truth I wouldn't have been able to tell her. After everything that happened, going to law school and all my indebtedness as a result, how going to law school ultimately made me feel like a fool and rearranged my life, my mind was in a different place. So I was sure it was better for her for me to let her go. It was better for me to go back to work.

Whirlwinds

My over the road truck driving career lasted almost seven years. It actually wasn't a career so much but just one more in a long series of diverse employments. Afterwards it was difficult to fill out employment applications because they usually require you to list all previous jobs, and to explain why you left them. There was so much instability in those seven years they are dizzying to recall. Like the rest of my life before then, they portray an unflattering picture of me, but in regards to trucking I can only be blamed for half the turmoil. I didn't want to break an ankle. I don't buy out smaller trucking companies because I'm greedy.

Whirlwinds began to blow after showing up in Iowa to drive for a different trucking company, my third. The Iowa company was like others in the industry, chasing profits, which meant getting bigger. Trucking mirrored the rest of the country at the time, caught up in a buyout and merger frenzy. Of course buyouts were justified, and understandable. Big fish are safer than little fish. It's better to eat than to get eaten.

The Iowa company fit the mold of other large trucking firms. Leaders at the top thought they could mix profitability with driver friendliness, when it only exhibited the same state of denial; it's concern for drivers was razor thin, on paper, and never genuine. No one questioned the systemic problems throughout the transportation industry - that always worked against drivers - when changes to the system would have threatened cost to benefit ratios. Instead, the bigger firms resorted to various schemes that amounted to smoke and mirrors; for example, driver appreciation days with accompanying parties, attended mainly by office personnel with a smattering of drivers, despite the fact if drivers were really appreciated they would know it and driver appreciation days wouldn't even be necessary.

The dispatchers at the Iowa trucking company habitually breathed down the necks of drivers, always pushing them to drive more miles, in willful ignorance to regulations that restricted the number of hours they could drive legally. Dispatchers and office personnel went home every day, for weekends, and had holidays, sick days, and paid vacations, but they had no empathy for drivers who drove over the road for weeks without a day off. Like the others, and the bigger the trucking company the faster was the flow, the Iowa company had a continuously revolving door as drivers got fed up, and quit, and as a steady stream of new drivers arrived. Despite efforts to prop up appearances, the Iowa company was the least friendly company that I drove for.

It had a rider policy. If a driver was willing to have a fee deducted from their paychecks, they could take a rider with them out over the road. I enthusiastically signed up. The company claimed the fee compensated for its increased insurance costs. Fair enough. I didn't mind.

When my child was on summer vacation, and out of school, I informed a dispatcher that I was taking my child with me for a month. Unlike me, my child was not going to go without showers or eat out of vending machines for days. Upset that he couldn't push me harder, though the difference in miles driven was slight, the dispatcher complained so much about company inconvenience he diminished the pleasure of what should have been a great time for a dad and his teenage child. He went so far as to send nasty critical messages over the dash mounted Qualcomm (a forerunner to portable laptops) that my child read back to me as I drove. We had a good month, but it would have been so much better with a modicum of respect, and common courtesy.

Later that year, in winter, while pulling a load of breakfast cereal going to Cherokee, Iowa, I stopped driving in the early afternoon. I'd run out of legal hours. There was more than enough time to make the delivery early the next morning. An irate freight coordinator, not a dispatcher, sent a message on the Qualcomm that had a two-way signal, that allowed him to monitor the location of every truck, which he always did. His message to mc was "What the fuck are you doing?" Freight coordinators had a lot of control. They could feed drivers with long distance loads and better pay, or starve them. This freight coordinator constantly blurred the line between what was expected and what a driver could get away with. It was a challenge to drive legal in normal circumstances. That's why drivers often referred to their logs as comic books. Midwestern states, and especially Missouri where I was driving, were notorious for checking log books when trucks drove through their weigh stations.

Shortly after I stopped driving, regulations governing driver hours were updated and changed, testimony that the old set of rules wasn't working. Under the previous system, driving strictly legal was for all practical purposes impossible. If drivers claimed they always drove legal, I was convinced they lacked credibility. And old timers agreed with me. When drivers were getting paid for more than 10,000 miles a month (me too), if they were strictly legal, and properly logged all of their time attached to a truck, and their job, they'd have been lucky to make half of that.

The next day, after delivering my load of cereal and getting the "What the fuck are you doing?" message, I woke up in Iowa on a Saturday morning at an oversize gas station, and mini truck stop, somewhat common to the rural Midwest. I was on a two-lane farm road connecting small towns. During the night a winter storm left wet snow on top of a thick sheet of freezing rain. In the aftermath of the storm, there was a steady wind with gusts in excess of 60 mph.

The only sensible thing to do was to remain at the truck stop and not head east to pick up the new load, to which I'd been dispatched, even if it meant sitting idle until Monday. The result was my fault for not listening to the rule that says in one ear and out the other. But with the freight coordinator's message playing in my head, not wanting to incur more of his wrath, I felt provoked into at least trying to pick up a load.

There was no way to control the truck and trailer against the forces of nature. Immediately after heading out, I felt the wind swatting the empty 53-foot trailer with all its surface area back and forth. The two-lane road offered no intersections, no driveways, and no chance to turn around before a violent gust of wind slammed into the side of the empty trailer. The trailer slid all the way around and slammed into the cab causing a jackknife accident.

The cab was destroyed. I suffered no physical injuries. Emotions were another matter. If I had been a tougher minded man, which I'm not and that's my shortcoming, I wouldn't have moved the truck. The only way to have avoided that accident would have been to refuse to drive.

The Iowa trucking company solution was simply to give me another truck. My passive-aggressive solution, after stewing in my own juices for a week, was to seek new employment. That's how I got lucky and found myself driving for an Alabama trucking company, my fourth, that may have been the most driver-friendly trucking company in America. That's why it had a plethora of veteran drivers that drove for them for years.

The Alabama company handled freight to and from New York City, the dreaded hell for truckers, but it wouldn't force a driver to go there. And if a driver was willing to venture into the five boroughs, every stop paid an extra $100. If a driver picked up a loaded trailer and moved it to anywhere, the driver was paid a minimum of $350. The Alabama company understood that drivers wanted to drive, and not get bogged down hitching and unhitching trailers. It only operated in the eastern half of the US, which was a bit boring, but it had a bright line rule: it never let a driver stay out over the road for more than two weeks. Then when it got you a load going home, your dispatcher would tell you to give him a call when you were ready to drive again. Giving respect to a truck driver was like giving heroine to an addict.

Respect was great but it wasn't a priority or my reason for driving a truck. When I started with the Alabama company, I had been without a residence for three years, since graduating from law school. Granting me regular home time made me want a home to go to. No longer spending time off in Miami, it seemed to make sense to rent an apartment, and in Tampa, in the bay area where my ex-wife and child lived. But then I double-faulted.

At home one day, basking in luxury within four walls, my walls, and perusing the newspaper and classified ads, my thoughts were provoked into making a mistake while reading an ad from a local land surveying company. Driving a truck was not a natural fit or a job of choice. At least surveying was more fun. Or so I thought. I applied and was hired at my seventh, or ninth, land surveying company, depending on what counts.

As it turned out the land surveying company was not a good fit either. Ninety nine percent of the work we did was to stake out concrete slab locations for new houses in subdivisions. More than boredom, it made me feel like a lackey for rich people, those who could afford to live in one of the new houses we were staking out, the costs of which were well above my income level. The land surveying people didn't like me especially well, and they were right not to as my attitude towards their work gradually declined. It was also true that my wage was not enough for me to cover my debts comfortably. So, I bit a bullet, lost face, and called up the Alabama trucking company again. They graciously took me back.

At least with an apartment there was now a place to call home, even if it wasn't a home. Since the age of seventeen, home to me was where my shoes came off at the end of the day. Still, it was nice to get mail somewhere other than from a box at the post office. It felt like a waste of money to pay rent for an apartment only to spend a few days there each month. Nevertheless, it was progress of a sort.

The second tour with the Alabama trucking company came with a snag. In the interim, while I was working for land surveyors, about three months, it too was bought out by a bigger trucking company, a mammoth company, one of the biggest in America. And it wasn't a happy marriage. An ongoing transition was in progress. At first there was a mix and match of Alabama generated loads and mammoth company procedures. Then there was a palpable feeling of slowly being swallowed up. Like other large outfits, the mammoth company made a pretense of being driver-friendly, but it was too big, bureaucratic, and insincere to make good on that alleged goal.

For example, there was a requirement that a driver had to call their dispatcher every morning. Then when I called in, I was identified not by name, but with a 5-digit employee ID number. The mammoth company would send drivers into New York City with no right of refusal, or additional compensation. All the perks that Alabama drivers had were promptly eliminated, while mammoth company drivers had benefits Alabama drivers didn't qualify for.

The worst change was trying to work with what the mammoth company proudly boasted was the most advanced computer in the transportation industry. The computer made most of the decisions relevant to drivers, including load assignments. While driving, it felt like the computer was actually holding the steering wheel, and the computer was not as smart as advertised.

If a load was going to New York City, and it was picked up in New Jersey, the computer expected you to deliver it in the same amount of time as if you were driving in rural Kansas. The computer once allotted me 15 minutes to pick up a loaded trailer in a humongous Chicago railroad yard. I spent more than two hours driving up and down endless rows of trailers trying to find one of theirs with the right number on it.

One day the computer sent me to Sioux Falls, South Dakota to pick up a load. When I got there the bill of lading had a bold stamp across the page that said not to let the *name of mammoth trucking company* transport this load. I didn't know what the issue was, and never found out, but shippers didn't want to put the load of plastic liners in my trailer, and wouldn't, until I convinced them I was an Alabama driver which was different. I then smoothed the situation over with the receiver in New York City by calling them (against company rules), and promising to have my truck at their dock on time Monday morning.

It was serendipity for me to return to South Dakota. Through the truck stop grapevine, I learned that the son of the owner for the original flatbed company, had started his own trucking company, presumably because he was not barred by a non-compete clause in the buy-out contract. Back in South Dakota, I decided to give him a call. We talked, negotiated, came to terms, and I consented to pull flat beds again.

It came with a risk, but after two years of recovery I was reasonably confident my ankle was healed enough to handle flatbed freight. I preferred flatbeds, a smaller trucking company not addicted to a computer, as well as driving for an irregular carrier that operated throughout the entire country. That was the incentive I needed to make a change. So, I officially filed for divorce from the mammoth trucking company.

Approximately two weeks later, a load took me to Alabama and I returned the mismatched green cab and orange trailer at the terminal of the Alabama trucking company. I expected to defend my decision to quit but as it turned out words weren't necessary. A sad looking woman behind a counter told me to drop the trailer, then park the cab out in back with the others. She wasn't surprised, but I was surprised, to see an ocean of discarded green cabs thrown into the sea by the plethora of veteran drivers that already quit.

In summary, from January of 1995 to September of 2001, after graduating from law school, I went to truck driving school, started with a company pulling vans out of Georgia, was an office secretary for a month, drove for a flatbed company out of South Dakota, broke an ankle and had a six-month hiatus while collecting Workman's Comp, then drove for an Iowa company that bought out the flatbed company, was in an accident and quit, then drove for an Alabama trucking company, briefly tried land surveying again, then went back to driving for the Alabama company, and then it too was bought out by a bigger trucking company. So, when opportunity knocked, I agreed to pull flat beds out of South Dakota again because I liked it better.

Try fitting that on an employment application. Lots of luck as you wait by the phone for the call that tells you you're hired.

Rich and Famous

After two more years pulling flatbed freight for the trucking company in South Dakota, it was time to do something else. My child was an emancipated adult. Child support payments were no longer required. Inexplicably, they never kept up with inflation and should have cost me more than they did. Call me greedy, but I didn't feel it was my job to point that out to a bureaucracy. After consolidation, the only burdensome debt I had left was a monthly student loan payment. I'd managed to put some money in a savings account as a safety net. Once again, what the future held for me was a blank page, but there was only one more serious obstacle in my way.

Due to stress, I assume, while driving a truck a bad smoking habit got much worse. It wasn't just an addiction; it was a stranglehold. The first act when waking was to light up a cigarette, and the last act before shutting my eyes to sleep was to stub one out. An on an off smoker since military service, with a lot more on than off, as a truck driver I smoked three packs of cigarettes a day, more than a carton every four days, every cigarette down to the filter. Meanwhile, due to a flurry of law suits and government hysteria, taxes on cigarettes were rising faster than desert temperatures in August.

A side benefit to driving a truck was the time it gave a driver to think, enough time for me to put two and two together. I was spending most of my earnings on cigarettes and life's necessities at truck stops, and paying exorbitant truck stop prices. So that, if I stopped driving and at the same time stopped smoking, minimum wage and forty hours a week would put me at nearly the same level of income. Philip Morris was getting more out of my driving a truck than I was! All I had to do was quit smoking and find another job, any job. That was the plan anyway.

Easier said than done. Especially since ten days after I stopped driving and began living in my Tampa apartment full time, I was crushed by the tragedy of 9/11. It was a devastating disaster for me personally, the reasons for which will be explained later. Like so many others, I stayed glued to the television, that was dusted off after being retrieved from a storage locker in Tallahassee, trying to make sense out of madness.

Weeks after 9/11, when it was clear the media was just beating a dead horse, the way it always does when exploiting disasters, showing the same gruesome footage over and over without new information, it was time to do something radical. I stubbed out my last cigarette, staved off personal madness, and ran through the gauntlet of emotions known only to heavy smokers who quit cold turkey; emotions I never knew I possessed. The wild ride was worse than a run up the New Jersey Turnpike on a Monday morning.

The first diversion that helped was a basketball. The hoops at the apartment didn't have nets but shooting baskets wasn't necessary. For inexplicable reasons, hard dribbling alleviated anger caused by nicotine withdrawals. Every time I felt uncontrollable anger, on average once an hour, I walked over to the court to pound a basketball on asphalt.

The second diversion was pure foolishness; although it took me a few weeks to figure that out. I tried to get a job through the wrong kind of employment agency. The head of the agency, that apparently had only two employees, indicated that with my level of education it could help me land a job paying $80,000 a year. Literally a pot of gold in my case. I was skeptical but paid their $4,000 fee.

The agency's other employee was an advisor. It was his job to lead me down the yellow brick road. At every appointment with him, he told me to revise, enhance, and improve my resume. This went on for a few weeks until I became convinced, I was stretching the truth so much I was lying. The way to land a really good job, it seemed, depended on presentation, which depended on how an individual looked on paper, requiring gross exaggeration. I might be just a working stiff but I only do honest work, except for driving a truck when honesty was squeezed out of me.

When the picture came into focus I wrote a letter to the advisor, implied that he should share it with his corporate office, wrote the $4,000 off as a loss, and proceeded to hunt down a job by myself. That's how I found myself driving a box truck for a Tampa paper company. So basically I traded in a big truck for a short truck.

The time and money spent at that employment agency, however, that wasn't an employment agency at all, was not wasted. Along with hard dribbling of a basketball, the second diversion provided time for nicotine to work its way out of my body, and my brain. The three months it took me to stop smoking, to mess around if you will, was one of the most productive periods of my life. It's easy to see why. As heavy a smoker as I had become, without kicking the smoking habit more than two decades ago, I might already be dead.

Having a local job meant I got to live like normal people, even if I was never normal. I went home every day, had weekends to myself, paid holidays too. To earn my keep all I had to do was make deliveries up and down the west coast of Florida from Ocala to Naples. The job paid by the hour, so that unlike over-the-road trucking, every hour counted. Although sometimes the hours were elongated and bent out of shape. Once I punched in on a time clock at 3 a.m. Friday morning, and punched out at 1 a.m. Saturday, for a 22-hour workday. Often I worked two-hour shifts inside the warehouse to make it to 40 hours and a full paycheck.

All in all $9.50 an hour without overtime, since it wasn't allowed, was a good living, even if it didn't make me a rich man. I made enough to cover the cost of rent, a phone, to keep an old automobile running, and once in a while to take seasonal bird watching trips in the Florida panhandle. I also had access to bookstores with better selections than what was available at truck stops. Mostly there was time left over after working to enjoy the simple pleasures of life, which are always the best pleasures, that were sorely missing for a long time.

After four more years driving a box truck, and fighting urban traffic, I accepted a pay cut and requested to work in the warehouse instead. There were a few reasons behind the change, including a lot of years in motion, advanced age and wanting to slow down, boredom and a desire to do something different. So I pulled orders using a pallet jack, loaded and unloaded trucks, and sometimes operated a forklift. Warehouse work at the paper company lasted three more years until a classified ad in the paper flashed before my eyes. That's how I found myself working for the rich and famous.

The ad was from a gated community known locally as "where the rich people live." They were advertising for security guards. To give myself a better chance, I used a week's vacation, took a class at the community college in Ybor City, and obtained a security guard license. The class was easy and a waste of time. The security license wasn't. I applied and soon afterwards was hired. The result was upward mobility that hadn't happened to me since I was drafted into Little League.

Everything was better. The gated community was within walking distance of my apartment, which made owning a car unnecessary. Eventually I was able to save money by going without one. The working environment was more attractive than a warehouse. The job paid more, had great benefits, and guards were given generous end-of-year bonuses. Security guards worked in temperature-controlled booths and patrol vehicles with air conditioning, so I no longer had to sweat for a living. The executive director even appreciated good employees and personally thanked them when she was pleased with their work. The gated community job seemed too good to be true, and it nearly was six months later when it fired me.

From the gated community's perspective, I had refused to give them a photo. The photo was requested for what was essentially a promotional brochure given to residents during the holiday season. Actually, despite being photo averse, I did provide a passport photo as requested. But a man with a big ego sabotaged me. He didn't pass the photo on to the property owner's association. That was because he had told me the photo was mandatory, then he was apparently offended when, along with the photo, I included a letter in which I pointed out it was illegal, especially under Florida law, to force employees to submit to photos against their will. Employees own their own faces after all. I wasn't trying to make a federal case out of it; although immediately after getting fired and sending them an email, the American Civil Liberties Union backed me up. It sent me a letter apologizing for not having the resources to represent me, but it included a long list of attorneys who might be able to help.

It all came out in the wash anyway. A mere six weeks after firing me, my replacement was so bad he made my employers miss me. The gated community hired me right back. Then I spent almost ten years, an eternity for me with the same employer, working at the best place I ever worked. Among other intangibles, a security guard there, with access to movers and shakers, and to be honest all kinds of wicked gossip, could feel the ebb and flow of the greater Tampa community.

The job title was security guard but mostly the job amounted to customer service, doing whatever was necessary to keep wealthy residents satisfied, quiet, and most importantly complaint-free. The community teemed with million-dollar mansions, some of them owned by famous people, including household name athletes. It was eye-opening and educational to see how athletes lived after they signed million-dollar contracts, or a businessman once he'd climbed to the top of the corporate ladder, or attorneys (perhaps) after they'd sued enough people to reach the promised land.

Balancing out the picture, though, in my years working at that community, I discovered that rich and famous people, except for their money, are fundamentally no different than anyone else. Their emotional tendencies and personalities are exactly the same as one would expect from the general population. This should have been obvious beforehand, but it's one thing to intuitively believe they're the same, and quite another for someone from my background to see it in real life.

Incongruent is the word that comes to mind. The rich residents had a lot of money. Comparatively, I had none - to start with but I did begin to save while working there. They drove expensive automobiles. I didn't even own a car; depending on mood and weather half the time I rode a bicycle to work, the other half I walked. Many of the residents were born into wealth and privilege. My parents were alcoholic high school drop-outs. Gated community residents lived in huge mansions. I lived in a one-bedroom shoebox-size apartment. And while some of the residents had emotional issues, it's not likely many of them had ever been Baker Acted. Yet there I was keeping them safe while they slept at night.

Nevertheless, even if they didn't know it, the well-to-do were right to rely on me. Whether it meant stomping through the Everglades, typing letters as an office secretary, hauling freight across country, or sweating in a warehouse, I always did my job.

Working at the gated community checked every box in the description of a good job. Only a fool like me would walk away from a job like that, especially considering how it compared to all the bad jobs. But I was living in a place where I didn't want to live. I'm still a country boy at heart. Though okay to work in and live in temporarily, Tampa, the same as Miami, was too urban for long term comfort. My child, as an adult, had already left the state to live elsewhere. Most significantly, approximately two years after settling in to employment at the gated community, I'd reached a life-changing milestone.

Knowing I was getting up in age, not having a 401K account or similar investment, I'd paid more than the monthly minimum on my student loan obligation, and paid it off in full years ahead of schedule. That allowed me to put money into a savings account instead. The last student loan payment closed one chapter and it opened a window to a new way of thinking.

Pursuit of law school, going to law school, and paying for law school, took a forty-year chunk out of my life. When it was finally over and done with in its entirety it begged the question: What next?

Return of a Native

Riding the Gravy Train

Florida was a great state for me to devote forty years of my life. I went there to sever ties to a childhood past and to establish a life of my own. Florida gave me that opportunity. Yet despite appreciation for everything Florida had given me, a onetime wayward child, despite intimacy with every square mile of the state from Pensacola to Jacksonville and down to Key West, in the back of my mind stemming from arrival on a bicycle in 1979, Florida was always alien territory. Emotional attachment was thin. Without roots there, I didn't want to die there. So I tried to put together an attractive picture of where to go next.

Most of my hours working at the gated community were at night. Most of the nights were spent at one of the entrance booths making sure no one entered the community without authorization. Traffic usually tapered off, roughly between 2 a.m. and 5 a.m., giving me dead time to fill in the middle of the night. As long as there weren't any special events that kept me busy, it was a reader's paradise. Then, later than most, I joined the rest of the human race and purchased a smart phone that allowed me to roam the internet.

Somewhat between a pastime and an obsession, I fiddled with the smart phone while looking at real estate web sites and home sales from around the country. Without a family, I had no limitations for places to retire. Also, per usual, I relied on myself without seeking advice or assistance.

Looking for a place to settle down, night after lonely night in one of the entrance booths, I scoured real estate web sites while scrutinizing and comparing potential destinations from Tucumcari to Presque Isle and everywhere in between. Experience as a truck driver taught me a lot about the country, and helped me focus my attention on locations that I liked. Affordability, though, was the most important factor. Never a rich man, by living cheaply I had just enough in savings to give myself a few options. It's why I went without a car, a big screen TV, other luxuries, and why I was willing to live in the same one-bedroom apartment for twenty years. If possible, my preference was to buy my own home, even if it was just a trailer in a mobile home park.

Other considerations still mattered, especially peace of mind. So I compared crime statistics, population densities, and economic indicators that shed light on quality of life. I'm an enthusiastic bird watcher, but, for those inclined to notice them, there are interesting birds to see everywhere on the planet. Bird watching is also an incredibly inexpensive hobby. So I was hoping to find somewhere uniquely different that might satisfy curiosity in other ways.

Late fifties is not a good age to develop a retirement plan, but I had been economically squeezed into a corner. On the other hand, with a good job and a steady income, there was no sense of urgency; I had all the time I needed to do more searching, more contrasting, more scrutinizing. Searches were not limited to the United States and its territories. Seeing it as an advantage for the dispossessed, Ireland, Argentina, the Azores, Central America, and Australia were also potential retirement locations. I had a gut feeling that if I kept looking, at some point the right opportunity and the right fit would present itself.

A filter obstructed my vision at first. There was a sense among Floridians that New York was too expensive, its taxes were too high, it was a state in decline, and its winters were too cold. However, that wasn't what discouraged me from considering a retirement in New

York. I knew that living standards among people are vastly different. Depending on lifestyle, one person may thrive where another can't live at all.

My resistance to New York was entirely psychological and related to leaving the state under duress, because I needed separation, something just shy of complete estrangement from my parents. It needs to be repeated, though, I fault them for nothing. I was also estranged from my sisters, whom, to my knowledge never returned to New York. There was nothing for me there except a vague feeling of familiarity every time I found myself driving a big truck through upstate New York. Gradually, with something akin to a gravitational pull, reluctance broke down. Only then did it occur to me my reasons for avoiding New York were no longer valid. Only then did it occur to me, it made sense to die in New York. Not that I was in a hurry to reach the finish line.

After reluctance to retire in New York was overcome, I tried to buy a house in Norwich, a small town in the central part of the state. But a deal could not be consummated. Disappointed, I went back to exploring more real estate sites. Eventually an opportunity presented itself and I was able to buy the house I currently live in. It's a small old house. It's more than I need. It's mine, it's paid for, and there's not a doubt in my mind that I earned it.

Knowing I would also need another job, I consulted online employment sites in tandem with real estate sites. On one of them advertising job openings near here, a posting appeared for months on end. A dairy farm was constantly seeking people to milk cows. The job paid well enough for me to make ends meet. Although I didn't have experience, I figured that with my track record of hard work, I stood a good chance of getting that job. Even though I found a different job with a shorter commute, the ad was crucial to giving me the confidence I needed to pull up stakes and return to upstate New York. Nevertheless, the idea of milking cows for a living had its appeal. After all, one never knows what the future may bring, so it's never too late in life to pad one's resume.

Since returning to New York I've made my final plans, bought a burial plot and a monument to go with it. Whatever remains of this life is just gravy on the potatoes.

Forced to move downstate at the age of seven, when everything went to hell in my opinion, there were some cousins here that were part of a previous life. Their clan often visited our clan and vice versa. Since returning to New York, after being separated for fifty years, I've made contact with a few of those cousins. It's evidence I used to live here anyway. Also, seeing four picture-perfect post-card-quality seasons every year, that comprise the natural cycle of life, is in my blood. I had forgotten what it was like to belong some-where. Now I remember.

Through the Looking Glass of Time

At this late stage of life, neither money nor fame are of any value to me, and I never wanted them anyway. After processing, and regurgitating, my life repeatedly over many years, I also don't need a catharsis. Sharing my life with strangers gets me almost nothing for myself. But I would like to help people if I could, especially those who fight every day to escape their childhood past.

Why should anyone read about me? All I've amounted to was a life-long student trying to figure out what it means to live on our planet. Someone who made a lot of mistakes (and there's not enough paper to enumerate all of them). Someone who will never earn enough credits to graduate.

My father looked at me and saw a failure. He might have been right. I'm a social outcast who has lived, for the most part, on the periphery of society. As an old man I've gravitated to the lifestyle of a recluse. There are no great achievements to my credit. I haven't invented anything. Mine is not a rags to riches story. However, maybe I do have something to offer, in particular to individuals with similar origins. And I am sure there are many others among the voiceless who the world seldom hears from, or notices. I also need to communicate with my descendants.

Subconsciously, subliminally, personality traits and social habits are often passed down through generations; they can even skip a generation and then reappear. Children shouldn't have ancestral history forced on them, in my view, because they have a right to develop their own lives with no strings attached. But, descendants have a right to know about their origins in detail, if the details are available, if they care to know about them. Sooner or later most people become curious about relatives who came before them, so that they can better understand themselves. One reason to write about me, the most important reason, is to provide information linking myself and my past to my grandchildren. Whether it's good or bad they deserve access to the truth.

For a myriad of reasons, information about me and my past wasn't available to my child growing up, or my ex-wife, when they had a right to know about them. That's because I didn't understand my origins. Nor did I understand who I was as a person, which happened to be two persons, one in a false persona with a state of denial. Also, my past was so convoluted it was at times impossible to discern what was relevant and what wasn't. Deep-rooted shame also hindered communication. Closing the gap of information with my adult child and ex-wife, hoping it provides a modicum of closure and more peace of mind, is also a compelling reason to write about me.

Truth be told, there is one self-serving reason. No one wants to end their life as a nothing, having never amounted to anything. There is no one to validate me, no one to tell me before I die that I was a good man and a decent human being. So if I leave a written record, there's at least a chance that I can finally receive that validation even if it's posthumously.

Borrowing a concept from Supreme Court Justice Potter Stewart, except for pure evil - which we know when we see it - I end life with no blame for any other person. That despite the burden I've had to bear. It's not a figment of my imagination. I've seen it too much, so often, and constantly throughout my life, even among those who have interacted with me the most and knew me best. There's an overwhelming tendency for people to look me in the eyes, prejudge me, draw false conclusions, and put words in my mouth and thoughts in my head that aren't mine. However, on the other side of this face, that apparently depicts weakness, it has taken a certain strength of character to start where I started, to endure, and to keep getting back up to carry on some more.

Other than one orthopedist in North Miami Beach, no one else, to my knowledge, has seen that in me. That's a hidden side. But I don't need validation for that, especially after the all-important discovery of self when I learned to live with my limitations, and the maturation process was restarted. I learned to accept realities and at the same time love the gift of life, no matter how others conceive of me.

It's incumbent on me to defend, if not rehabilitate, the reputations of my parents in the minds of my adult child, my ex-wife, and potentially with my grandchildren. I'm sure that despite the divide in years, my parents' good attributes have passed through generations and made positive contributions to the lives of their great-grandchildren. Despite their personal problems, they were nice people. They were well liked gentle souls with strong work ethics and strong moral values. They were the salt of the earth whose admirable qualities far outweighed their difficulties. As a result of their troubled souls, it was often difficult for me to see, especially when younger, but it's clear to me as an adult; my parents were wise and conscientious enough to know that children matter. Not just their children.

No one has had a greater impact on me than a second-grade teacher after moving downstate. She caused life-altering trauma that radically changed the trajectory of my life. As a result of the trauma, my psychological problems afterwards were not the same as my parents' issues, at least not directly. Although, as previously noted, I was already a psychologically wounded child before my life and that of the second-grade teacher intersected. Her motivation remains obscure but I probably represented something she couldn't deal with.

Strangely looking back, in one of life's ironic twists, the trauma the second-grade teacher caused me did not ruin my life. On the contrary, she improved it. Given my lowly station and poor prospects beforehand, it was better for me to proceed through life with less emotion, a heightened intellect, and more thoughtfulness.

Childhood trauma had a downside though. The trauma planted a suicidal seed inside me. The seed was destined to break the surface at an unpredictable point in the future. In the meantime, starting as a young boy, I'd unconsciously surrendered my original self and replaced it with a false persona and a state of denial. That put all my problems on a shelf, into a state of dormancy.

When the suicidal seed broke the surface during a period of personal struggle, I was able to see my two-personality make-up, come to terms with my past, and the root cause of my problems, and to finally understand myself which is the most important thing anyone can understand. Like an addiction, the suicidal seed never goes away and still exists inside me. But it's manageable. People live with far worse maladies than mine.

It's human nature to exaggerate weakness in others. That's what leads to rubbernecking, a fascination with dirty laundry, the lure of fostering dependency as opposed to independence in young children. But no one should ever feel sorry for me. I've had many apples off of Mr. Frost's apple tree. The fact is, I was a lucky boy. I am a lucky man.

The people who fear death the most are the people who have never lived. Don't put me in that category. My life was rich in experiences and adventures. Adversity once overcome enriches a life as well.

When they finally put me in the ground, no one will be able to say I got cheated. So don't stand over my grave and say rest in peace. For one, life is for the living, not for those already gone. Besides, for non-believers in an afterlife, the only peace that matters is the peace that exists here on earth, if we can find it.

As food for thought, there's something else worth mentioning. I always felt an affinity, distinct from admiration, for extreme people of all kinds, dare devils, gamblers, misers, workaholics, kleptomaniacs, pyromaniacs, even the Unabomber and Ted Bundy. That's because I know how people from unstable backgrounds can spin off in any direction. It was only circumstances and blind luck - not my luck but society's - that I spun off in a benevolent direction. But for a different childhood ingredient or two, any of the above might have been me.

It never made sense to me to tell other people what to think, how to feel, or what to believe. All individuals, in my view, have both the right and the responsibility to determine these factors for themselves. It's what makes mutual respect possible. More of that and we might actually have peace on earth for everyone. Asking others for advice often makes sense, but allowing others to make final determinations for oneself never does.

Atheism was a precarious belief for a young child of the 1960's. No one wants to be a pariah, as all Atheists at that time were. So I became a passive Atheist, keeping my disbelief to myself while trying to go along to get along. But it was atheism that gave me strength to endure in my darkest hour, when psychologists posing as experts tried to force-feed me a bible. Atheism allowed me to hang on long enough to make the most important discovery, myself, which was the key to understanding all the pieces of the puzzle.

Therefore, if I could give advice and encouragement to others, it would include this. First know who you are, what you believe, what keeps you grounded and feeling secure. Then whatever it is you believe in, be it reincarnation, science, a god, or multiple gods, hang on to that belief like a dog with a bone. Don't let anyone take your identity and fundamental self away from you.

My reasons to write about myself and my unconventional life do not include self-promotion. Obviously. I don't want an award, honors, or recognition, all of which are contrary to my values and philosophy. If my life has meant anything, it was about trying to live a decent life regardless of circumstances. I am proud to be among the little people, and proud to remain amongst them, without ever getting elevated to where elites appreciate me. Though they in my mind are just as free to live their lives and think what they will as I was.

Whether it's critical or complimentary, I don't care what people think about me, so I do not solicit feedback. I've already analyzed my past to death, pardon the pun. While I would be inclined to extend empathy, for an important reason I will not help others to figure out themselves, which again is their responsibility, and worth every effort. At this late stage of life, it's time to put the past and all the analysis behind me, and to finally live entirely in the present tense.

Compelled to put my story down on paper while I still have cognitive ability, what to do with it afterwards was not well defined. The first priority, as previously stated, was to link myself and my past to the lives of my grandchildren. Then perhaps at some point, maybe a distant future, what I have to say may reach a wider audience. Because I would like to encourage those who suffer as a result of their past to not give up, and to believe in themselves, and their future.

It's ironic and it's sad. In his final years, and until his life was upended by a catastrophic fire, in our phone calls my father often began by criticizing me, reminding me that a rolling stone gathers no moss. It's ironic because upon reaching the final stage of life, I have managed to gather a bit of moss. It's ironic, and it's sad, because he ended up with none. It's also a tragedy because he was a good man who lived a decent life, while struggling mightily against demons from his past.

My wish is that sufferers from childhood trauma can use my story to reflect upon their own lives. You don't have to land on millionaire acres. Life gives you many chances and not just one. You can always reinvent yourself if something isn't working.

There was luck on my side, but I navigated through the obstacle course of life with hardly any money, without a family safety net, without god, without self-confidence or courage (of the genuine variety), with no talent to speak of, and until the very end without a place to call home. And by my standards and to my satisfaction, I managed to land in a good place.

If you suffer from demons, known or unknown, don't get too caught up listening to self-proclaimed experts telling you that you need those attributes and assets that I lacked. If you trust in yourself and your core values, especially if they're down-to-earth values, there's a good chance that's all you need. In any case, if you're struggling to see through the fog of life, and you read about me, I hope my story helps to improve your vision.

A Godless Reality

As often as atheism was invoked in this narrative, and as much as it has meant to me personally, my life story would be incomplete without a more detailed explanation of what it is exactly that I believe in. Like other subjects my amateur opinion and theories are debatable: this is not an effort at persuasion. It's just me speaking for myself without wanting to criticize others for what they believe.

That said, the faithful have a trick they often use with non-believers. They'll ask, "What do you believe in?" If you give them an answer, any answer, they'll counter by saying, "You believe in the same thing I do just with a different name." That's their belief, not mine. There's another ruse whereby the faithful will say, "You have doubts." No, personally I don't. I have as much confidence in what I believe as Billy Graham ever had in his faith.

An anecdote might help to illustrate this. At a monthly meeting among Atheists once, a question was asked of attendees, "How would you feel if Jesus suddenly materialized in the middle of the room?" There was a great deal of anger directed at this imaginary Jesus, and that did surprise me. However, when it was my turn, I responded that I would have no problem walking over, shaking hands, and admitting that all these years I was wrong. But I've never been afraid of being wrong.

With deliberateness, the faithful typically foreclose the possibility of other explanations for life on earth. Also, the faithful seem to care a lot about the nonbelief of Atheists, while Atheists, of whom I've known several, seldom care what the faithful believe so long as they practice reciprocity and the same degree of toleration. Are the faithful afraid that they are wrong? I've often wondered about that.

My atheist perspective has two components. It requires a small amount of science and a bit of thinking outside the box to see and understand it. Though I suspect most won't want to, and that's fine with me. I've been battle-tested and am not afraid to stand alone.

In the first component, I borrow from something I learned from the expertise of Richard Dawkins as an eminent biologist. Mushrooms are biologically closer to animals than they are to plants. Let's just say they're between the two. It's well established that humans retain a reptilian section in their brains that makes them at their core animals too, related to mushrooms, and plants. It's known that trees compete with other trees for sunshine, water, and space, which are the essential means of their survival.

That's because all living things have the same built-in biological program. Animals, mushrooms, plants, and humans, insects and microorganisms too, devour resources for nourishment, reproduce, and will continue to destroy more of their environment in order to devour more resources so as to reproduce more, in competition with other living things. There's nothing that distinguishes humanity other than an ability to dominate other living things and a dearth of humility. Humans will continue to nourish themselves, reproduce, consume, and destroy their environment, and dominate other species until something stops them, if not themselves, or they run out of environmental resources.

Other living things would do the same if they could, but they're confronted with too much competition. Even sparrows would rule the world if they could get away with it. While some individuals and groups of people claim there's a way out of the predicament (as they sound a lot like preachers telling everyone else how to live), to save humanity from its built-in biological program they would need a way to persuade or subjugate all the rest of humanity, and then still separate humanity from its biological constraints.

In economic terms, humanity can't live without economic growth. Economic growth is not possible without growing the population. Stretching economic theory there might be another way, but no persuasive economic model that I've seen has taken population growth out of the equation, while at the same time keeping the human race vibrant and satisfied.

The second component to my atheist perspective holds that there is no extant explanation for human existence. Therefore there is nothing special about life on earth. We are here and alive. That's it. However, and this is the hardest part to see, and the most important part to grasp: If there's nothing special about life, that also means life is very special and we are all lucky to be alive. To understand and to fully appreciate life on planet earth, it's necessary to see both polar opposite concepts simultaneously. That life is not special and therefore very special. That's what makes life fragile, precious, worth worshipping. That is what I believe.

A built-in biological program that is destined to snuff out humanity someday is an ugly reality. Any other explanation is preferable to that naked truth. No one wants to believe that all human accomplishments are futile. Everyone wants to believe their lives and their work matter; it's daunting to confront one's meaninglessness. That creates an opening for a few who are perhaps misguided, self-serving, good-intentioned, maybe right or wrong (who can say?), to exploit or reassure the fearful. Some individuals are in great need of an alternate reality. But life is hard for everybody. Which is a good reason not to criticize others and to respect all viewpoints and explanations for human existence.

As for the built-in biological program, there's no reason for anyone to worry about that. Not currently. Not yet, anyway. At some point in the future, a far distant future hopefully, humans at the end of the road may run out of resources and have to deal with the end of humanity. Perhaps as a species we are already seeing that reality. In any case, we all take our chances after we come to terms with our birth, then try to get what we can out of life while living within our personal subsets of beliefs and values, knowing that life is a big risk and some are luckier than others. Other than to change (or distort) perception, that immutable reality exists regardless of religion or atheism.

If the faithful can ever show me with substantive proof that the initial spark to life began with divine intervention, I'll reconsider my atheism. In the meantime, I'm not going to worry about the inevitable end of humanity, about what the faithful believe, or what the faithful believe that I need to believe.

Bridgework

Subconsciously as a child, between the ages of seven and nine, I reinvented myself. Untethered, lacking supervision, I was an open book trying to teach myself how to live. From childhood influences, somehow, I absorbed a few values that would govern the rest of my life. Fueled by physical activity, that was both work and a means of escape, one of those values led to the necessity of employment. Another was an emphasis on responsibility towards others. No responsibility was ever clearer to me than the responsibility parents have towards their children. Therefore, after my child was born, nothing was more important to me. My child was my son.

From the vantage point of old age, it's not from sentimental feelings but from objective analysis that I see, and can state, that my father was, and my son is a better man than myself. They have been more mature, less insecure. They made good career decisions, obtaining at least the means to higher standards of living with more disposable income. They have both demonstrated genuine courage. My father and my son both served in the Army in times of war. Both were military heroes.

By comparison, after seven years of marriage, I was divorced. Then I began drifting towards the lifestyle of a recluse. I've been stifled by an arrested development with accompanying psychological difficulties. My military service was in peacetime, and unremarkable.

My shortcomings are a major factor why I have enormous respect for my son, as I had respect for my father even if he never knew it. Nevertheless, life is full of irony and contradictions.

My father served in the Army during World War II. When he did talk about his time in the service, which wasn't often, he proudly identified as having been a former doughboy, like his father was in WWI. He venerated Douglas McArthur and praised West Point officers in general, which he claimed were always the best officers. My father showed little respect for me. It was as if fate had dealt him a failure of a son and not the manly son he hoped for. How ironic then, that my son, the son of his failure of a son, went to and graduated from the academy at West Point. I can't imagine my father's thoughts in his final years as he had to wonder how that was possible.

Ironically, I hated to see my son enter military service in any capacity. I can't speak for my ex-wife, but I have reason to believe that she, like me, looked forward to seeing our son go to a university after high school. She probably shared my chagrin upon learning of our son's determination to enlist. When our son was young, I told him that if he wanted to paint houses for a living that was good enough for me. I believe in allowing children to determine the course of their own lives, and to do whatever it is that keeps them satisfied and feeling wholesome. Entirely on his own initiative, our son enlisted, requested Special Forces, and became an Army Ranger.

That's why the tragedy of 9/11 was a disaster for me personally. On that day, our son was between Army basic training and training to become an Army Ranger. 9/11 was a brick to my head that told me my son was going to war. By December, he was in Afghanistan. He went to Afghanistan on a second tour, then to Iraq for Shock and Awe. Then he applied to and was accepted at West Point. After graduating from the academy, he went back to Iraq for another tour.

He, not I, was the fighting soldier bearing unimaginable burdens. However, his active-duty years were gut-wrenching for me. They gave me a roller coaster ride with tension-filled times when he was deployed, relief when he came back, always feeling guilty, thinking I must have influenced him the wrong way when he was young, giving him heroic aspirations that led him to put himself in harm's way. I second guessed myself, wondered where I went wrong, but kept my guilt to myself so as to support him as he put his life at risk.

There's more irony, I believe, in that based on what I know in the aggregate, my formative years were better than those of both my father and my son. It's also true regarding my ex-wife. I wouldn't have wanted to trade places with any of them. Compared to all three, at least in the latter half of childhood, I alone could run around unhindered like a wild child, while enjoying the unlimited fruits of freedom.

As a child, my father lived through the Great Depression and in numerous locations, Brooklyn, sometimes hauled down to Texas where his father worked as an oil driller, on a chicken farm upstate. At age eleven he had a virtual job, probably (my guess) working to please his domineering father. From his adult demeanor and behaviors, he obviously suffered from something devastating in his past.

Whereas my youthful years were spent at two locations, both rural, my son was bounced around and lived in many places, by my standards all of them urban jungles. He had so many preschool arrangements and attended so many public schools, I could never count them. He had to endure and to process divorce between his parents, which I didn't have to deal with due to my parents' willingness to stick it out through thick and thin. There are many reasons for me to conclude, compared to my father, son, and ex-wife, I as always was the lucky one.

An information gap separating my past from my son eventually made a relationship between us difficult. For example, he never met my two sisters, both of whom had moved out of New York before I rode a bicycle to Florida. He also didn't have a meaningful relationship with my parents, his grandparents, both of whom were still living during most of his childhood. As a result of my estrangements, everyone related to me was alienated from my son. A child must process a nebulous past of a father somehow. Awkwardness was exacerbated further by my psychological struggles. It was always beyond my abilities to present a picture for him to understand my past, and my relatives, let alone to explain my thought processes and psychological difficulties.

Meanwhile my ex-wife, with her relatives, offered a reasonable familial lifestyle that he naturally gravitated towards, which contrary to making me jealous pleased me knowing he had that alternative. Coupled with our physical separation, however, his comfort level with her relatives added to our awkwardness, and, I believe, hastened our drifting apart.

Gradually our relationship went through stages. We started out with a very strong bond, which lasted until his move to the other side of Florida. Then we went through a middle period simultaneous with my paralyzing depression, when it required effort to maintain a positive relationship. Then we began drifting farther apart as he matured.

The first time my son met my father was when I took him to see my mother before she died. My mother had reached out to my son, sending him cards and gifts for his birthdays and for Christmas. Before the end of her life, that was the only contact between my son and my parents. Estranged from her two daughters, my mother desperately wanted to be a grandmother. But consistent with the rest of her sad life, her efforts went for naught. As was the case with my father, I was almost totally estranged from my mother, and before she was dying I couldn't afford to bring my mother and son together, and wouldn't have been able to without law school student loans.

My father and son met a second time, that I'm aware of, when my son was at West Point and he was able to borrow a car from a friend. He visited my father at a nearby assisted living facility. I gathered that their meeting was awkward. As the man in the middle that didn't surprise me.

Oddly perhaps, or perhaps not, my father and son seemed to have more in common with each other than either of them had with me. Apparently I was the knot in the woodwork. My father and son were both an only child. Both received love and support from two parents - I believe in my father's case despite it being concomitant with abuse. They were both centers of attention among relatives. They had common interests and material values that I don't share; for example, a fascination with armaments and new technology. As compared to me, my father and son have been pragmatic, whereas it's fair to describe me as a confused mix of working stiff on the one hand, an egghead and a bookworm on the other.

The difficulty I had communicating with my father was replicated with my son. My familial past was too difficult to explain. Nor could I describe my divided soul, before or after I discovered and came to terms with it. But for blaming me for estrangements, and I was not the only child that chose that course, and my psychological difficulties, which of course I didn't want, the gap in communication between my son and myself was not his fault or mine.

Also, my father, myself, and my son all had challenging childhoods in vastly different ways. Making it little wonder that our abilities to communicate with one another were stifled. That, I believe, is why my son and I were already drifting apart before our denouement.

The germ of the idea started many years before with a billboard ad outside the Seabee base in Mississippi. The ad was an attempt to lure new sky divers. My roommate and I often discussed the ad. Like a mountain that entices a mountain climber, sky diving had a unique appeal. It was the ultimate challenge for a born (or manufactured?) coward like me. With the passage of time the sky diving fantasy faded away and was forgotten.

My son learned to sky dive as an Army Ranger. Then he took it up as a form of recreation. When he invited me to go sky diving with him, and offered to pay for the initial jump, it brought an old idea back to the surface. With reservations, I decided to try it. In a lifetime full of bad days and bad decisions, if there's one I could have back, this was the one. I didn't anticipate the withholding of information. Sky diving might not have been a good idea for someone with a peg leg, but if there's a silver lining that worry wasn't put to the test.

When we got to the drop zone there were preconditions. My son and I would not jump together, or from the same plane. An instructor was assigned to me, who I had to accept unconditionally. As was the case with all sky divers on their first jump, the instructor would harness himself to me in a specialized suit that held both of us. The instructor given to me, as it turned out, was half my age. A kid. I could tell instantly that he read my face and drew conclusions. That's why he decided to ignore me.

When I tried to ask a question, he put his hand in my face, said, "Wait," and then walked away to chat with a buddy. It happened a second time. He came back just as it was announced there was a delay before our plane could take off. I again tried to ask a question. Again, he said. "Wait," and walked away to chat some more. When our plane was finally ready we had to scramble to get on. He zipped up our suit on the ascent.

As soon as our plane reached its apex, one after another half a dozen divers jumped out through an open door. Apparently I was supposed to jump after them, without answers to questions. One of which was the proper procedure for jumping. Another question was what to expect in the first seconds of free-fall. It didn't seem like too much to ask. Apparently I was supposed to take a blind leap of faith while attached to someone who openly disdained me. I was confused, only a second or two had elapsed, when the kid instructor shouted in my ear that if I didn't jump he was going to throw me from the plane.

The thumbs down I gave him was a reflex triggered by anger. Yes, I'm tolerant, but on the other side of a facial appearance that depicts weakness, I have an analytic mind that does not suffer fools gladly. I wasn't willing to put up with crap like that. For the rest of my life, I will blame myself for not jumping, even if it was a gut reaction.

Back on the ground I was so distraught I could hardly breathe. Meeting up with my son after his jump, I knew that our relationship would never be the same. The damage was irreparable. Nothing was his fault, although he too misread my face, and my emotions, that day. I can blame myself until the day I die but it doesn't provide a remedy. This long narrative is the only chance I have to explain the reflex and the gut reaction.

A strain had already infiltrated our relationship, which may have been, and likely was due to things I had said, or didn't say, did, or should have done. However, there was an additional factor unique to me. My lifetime of commitment to the interests of my father and my son, sacrificing my interests for theirs, made it unsustainable for me to feel comfortable around them once respect was lost, no matter how justified.

For my father, an alcoholic and needy man, throughout childhood I was his right-hand assistant, his on-call laborer, his peacemaker with those he angered, his ever-ready companion for emotional support. I was the one he could always count on. The constant need to serve him first, then flee from him, cost me any chance I had to pursue a future for myself until after childhood.

For my son, in a voluntary role reversal, I had devoted myself to his development in his formative years. Later I endured what felt like manipulations from my ex-wife without making him an object of contention between us, knowing it's among the most destructive harms parents can inflict on their children. I elevated his interests above my own when they compromised my career goals.

There are days when I reflect back and it feels like I was torn between two heroes and left feeling like a fool. It's better to remind myself, however, that there are always two sides; there's always irony. My father and my son have enriched my life. They've given me knowledge and experiences I wouldn't have had without them. They've given me a greater sense of purpose. Despite his flaws my father was a good man. And he was a hero. My son is also a hero. In fact, he's my hero. He's everything I wish I could have been. I am but a conduit between them and I wouldn't have wanted to go through life any other way.

In regards to my son, my one burning desire was to see him free of the demons that handicapped my parents, preventing them from getting more out of life if they weren't trapped by whatever happened to them when they were children. I wanted a bridge and safe passage between their generation and his. That bridge exists. I have seen it. My son is not like my mother, my father, or like me. My ex-wife did as much if not more to construct that bridge than I did. As long as it's there though I have what I need for peace of mind.

It bears emphasis that my ex-wife was always devoted to our son and worked tirelessly on his behalf. I always knew the actions she took were out of necessity. We had our differences, but we were in harmonious agreement in wanting our son to have better opportunities in life than what we had had. My ex-wife has earned my respect and appreciation many times over.

Our son is a high achiever. He was before and during military service. He is again as a civilian. And although as of this writing I haven't met them yet, he is as a dad to our grandchildren as well. I'm sure. He stared back at adversity, overcame odds, and made the most of his opportunities. Our son is 100% a self-made man.

My father lived until age 87. He was one of the last survivors among exceptional WWII heroes. After he died, over the phone, I was told he would be given a 21-gun salute at his burial. My son and I discussed going, and we wanted to go, but it happened too fast for us to make it. Certainly Father deserved recognition even if he was just one of the little people. Like my mother, he lived the last part of his life alone. It's likely that he was given his 21-gun salute alone at an unattended burial.

He seldom talked about his time in the service, but I spent so much time with him, I was able to put together enough scraps of information to paint the picture. He was never the type to be popular in a group, which is why he was withdrawn, and why he always had only one after work drinking buddy. That made me think he was more expendable and vulnerable than the average soldier. That was just my own deduction and nothing he would have ever said himself. A lack of courage was never one of his issues.

In any case, when the atomic bombs were dropped on Hiroshima and Nagasaki, Father was nineteen, a private infantryman on a troop carrier in the Pacific Ocean. Instead of an invader in combat he became an occupier after hostilities ended. Then he came home with respect and admiration for the Japanese people. He was after all a fair-minded man.

So, if Harry Truman didn't okay the dropping of those bombs, that killed thousands of civilians, Father might not have survived the war. If he didn't survive, neither my sisters, myself, or my son would have had any life at all. In his final years, when he was living at assisted living facilities, and he went outside to smoke, was Father thinking about that?

Final Irony

My mother spent the last half year of her life dying in a hospital. My father spent his final years in assisted living facilities. My parents died alone and alienated from everyone in their past. As a child, I used every excuse to escape our abode and spent as little time with them as possible. As an adult, I put continental distances between them and myself. It's ironic, then, that despite all my running around, I'm ending my life alone and alienated from everyone in my past. I see it clearly now. Our differences were only cosmetic. In the ways that are important, in the ways that matter, my parents and I were always a lot alike.

Acknowledgments

Without Adriana and her team of professional typists at Vanan Services, who somehow managed to convert my chicken scratch typing into something useful, and without Lil Barcaski and her team at GWN Publishing, a book with my name on the cover would have never made it down the runway, let alone off the ground. Words are not strong enough to express how much I owe them.

I owe posthumous thanks to my mother and father. By being nice people, despite the stress they felt, and were under, they set an example worth replicating. I at least tried to live up to that standard.

Also, reaching back in time, there are many childhood friends to mention. Helen W., John C., Phil H., Greg E., brothers Phil and Ed M., Chris C., Dickie W., Mark D., Danny L., Bill K., Lisa L. who lived next door, and brothers Bob and Steve M., are among those who invited me to their homes, allowing me to see how their families lived, giving me the chance to see a better way to live than the lifestyle that existed at my childhood abode. I thank all of them.

Many others over the last fifty years were simply decent people that assisted me in times of need. For example, military comrades tolerated my ignorance and naivety, provided me with examples of maturity, and on more occasions than I care to recall, covered up for me and kept me out of serious trouble. My appreciation for them increases steadily with the reflection that comes with age.

Deanna, whose sage advice lifted my roommates and myself out of legal jeopardy, Mary, who gave me rides in her VW when I was immobilized, Saul, the road tester who alleviated my nervousness and helped me to obtain a CDL, and my son who gave me so much of value without ever giving me any trouble, are among those who propelled me forward.

My ex wife deserves praise too. She shared childcare values with me that, in my humble opinion, made all the difference in the world.

If there were more individuals that feel they should be mentioned here, and are not, blame me. Likewise, all errors in this narrative, and all the controversial opinions expressed, are mine alone. In addition, stubbornness and an independent mind led me to express myself in my own brand of grammar, often while rejecting recommendations. From the first page to the last word, anything between the covers not right, or not liked, is either my fault or entirely attributable to me.

No one, and not even a stubborn and independent soul like me, can get through life, and live long enough to write a book with my name on the cover, without a lot of help. Many of those who aided me were little people. Whether among the little people, or not, everyone who assisted me in the effort to find my way through the fog of life, will forever remain big in my eyes.

www.ingramcontent.com/pod-product-compliance
Lightning Source LLC
Chambersburg PA
CBHW051756050726
47598CB00006B/2311